AN
INTRODUCTION TO
THE HISTORY OF
EAST AFRICA

AN
INTRODUCTION TO
THE HISTORY OF
EAST AFRICA

BY
ZOË MARSH
&
G. W. KINGSNORTH

CAMBRIDGE
AT THE UNIVERSITY PRESS
1965

PUBLISHED BY
THE SYNDICS OF THE CAMBRIDGE UNIVERSITY PRESS

Bentley House, 200 Euston Road, London, N.W. 1
American Branch: 32 East 57th Street, New York, N.Y. 10022
West African Office: P.O. Box 33, Ibadan, Nigeria

First Edition	1957
Reprinted	1958
Second Edition	1961
Reprinted with amendments	1963
Third Edition	1965

Printed in Great Britain at the University Printing House, Cambridge
(Brooke Crutchley, University Printer)

LIBRARY OF CONGRESS CATALOGUE
CARD NUMBER: 65–17203

CONTENTS

CONTENTS

CONTENTS

CHAPTER IV. EUROPE HEARS OF AFRICA

CONTENTS

CHAPTER V. MISSIONARY SOCIETIES AND THE DEVELOPMENT OF EAST AFRICA

CONTENTS

CHAPTER VI. THE SCRAMBLE FOR AFRICA AND THE FIRST PARTITION OF EAST AFRICA

I. *The scramble for Africa*

II. *The first partition of East Africa*

CHAPTER VII. THE HISTORY OF UGANDA

UP TO 1890

CONTENTS

CHAPTER VIII. KINGDOMS AND LEADERS

CONTENTS

CHAPTER IX. ZANZIBAR UNDER BRITISH
INFLUENCE

CONTENTS

CHAPTER X.   THE RAILWAY AND THE ECONOMIC
DEVELOPMENT OF KENYA

East Africa's contribution   *page* 178
The Swynnerton Plan   178
Land tenure   179
Settlement schemes   179
Post-war industrial development   180

CHAPTER XI. THE SOCIAL AND CONSTITUTIONAL
DEVELOPMENT OF KENYA

Introduction   182
Policy of the British Government   183
Beginning of central government   184
First Legislative Council   184
Introduction of the franchise   184
The Indian community—Devonshire White Paper   184
Advances in self-government   185
Urban development   185
A new way of life   186
Problems created by social change   187
A State of Emergency   188
After the emergency   189
Changes in local government   190
The Lyttelton Constitution and the Council of Ministers   190
Lancaster House Agreement   191
Between conferences at Lancaster House   192
Independence   192
Outline of government, 1964   194
Post-war social development   195

CHAPTER XII. THE LATER HISTORY OF
UGANDA

The Mohammedan rising of 1893   197
The invasion of Bunyoro   197
The years of peace, 1894–7   198
The rising of the chiefs, 1897   198

xiv

CONTENTS

CHAPTER XIII. THE LATER HISTORY OF
TANGANYIKA

CONTENTS

LIST OF MAPS

PREFACE

While books of various sizes have been written on Uganda alone, Tanganyika alone, Zanzibar alone, and Kenya alone, to the best of our knowledge no book has previously been written which deals specifically with the history of East Africa as a whole, giving roughly equal weight to each territory. The purpose of this book is to fill that gap by supplying an outline of the history of all the East African countries.

As Uganda, Tanganyika, Zanzibar, and Kenya each have their own clear characteristics as a result of their widely differing processes of development, we have been at pains to stress the separate histories of all four countries. On the other hand, the story of their development is so much of a unity that at some points in their history it seemed necessary to pursue a theme in relation to East Africa as a whole. The chapters on Exploration and Partition may be taken as examples of this. But East Africa is not an isolated unit unconnected with other countries of the world or separated from the rest of the African continent by some magic barrier, and the significance of its development cannot be gauged unless it is seen in a wider frame, especially in its relation to the rest of Africa. Therefore, in the chapters on Slavery, Partition, and Lord Lugard, we have tried to present the picture in its true perspective by exploring beyond the boundaries of East Africa.

For most of us the words 'school text-book' have disagreeable associations, and it is hoped that the general reader will not be repelled by the fact that this book was primarily designed for students in connection with the Cambridge School Certificate syllabus on 'The Development of Tropical Africa'. It was written with the hope also that the story of East Africa's growth would prove sufficiently interesting and readable to appeal to many others. But because we were thinking especially of schools, emphasis has been laid on the biographical presentation of material, and, because the book is meant to be used for School Certificate purposes in conjunction with the companion volume by W. D. Hussey (*Discovery, Expansion, and*

Empire, also published by the Cambridge University Press), an effort has been made not to duplicate material given there. As a general history of East Africa, however, this book stands as a self-contained volume.

We have worked closely together throughout the writing of the book, and share responsibility for the work equally. Authorship of particular chapters is as follows: by Z.M., I, II, V, VI, X, XI, XII; by G.W.K., III, IV, VII, VIII, IX, XIII and XIV.

Specialist checking and criticism of parts of the draft have been most kindly given by Mr H. B. Thomas, O.B.E., Miss M. Perham, C.B.E., Dr R. Oliver, Mr J. R. Moffett, Miss D. Middleton, Mr J. Smart, M.B.E., D.P.A., and Sheikh Mubarak Ahmad. We should also like to thank Mr C. G. Richards of the East African Literature Bureau, Mr G. Hazeldine of the Macmillan Library, and Dr D. A. R. Kemp, librarian at the Royal Technical College, for their invaluable co-operation throughout. So many people have helped us that it would be impossible to thank them all here, but special thanks are due to Mr F. H. Goldsmith of the Prince of Wales School, Nairobi, and Miss Goldie late of the Kenya High School. Mrs B. M. Weller and Mr J. A. Boxhall have also given us special help. Particular thanks are due to Miss S. White, Principal of Machakos Girls School, who not only gave us much valuable criticism but also drew some of the maps.

Z. M.
G. W. K.

Nairobi
31 March 1956

PREFACE TO THIRD EDITION

Advancing years bring changing perspectives, requiring adjustments of emphasis. Since the second edition of this book was published in 1961 the four countries which make up East Africa have all attained independence; two have since amalgamated. In addition, research has begun to provide a clearer outline of events before the mid-nineteenth century.

As far as possible the familiar framework of the book has been retained; but the amalgamation of the two chapters on the slave trade has led to renumbering from chapter IV onwards. References made below are to the list of contents in this edition.

Chapters I, VIII, X and XI have been substantially rewritten. 'Post-war changes in Kenya' (previously Appendix I) is incorporated now in chapters X and XI; and an account of the development of local government in Kenya has been included in chapter XI, Appendix II being omitted. The description of events in chapters IX to XIII has been carried down to 1964. Lesser revisions have been made throughout. Authorship of particular chapters is now as follows: by Z.M., I, II, IV, V, IX, X, XI; by G.W.K., III, VI, VII, VIII, XII.

Z.M.
G.W.K.

September 1964

CHAPTER I

EARLY HISTORY OF EAST AFRICA

Link with geography. The study of history is connected with that of geography. Hence a map is useful in explaining why the north and south of Africa have been more closely linked with Europe than has either the west or east. It also explains why the early invaders of West Africa from overseas came from Europe, and those of East Africa from Asia. The map shows that the link between Europe and the north and south of Africa is partly due to the climate, which in both these latter areas is sub-tropical and therefore attractive to Europeans. It also makes it clear that the Sahara Desert was an obstacle in the way of an overland route from Europe to any part of Africa except the north. A more serious barrier to trade with West Africa was the equatorial forest which stretched from the coast to the centre of the continent. This was dense and unhealthy, and so was avoided by the desert riders of camel and horse alike. Moreover, the tsetse fly, which carries *nagana*, is to be found not only in the equatorial forest but also in about 40 per cent of East Africa. In these areas, therefore, it is very difficult to keep horses and cattle and, until the development of mechanical power, transport depended on human beings. There was another obstacle to the penetration of East Africa from the north; this was the Nile Sudd which blocked the river in the southern Sudan.

But, although East Africa has not been an easy place to reach by land, it is not so inaccessible by sea. Before the Suez Canal was cut the shortest sea route from Europe to East Africa was over 8000 miles. By contrast, the distance from Zanzibar to Bombay is only 2500 miles (about the length of the Mediterranean Sea). Therefore, while early visitors to West Africa came mostly from Europe, those to East Africa came from Asia. These visitors to East Africa were helped by the fortunate direction of the monsoon winds, which start to blow from the north-east in December and from the south-west

Map 1. The Indian Ocean.

in March. Very early on the Arabs realized that this meant that their dhows could be blown south to East Africa by the monsoon in December, and a few months later driven back by the same wind, when it had changed direction. The dhows were similar to those which today still use the monsoons to sail up and down the east coast of Africa. Most of the places mentioned in this section can be found on the map above; others will be on page 18 or page 161.

Early visitors. The monsoon also helped the Hindus, the Phoenicians, and possibly the Assyrians and the Jews to reach East Africa. As these traders were coming before the birth of Christ, we do not know much about their early voyages, we do not even know enough to be sure that the last two peoples came to the shores of East Africa; although we are certain that the Hindus and Arabs did. And we do not know for certain whether the land of Punt, to which the Egyptian writings say Egypt was sending traders, really was Somaliland or not.

Greek ships probably first sailed to the south round Cape Guardafui searching for ivory in the time of Ptolemy III, who reigned in Egypt from 247 to 221 B.C. In A.D. 45 a Roman sailor Hippalus discovered the regularity of the monsoon winds, and books were afterwards written in Greek and Latin telling of the Indian Ocean and its ports; but at some time between the late fourth and early fifth century direct contact between the Mediterranean and the Indian Ocean stopped. We know very little about this, as the period from then until the late seventh century is still very obscure. After that, contemporary Arab geographers provide an outline of the history of the east coast from the tenth to the thirteenth century, from which we gather that it remained a largely non-Islamic, Negro area.

By the tenth century Arab dhows were trading regularly with China, but the Chinese still regarded trade as something inferior. They liked to think of the 'Barbarians', as foreigners from overseas were called, bringing tribute to the Emperor of China, after which they were allowed to trade. The more foreigners who came, the greater was the glory of the Emperor. So in the fifth century A.D. a series of expeditions was sent overseas to bring back the luxuries which the Chinese court enjoyed. The fifth of these expeditions went to Kenya, because of a giraffe which had been presented to the Emperor. The Emperor regarded it as a very good omen and saw that the ambassadors who brought it were escorted back to their home in Malindi.

Early trade. All these visitors came for the sake of trade. They hoped to get from East Africa spices, ivory and slaves, for which they would usually trade beads and cloth. In those days spices were valued

3

as preservatives, as well as for the flavour they gave to food, and these spices were obtained from the area round Cape Guardafui. Africa has always been the chief source of ivory, because the elephants there are not used for work and are, therefore, hunted for their tusks. Unfortunately Africa was also for centuries the centre of the slave trade, and one of the centres for distribution was the East African coast where trade caused town life to develop. In the towns the influence of Arab, Indian and Persian traders may have spread the Mohammedan faith. At any rate, when the traveller Ibn Battuta revisited the coast in 1331 he felt that he was among fellow-Muslims. By the fifteenth century there were 37 towns along the coastal strip between Kilwa and Mogadishu and on the eve of the discovery of the route round the Cape to the Far East, these towns were at the height of their prosperity.

Mohammed. Written records of coastal history are rare—less than eighteen foolscap pages would probably hold them all. Before the coming of the Portuguese much is, therefore, only guesswork. The first recorded happening stems from an event of great importance in the history of civilization. This was the birth of Mohammed in Mecca in A.D. 570. He taught the Arabs to turn from heathen gods to the worship of one God. 'There is one God (Allah), and Mohammed is his Prophet.' Mohammed's teaching angered the rulers of Mecca, and in 622 he was forced to flee to Medina. His power and influence, however, continued to spread, and eight years later he was able to conquer Mecca. When Mohammed died in 632, practically the whole of Arabia had accepted the faith of Islam.

Effect of Islam. The chief political effect of Islam was that it united the tribes of Arabia, who were now determined to use their strength to convert as many people as possible to their new religion of 'Islam', which was the word they used for submission to the will of Allah. The Muslims believed that those who died fighting for their religion went straight to Paradise, and they fought bravely and with strict discipline; and in the first eighty years after the death of the Prophet they conquered Syria, Mesopotamia, Persia, and Egypt, and spread their empire through North Africa as far as Spain. At the head

4

of this empire was the Caliph (or successor) of the Prophet, and it was not long before disputes broke out as to who was the rightful Caliph. These disputes divided the Arab Empire, and caused some of those who had been on the losing side to take refuge on the pleasant coast of East Africa, with which trade had already made them familiar.

A really reliable account of events affecting the East African coast from the seventh to the tenth century has not yet been found, but there is some evidence for the following version. Among those who knew the coast well were the traders of Oman. Their land is in the south-east corner of Arabia and juts out into the Indian Ocean, with the Arabian desert behind it. Those who lived in Oman were therefore in a very good position for trade, and were quick to seize any chance to win independence. Among the lovers of independence were Suleiman and Said, who led a rebellion against the Caliph towards the end of the seventh century A.D. When this failed they had to flee to Zenjibar (*zenj* is a Persian word for black, and *bar* means coast), or the 'land of the Blacks'. They finally settled on the Lamu archipelago, where they lived by hunting, fishing and farming. After a time they became traders, and it is said that they eventually became the first slave-hunters to operate on a large scale in East Africa. Two other groups of refugees followed: the people of Zaid, who left the Yemen because they hated the Caliph, and the Seven Brothers of El Hasa. The 'Seven Brothers' were probably the seven leaders of a large group of warriors who left El Hasa, which at that time was the capital of a state in southern Mesopotamia. They conquered the whole coastal strip down as far as Mombasa. Finally Hasan bin Ali and his six sons set sail from southern Persia in A.D. 975, in seven ships, and each shipload founded a settlement. Four of these settlements are known: Mombasa, Pemba, Johanna in the Comoro Isles, and Kilwa. It was at Kilwa that Hasan bin Ali himself settled.

The Zenj Empire. Thus the Persians and the Arabs settled on the east coast of Africa and gave the people who lived there a cosmopolitan character which distinguished them from most of the Africans

5

in the hinterland. The period from 975 (when Hasan bin Ali and his sons took refuge there) to 1498, when Vasco da Gama sailed to Mombasa, is often called the time of the Zenj Empire. This is a somewhat misleading title because the thirty-seven towns between Mogadishu and the Kilwa group never coalesced into a single state, although Kilwa took the lead and was the centre of a network of trade connections. The chief coastal settlements were Kilwa, Tumbata, Pemba, Zanzibar, Vumba, the Lamu Archipelago and Mogadishu. Most of the towns probably began in the twelfth or thirteenth century. By the fifteenth they were well laid out, with streets in which there were houses of stone and mortar surrounded by land cultivated by slaves. In between the towns there were probably smaller settlements with only a mosque and perhaps a headman's house built of and cemented with coral lime.

The map on page 2 shows that many of these places were on islands, although some of them, like Mombasa, were only separated from the mainland by a narrow stretch of water. This was because many of their settlers were people who were used to making their way as traders on the sea. These islands were also all fortified, and gradually towns grew up behind their defences. From the appearance of the ruins of these, we think that many of their inhabitants were influenced by memories of homes in Arabia and Persia. To Kilwa, for instance, the knowledge of how to build in stone, carve wood and weave cottons seems to have been brought from Persia. Although the towns were always quarrelling among themselves, now one and now another taking the lead, Kilwa always had an important position from the time when it was bought by Hasan bin Ali from the Africans. Guessing that the Africans meant to come back later and recapture it, Hasan dug a channel between the town and the mainland, thus making Kilwa an island, not only at high tide, but at all times. When he had also added fortifications, Kilwa became a strong point from which Hasan went on to control the coast from Sofala to Pemba. Its leading position at this time is illustrated by the fact that, in the reign of Hasan's son Ali, it was possible for Ali to appoint his son Muhammad to be governor of Mombasa.

Decline in Arab trade. From earliest times southern Arabia was the market for goods from the East, and the north-eastern monsoon brought Arabian dhows to the coast of East Africa. In the second century A.D. this trade decreased. First, the irrigation of south-west Arabia was seriously disturbed by the bursting of a large reservoir which reduced the prosperity of the whole of the area. Secondly, the Bantu people had begun to appear on the coast and, as they were fiercer and better armed than the original peoples, the Arab traders were further discouraged. Trade revived with the rise of Islam and the arrival of Arab settlers on the coast. By the twelfth century Kilwa had control of the gold trade from Sofala to the north and had contacts with the interior that may even have stretched as far as the Mali Empire on the west coast.

Trade in the Indian Ocean. During the period of the Zenj Empire southern Arabia was the centre of the valuable maritime trade between the Far East, Mesopotamia and Persia and the countries bordering the Mediterranean Sea. Chinese silks, Indian cotton cloth, rhubarb from China (valued for its medicinal properties), precious stones, pepper, nutmeg, mace, ginger and cloves were brought there by sea and sent thence by caravan across the desert, or transhipped up the Red Sea by the Arabs, who monopolized its navigation.

As well as being an important market-place for the traffic between East and West, Arabia annually sent a fleet of ships down the east coast of Africa to carry on the trade in ivory, slaves, spices, tortoise-shell, skins, iron and millet which had attracted the Arabs. While Africa was the chief source of the first two, the only spices that were then obtained from East Africa were frankincense and cinnamon. Other spices, such as cloves, which came from the Molucca islands, and pepper, from India, were obtained in the Far East, where the merchants of East Africa and Arabia paid the local rulers for the right to have factories and agents. There was also a fair amount of East African trade in ambergris and gold. This last had its centre at Sofala, the nearest port to Zimbabwe. The Indians, also, who owned a good deal of the ocean shipping, shared in this trade, and by the end of the Middle Ages trade relations between India and East Africa may have been as important as those between the East African coast and the Persian Gulf. Indians were probably the experts who dealt with finance and with the retail trade, for this is work for which they, unlike the Arabs, have long shown ability. Neither Indian nor Arab showed any desire to explore the vast continent which lay behind the coast. They were content to exchange the goods they brought, their beads, glass, metal-work and cloth, for the ivory, ambergris, slaves and gold. This exchange involved sending caravans into the interior and sometimes fighting to keep a trade-route open. But unless it served the interests of trade, the Arabs were not to be found in the interior.

Life on the coast. On the coast the Arabs intermarried with the Africans. The result was the birth of the Swahili people, who shared the faith of Islam and much of the Arab way of life. A report from Ibn Battuta, when he visited the coast in the fourteenth century, suggests that they ate well. The usual meal seemed to be a large dish of flesh, fish and fowl, laid over rice with milk and fruit added. It is not surprising that Ibn Battuta noticed how fat they were. As he remarked, 'One of these people eats as much as several of us. It is their custom.' This life on the coast was dependent on slaves who had been captured in the interior. Those who survived this journey to serve Arab masters in their plantations and homes were relatively fortunate, for the Koran taught Muslims that kindliness to slaves was a virtue, and many were as well treated as slaves can be. The more unfortunate were those who had still to face the horrors of a sea-passage in which they were packed so closely together that they could hardly turn round. These included those who were shipped to Oman (where the slaves made up a large portion of the population), to India and probably to China.

Although it is thousands of years since the monsoon blew the first Arab dhow into an East African harbour, we are able to get a picture of life on the coast before the Arabs had made a permanent settlement there. After the discovery by Hippalus of the regularity of the monsoon winds, the knowledge soon spread and books were written in Greek and Latin telling of the Indian Ocean and its ports. One of these books was a guide-book to the Indian

Ocean. Its title was *Periplus* (circumnavigation or sailing round) *of the Erythraean Sea,* as the Greeks and Romans called the Indian Ocean. This book still exists today, and in it we find references to East Africa, where there lived along the coast 'men of piratical habits, very great in stature, and under separate chiefs for each place'. To the coast there came 'Arab captains and agents, who are familiar with the natives and intermarry with them and who know the whole coast and understand the language. There are imported into these markets the lances made at Muza especially for this trade, and hatchets and daggers and awls, and various kinds of glass.' The *Periplus* tells us that the Arabs also imported a little wheat, not so much for trading purposes as to secure the good will of the native inhabitants of the coast, for 'there are exported from these places a great quantity of ivory . . . and rhinoceros horn and tortoiseshell . . . and a little palm oil'; while from just below Cape Guardafui there were exported 'slaves of the better sort which are brought to Egypt in increasing numbers'.

Early Mombasa. There is another very interesting description of parts of the East African coast. This was written much later, at the beginning of the sixteenth century, by Duarte Barbosa, who writes:

There is a city of the Moors, called Bombaze (Mombasa), very large and beautiful, and built of high and handsome houses of stone and whitewash and with very good streets, in the manner of those of Quiboa. And it also has a king over it. The people are of dusky white and brown complexions, and likewise the women, who are much adorned with silk and gold stuffs. It is a town of great trade in goods, and has a good port, where there are always many ships, both of those who sail for Sofola and those who come from Cambray and Melinde, and others which sail to the islands of Zanzibar, Manfia and Pemba, which will be spoken of further on. This Mombasa is a country well supplied with plenty of provisions, very fine sheep, which have round tails, and many cows, chickens and very large goats, much rice and millet, and plenty of oranges, sweet and bitter, and lemons, cedrats, pomegranates, Indian figs, and all sorts of vegetables, and very good water. The inhabitants at times are at war with the people of the continent (Mombasa itself is an island) and at other times at peace, and trade with them and obtain much honey and wax, and ivory.

Arrival of Vasco da Gama. Such was the life lived in East Africa when Vasco da Gama rounded the Cape of Good Hope on his search for a new route to the spice islands of the East, the old overland routes having been blocked by the Turks, who had captured Constantinople in 1453. In 1498 da Gama saw the prosperous town of Malindi and was greeted by a king, 'wearing a robe of damask trimmed with green satin, and seated on two cushioned chairs of bronze'. He proved helpful and supplied Vasco da Gama with a good pilot to guide him across the Indian Ocean to Calicut. This reception was the beginning of a long friendship between the Portuguese and Malindi, and was partly due to the bad feeling that existed between Mombasa and Malindi. Once it was known at Malindi that Vasco da Gama had been received badly in Mombasa, the king was eager to welcome him.

D'Albuquerque's plan for the Portuguese conquest. In 1499 Vasco da Gama returned to Portugal and told of his great discoveries. Portugal was quick to see the importance of these, and ten years later she had conquered the east coast of Africa and was able to appoint Dom Duarte de Lemos as governor of all the Portuguese possessions in Africa and Arabia. This conquest of the East African coast was part of the great plan of the ambitious Portuguese d'Albuquerque, who had worked out his ideas before he became Viceroy of India in 1509. At that time the Portuguese merchants were dependent for their share of the valuable spice trade on the good will of the local rulers in India, who allowed them to maintain warehouses and agents on their soil. D'Albuquerque realized that this precarious foothold could be converted into a maritime and Christian empire only if Portugal had a permanent fleet in the Indian Ocean. This meant that Portugal must have fortresses which would command the chief routes of the Indian Ocean trade. Once these had been gained, she would cease to be dependent on an interloping commerce with a far distant base in Lisbon and would rule a secure commercial empire covering the whole of the Middle East.

Its centre was to be at Goa in India, where the chief representative of Portugal, called the Viceroy of India, would have his headquarters.

and control the trade of the west coast of India. To guard the routes to India, d'Albuquerque reckoned that he must gain control of three places: Socotra, which was to be a base for ventures into the Red Sea and so useful for the interception of spice cargoes (he would have preferred Aden, but it proved impossible to capture); Ormuz, which controlled the entry to the Persian Gulf and was one of the most important markets in the world for eastern products; and Malacca, which was the western end of the Chinese trade and the only place from which the Portuguese could control all the trade, mostly in spices, across the Bay of Bengal. But it was not enough for Portugal to conquer these places only; she had to think also of supplying her sailing ships on their long voyages to the East. For this it was essential for Portugal to conquer the East African coast, and between 1500 and 1509 this was done with great savagery.

Beginning of the Portuguese conquest. The first step was taken by Vasco da Gama on his second voyage to India in 1502. He called at Kilwa and forced the sultan to pay a yearly tribute to the King of Portugal. This was typical of Portugal's dealings with the coast. Tribute was demanded and unless it was paid the town was destroyed. If it was paid the local sultan was usually left in peace, provided he carried out the wishes of the Portuguese. After Kilwa, Zanzibar was the next place to suffer from the Portuguese. In 1503 a Portuguese commander called Ravasco showed the power of guns by using two boats with cannon to defeat canoes carrying 4000 men. These canoes had been manned by the ruler of Zanzibar in protest against Ravasco's unprovoked attack on a number of small local ships carrying goods that Ravasco wanted.

D'Almeida. This was only the beginning. In 1505 a fleet of more than 20 ships set sail from Portugal for India. The newly appointed Viceroy of India, d'Almeida, was in command, and his first task was to gain control of three key places on the coast of East Africa: Sofala, Kilwa and Mombasa. Sofala was important to the Portuguese because it would give them control of the gold supply. It offered hardly any resistance, and a fort was built to protect the Portuguese colony that now replaced the old Arab settlement. The same fate was shared by Kilwa, which once claimed to rule the coast. D'Almeida's fleet then sailed away to deal with Mombasa, which of late had secured a larger share of trade than Kilwa; so that by 1505 Kilwa had only 4000 inhabitants, compared to Mombasa's 10,000. Unlike Sofala and Kilwa, Mombasa did not yield without a fight, and throughout the two hundred years during which the Portuguese ruled in East Africa, she was to be a thorn in their side, an island well named the 'Island of War'. But the bowmen of Mombasa could not long resist guns and armour, and Mombasa too was conquered and set on fire.

Not one of these three places, Sofala, Kilwa and Mombasa, however, was to be the headquarters of the Portuguese on the east coast. They found it more convenient to rule from Mozambique, which was 'colonized' in 1507. 'The Portuguese representative on the north of the East African coast was the Captain of Malindi.'

Bases of the Portuguese Empire. When d'Albuquerque died in 1515, six years after the first Portuguese governor-general of the coast had been appointed, he left Portugal ruling an empire in the Indian Ocean which had its supply bases on the east coast of Africa, the chief of which was Mozambique. The headquarters of this empire was at Goa, the most important of the Portuguese trading stations on the west coast of India. It included Malacca, parts of Ceylon, a number of places in the Malay archipelago, Socotra, Muscat in Oman and Ormuz, which guards the entry to the Persian Gulf. Aden alone had successfully resisted the Portuguese. The importance of their conquests either as trading centres or as forts guarding their empire is shown by the map on page 2.

Results of the Portuguese conquest. From the beginning the Portuguese found the East African part of their empire disappointing, because it never brought them the wealth they had expected. They had hoped to secure this by cutting off Arab trade with India, and by attacking the Arab coastal trade, both on sea and on land. They intended to deal direct with the Africans themselves, and no share of their profits was to be taken by Arab or Indian middlemen. So the Portuguese were content to fill their warehouses with calico and beads from

India and wait for the Africans to bring gold, ivory and slaves from the interior. The Arabs too had had their headquarters on the coast, but they had also sent out caravans into the interior to encourage trade. The Portuguese underestimated the part played by these caravans, and in the event lacked the men to staff them. So the supply of gold, ivory and slaves dried up, and the old Arab settlements, which had been taken over by the Portuguese, became poorer and weaker. This was most marked in the south, where Mozambique, Kilwa and Sofala had their Portuguese garrisons and forts. Things were a little easier in the north where local sultans were still allowed to rule, provided they paid the annual tribute, but even here the conquerors were hated, and the Africans called the chief of the Portuguese 'Afriti' or devil.

Unrest in Mombasa. Mombasa was the leader in most of the trouble that arose from this hatred, and as she was unpopular with some of her neighbours, for example Malindi and Zanzibar, they sometimes helped the Portuguese to punish her. In 1528, for instance, both Malindi and Zanzibar helped Nuño da Cunha to attack Mombasa while he was on his way to India to take up his post as Viceroy. The result was that Mombasa had to pay a large sum of gold as tribute every year, and when the town tried to avoid this it was burnt to the ground. After this the 'Island of War' gave no trouble until 1586, when a Turkish pirate called Mirale Bey came sailing down the coast looking for loot. He told the people of Mombasa that he had been sent by the sultan to rescue them, and he did in fact drive the Portuguese out of most of their settlements. He then sailed away, and it was not long before the Viceroy at Goa heard from Malindi what had happened. Punishment followed swiftly, but the spirit of Mombasa was not crushed. Three years later the people again welcomed Mirale Bey on his return to the coast. The Viceroy of India also heard the news, and sent a fleet of ships to prevent another rebellion. Although Mirale Bey had come fairly well equipped this time, leading five ships, he knew that it would be very difficult to hold Mombasa against the Portuguese, and therefore accepted help offered by the Wazimba. This was a Bantu tribe which had been eating their way up Africa since they left their lands near Zululand (they were cannibals). They had captured Kilwa, and were certain that if they waited for their chance they would be able to cross to the island of Mombasa, and enjoy the feast that the fine town offered. Mirale Bey mistrusted them, but he could not resist accepting their offer of help against the Portuguese and allowed them to cross to the island. No sooner were they there than they turned on the inhabitants, many of whom flung themselves desperately into the sea, where sharks were waiting for them.

Fort Jesus. Although the Portuguese put down this rebellion of Mombasa, the island continued to give trouble, and so in 1592 they again attacked and largely destroyed the town. This time they deposed the sultan and put the sultan of Malindi in his place, because they hoped that, as Malindi had always been loyal to them, Mombasa under his rule would cease to give trouble. This they considered important, for there was no doubt that the town was in a very strong position, and with the change of rulers they decided to make it the capital of their East African lands. To guard their new capital Fort Jesus was built, looking out over the harbour.

The decline of Portuguese power. By the end of the sixteenth century the first English ships had begun to appear in the Indian Ocean. They were the forerunners of the British East India Company, and were disliked by the Portuguese, who dreaded any interference with their trade monopoly in this area, especially as they knew that their hold on the coast was weakening. There were several reasons for this. In the first place Portugal never had a large enough population to carry out all her colonial plans. Two million people were not sufficient to cultivate Portugal as well as control Brazil and their empire in the Indian Ocean. Such energy as they had was devoted to Brazil rather than East Africa, which was not a place where many Portuguese settled, even temporarily. In addition, many of the Portuguese settlers in East Africa died from tropical diseases. Others were killed in the continual fighting on the coast. In 1580 Philip II, King of Spain, inherited the throne of Portugal. Philip had already more lands to administer than he was capable of dealing with, and the affairs of Portugal took second place. Thus, by the end of the sixteenth century, Portugal's grasp on the east coast of Africa was feeble. She had long been hated in her empire, where the conquered people could not forgive her greed and cruelty. They were quick, therefore, to seize every chance of rebellion.

Serious revolts against the Portuguese. The first serious revolt to succeed was in Ormuz, where in 1622 the Persians drove out the Portuguese. When this news spread down the coast it encouraged a feeling of restlessness, and in 1631 Mombasa, as usual, was the first to rebel. The leader was the Sultan Yusuf, who had been brought up as a Catholic by the Portuguese and educated at Goa. In India he grew familiar with the Portuguese way of life, despising it. Soon after his appointment as Sultan of Mombasa Yusuf became a Muslim. In a few months he was complaining, with justice, of the way in which the Portuguese governor of Mombasa ruled. By 1631 he was plotting against the Portuguese, and then managed to lead three hundred of his followers into Fort Jesus, where he stabbed the governor. Although Yusuf followed this up by behaviour as savage as that of the Portuguese at their worst, his lead was followed by Pemba and other places on the coast. When it looked as if the forces from Goa would be successful in reconquering Mombasa, Yusuf himself dismantled the fort and destroyed it before sailing away to Arabia. Thus Mombasa lost its last sultan. The years of the Portuguese Empire in the East were numbered.

The British and the Dutch East India Companies were replacing the Portuguese traders on the eastern shores of the Indian Ocean, and one by one Portugal's strong places were taken from her. Oman had followed Ormuz in driving out her Portuguese conquerors. Even East Africa was not to be theirs long; for Mombasa was quick to appeal to the Sultan bin Seif, who as Imam of Oman was the religious head of his country as well as its ruler, to come to the rescue of his fellow Muslims. Sultan bin Seif answered this appeal by freeing Mombasa from the Portuguese. However, owing to revolts in Oman he had to leave the town to be recaptured, and it was his son, the Imam Seif bin Sultan, who finally captured Fort Jesus and became master of Mombasa in 1698. In 1699 he drove the Portuguese out of Kilwa and Pemba also, and this date is usually counted as marking the end of Portuguese rule in East Africa north of Mozambique, which they hold to this day.

Seif bin Sultan. Like his father, Seif bin Sultan was called back by one of the revolts which always seemed to break out when a ruler left Oman. He had, therefore, to leave various Omani Arabs to rule the different towns in East Africa. In Mombasa, for instance, he left the head of the Mazrui family.

The results of Portuguese rule. Considering that they ruled the coast of East Africa for 200 years the Portuguese had done very little for East Africa beyond introducing manioc, maize and the pineapple. This may have been due to the fact that there were never more than a hundred Portuguese living north of Cape Delgado. The hatred these inspired checked any impulse to imitate them. It may also have been because they were never really interested in the land except as a useful stopping place on the way to India. In fact the chief result of their rule was that it had crippled the old Arab settlements, which had lost their wide trade interests and become decaying towns off the main shipping routes, whose only political link with the outside world was that with the Imam of Muscat who ruled Zanzibar.

Invaders of the interior. Before the early traders from overseas saw the coast of East Africa for the first time there were invasions of the interior of the country by a Hamitic people who may have come from Arabia and pushed down into what Professor Coupland calls 'Negro-land, the mid-African home of the black-skinned, fuzzy-haired, thick-lipped Negroes'. We know few details of the past of these people, unfortunately, for they have no written records of their history. This is a gap which will have to be filled by the research of students, but the brief list of books we have given, which does not claim to be complete, may encourage readers to find out what is at present known about the history of the local tribes.

The chief link between the Bantu people is that of language, for while they speak several hundred languages, these are all closely related. In the same way Portuguese, Spanish, Italian and French are akin and together make up what Europeans often call the 'Latin' or 'Romance' languages. In all Bantu languages, for instance, the use of the suffix and prefix is similar and has an important effect on the meaning of the word. (The Negroes, on the other hand, speak languages which are not only different from those of the Bantu, but are also distinct from each other.) Their origin is still uncertain, although there is some evidence that it may have been in the lake region of East Africa. Today they live in the Sudan and in West Africa south of the Sahara Desert. The majority of the peoples of East Africa are descendants of a mixture, in varying proportions, of Hamite, Bushman and Negro.

The movement of populations. Descriptions of society in the interior of East Africa before the coming of Europeans largely depend on oral tradition, which varies in reliability. Although the story that is being pieced together still has large gaps, it is clear that East Africa has seen population movements on a giant scale.

In the late fifteenth or early sixteenth century, for instance, there was a movement southwards of the Nilotic Luo people into the Bantu-speaking half of Buganda. During the sixteenth century the Luo were also moving steadily up the Nile Valley towards a destination in the area now usually called Chope. They seem then to have moved further north to Acholi, westwards into Alur and eastwards into Lango country; and so passed on to the north-east corner of Lake Victoria.

Among the Masai, who are a Nilo-Hamitic people, there are legends of an ancestor called Maasinda who made a great ladder to help them climb up from Lake Rudolf to the Uasin Gishu plateau north of the Kitale. Tradition says that they then spread over the central part of the Kenya highlands, possibly at the end of the sixteenth century, and south down the Rift Valley into Tanganyika. In this migration they pushed past the Nandi group of tribes, who themselves have traditions of a southward movement. The Masai were travelling down a passage of pasture land, good for cattle but not much use to cultivators, and were only finally halted by the Hehe about 1830. As a result of this, the Barugya section of the tribe gave up pastoral pursuits and went in for agriculture. Eventually they joined the

Map 2. An area of major population movements.

Taveta on the south-eastern slopes of Mount Kilimanjaro. Another group turned northwards again and pushed through Kikuyuland to the rich grazing land of Laikipia. From their bases the Masai warriors raided far and wide—a distance of 300 miles was no obstacle; but even the Masai were checked by steep slopes and thick forests, and the Kamba, the Taita, the Meru, the Kikuyu, and others who were fortunate in their natural sanctuaries, all survived.

In southern Tanganyika until the middle of the nineteenth century many of the inhabitants were shifting cultivators; others were hunters and fishermen. This was a region which had not apparently been influenced by either the Nilo-Hamitic or Nilotic peoples. It was here that the last large-scale immigration before the coming of the Europeans occurred. The invaders were the Ngoni who moved away from Natal to avoid being absorbed in Chaka's cruel empire. They crossed the Zambezi in 1835 and the main body settled for a time on the plateau just above the south-east corner of Lake Tanganyika. On their journey they had been, often against their will, joined by the survivors of other defeated peoples. After the death of Zongendaba the Ngoni leader, they broke up into smaller raiding bodies. Some of these gathered up tribal groups which they found small and disorganized, and incorporated them into new Ngoni states. A number of their neighbours now sought strength through closer union. Among these were the Hehe. Others suffered from the hordes of raiders and refugees who were let loose; these formed bands of mercenary warriors, called 'ruga-ruga', who joined any leader holding out hopes of rich plunder. They usually wore red cloaks, feather head-dresses and ornaments of copper and ivory. Beyond building their leader's house and stronghold, they were not prepared to do any work. They reckoned to live on what their guns won for them; and by the middle of the nineteenth century there was a steady flow of these weapons from Zanzibar into the interior. These guns fascinated a young Nyamwezi warrior who was very successful in supplying his force of ruga-ruga with them. A man of great courage and clear aims, Mirambo, as the warrior was called, knew exactly what he wanted. He was also helped by speaking the language of the Ngoni, and may even have been brought up among them. His ancestors may have included the last ruler of a united Nyamwezi kingdom; but his father only owned Ugogwe. To this Mirambo added territory belonging to his mother's family. By 1880 he had managed to win control of the Ujiji road to Lake Tanganyika, having already obtained command of the main roads leading north-westwards to Karagwe and Buganda. Already his capital at Urambo was strong

Map 3. The peoples of East Africa.

enough to challenge the rival Arab market at Unyanyembe. Urambo consisted of a square enclosure the sides of which were made of a substantially built wall encircling nearly two square miles of ground, inside which lived about 15,000 inhabitants. When two sections of Ngoni, heading north, settled under Mirambo's leadership, the Ngoni invasions of East Africa were at an end.

The peoples of East Africa. The map on page 20 gives the present position of the chief peoples in East Africa, and the appendix lists the titles of several books dealing with the histories of these peoples. These histories are still being pieced together. It has, for instance, been suggested that the Embu moved up the River Tana from the coast and settled inland about 1425, and that earlier still the Kamba had travelled up the Athi River to their present site. According to this reconstruction of the past, the Kikuyu must have reached the Fort Hall area about 1545 and moved on to Kiambu about 1800. Age sets and traditional generations have been used for working out these dates; but the outline is still shadowy.

Archaeology, which is concerned with objects rather than persons and events, can fill some of the gaps, but our description of society in the interior of East Africa, prior to the middle of the nineteenth century, still depends largely on oral traditions—family records storing up the names of a man's ancestors back to the sixteenth century testify to the length of old women's memories; traces of eucalyptus hedges may supplement the tradition of an earlier settlement of huts, songs, ceremonies and place-names may provide clues. This is material that has to be examined cautiously; stories, for example, may be true of the people who tell them, but refer to some other place from which they have moved. But we do know that the East African environment was and is a harsh one; less than a quarter of the country has a good chance of obtaining sufficient rainfall to make it suitable for intensive arable cultivation. In this respect Kenya is the least fortunate area. Moreover, the soil is light and easily exhausted. Despite this, maize, millet, sweet potatoes, cassava and bananas were being grown in the nineteenth century and in some areas iron-working was carried on. Vegetation is unevenly distributed and in parts of the country there is an excessive tropical growth, while in others there are semi-desert conditions. One of the causes of the series of migrations in East African tribes may in fact be the nature of the soil. In large areas, this limited its occupation by peoples without modern agricultural knowledge. The environment also helps to explain the present distribution of the population, which is thinly spread over an area of 642,728 square miles of land (large parts of this are semi-desert and in addition there are 38,901 square miles of water), with pockets of considerable density. Of this compact block Kenya occupies 219,789 square miles of land, giving her (according to the 1962 census figure of 8,636,263 inhabitants) a density of thirty-nine inhabitants to a square mile of land, compared to approximately forty-eight for the world as a whole. Even today, therefore, East Africa has comparatively few people to the square mile; and there are good reasons to think that there were still fewer at the end of the nineteenth century. This may well have been due not only to disease but also to the slave trade and the wars between tribes that often went with it.

African society evolved to meet human needs within this environment, in which the mere existence of an individual depended on his relationship to the whole community. So long as he remained within it, he was sure of protection and assistance in time of need. Within this society there were outstanding individuals such as Kimweri, who ruled over the kingdom of Usambara; Mumia, who was Nabongo of Wanga when Joseph Thomson stayed with him; and Kivoi, who has been described as a Kamba merchant prince. Detailed accounts of their lives have, however, still to be written.

CHAPTER II

ZANZIBAR UNDER SEYYID SAID

Accession of Seyyid Said. An inscription on the arch of a mosque at the southern end of Zanzibar reads, ' This is what has been ordered by the high and very great Sheikh Ec Said Alu . . .'. The date given is Dhul Haj in the year five hundred (A.D. 1107).

Asian colonies of settlers were now established in Zanzibar and by the time the Portuguese invasion of East Africa began they were on sufficiently good terms with the local inhabitants to be able to leave their forts and develop plantations. Writing in 1512, Duarte Barbosa tells us that it was a very fertile island inhabited by people who 'live in great luxury and abundance, they dress in very good clothes of silk and cotton which they buy in Mombasa'. This life was largely restricted to the Arabs; three-quarters of the inhabitants of the island were slaves and heavy financial demands were made on the rest to support the Sultan of Oman in his war. The real foundation of Zanzibar's prosperity was laid by Seyyid Said, who in 1806, at the age of fifteen, became ruler of Oman, as a consequence of murdering his rival, this being a recognized Arab method of securing a throne. Power won by this means must be held firmly, and the young Seyyid saw the value of a British alliance in his struggle against both the warlike Wahabi of the desert and the Jawasmi pirates who had their headquarters in the Persian Gulf, where they attacked the shipping both of Oman and of the British East India Company.

Co-operation with Britain. These attacks finally became so serious that the British government of India co-operated with Said, and in 1810 it looked as if the power of the Jawasmi would be broken. They had recently accepted control by the Wahabi, who now came to their rescue; by 1814 Said had finally defeated the Wahabi. In this he had not been assisted by Britain, but he remembered with gratitude the assistance that Britain had given him earlier against the Jawasmi pirates, and, as the long war between Britain and Napoleon ended at

23

much the same time, the danger that Oman would be seized by one of the two was also at an end. Its value to either would have been as a base for attack.

The Moresby Treaty. Seyyid Said could now rejoice that he had the support of the victorious British. It was unfortunate, of course, from Said's point of view, that they were so determined to check the slave trade that he felt it only wise to sign the Moresby Treaty of 1822, thus limiting the profitable Arab slave trade. However, he was pleased to think that in exchange for this concession the British had recognized his claim to overlordship in East Africa. It was now time, he judged, to make good this claim.

Said's struggle with the Mazrui. This meant a struggle with the Mazrui of Mombasa, who had seized control of the town nearly a hundred years earlier, and were well aware that the Imam of Oman had ceased to have any real power on the coast, except in Pemba, Zanzibar, Mafia, and later Kilwa. In the early part of Seyyid Said's reign things had indeed become even worse; for the Mazrui family were no longer loyal followers of the ruler of Oman. They aimed at ruling themselves. When they seized Pemba it looked as if Oman's control of the coast was slipping away. So with the Moresby Treaty signed, the Oman for once peaceful, Said thought that the time had come to attack the Mazrui and make good his claim to the overlordship of the east coast of Africa, which his ancestors had freed from the Portuguese. To do this he had to capture Mombasa, which, by reason of its good harbour, protected by Fort Jesus, was still the key to the coast. The Mazrui, however, made a last desperate bid to remain independent of Oman by offering the Protectorate of Mombasa to Britain. Captain Owen, to whom the offer was finally made, accepted it in 1824 with a view to using the port as a base against the slave trade.

Protectorate of Mombasa declined by Britain. This was a bitter blow to Seyyid Said, who had so recently signed the Moresby Treaty with the one object of keeping Britain's friendship. Britain, however, did not want land in East Africa, and when Seyyid Said's protest was followed by evidence that the Mazrui only wanted to shelter under the Union Jack, and were not eager to accept British control, orders

24

were given that the flag was to be taken down and the small garrison removed. This did not end the ruler of Oman's difficulties. He still had to conquer Mombasa, which meant getting control of Fort Jesus. At first it seemed as though this was beyond his power. A split among the Mazrui as to who should be ruler of Mombasa gave him his chance. He got control of Fort Jesus in 1837, and in a few months he was the unquestioned ruler of Mombasa.

Said moves his capital to Zanzibar. During the years in which Said had been concentrating on the capture of Mombasa he had grown very attached to the island of Zanzibar, which had loyally supported all his efforts. By 1837 he was spending as much time at Zanzibar as at his other capital, Muscat. It was, however, a serious matter to shift the capital from Muscat to the island of Zanzibar from which it was separated by 2500 miles, especially as the dhows could only reach Zanzibar from Oman at the time of the monsoon. Said, moreover, meant to keep control in his lifetime of both Oman and the East African coast.

Assets of Zanzibar. In making Zanzibar his real capital in 1832, Seyyid Said knew that he risked loosening his hold on Oman, but he was a man with great commercial insight, and saw the possibilities of obtaining more real power in Africa than he had inherited as Imam of Muscat. Besides, Zanzibar was a green and pleasant land, with a delightful climate; and Muscat reflected the fierce heat of a sun-baked soil. It was also true that, until Seyyid Said developed Zanzibar, it was only an unimportant little town at which ships called for water and provisions on their way to the big centres of trade. It had, however, four very important assets. First, a good harbour, seven to nine fathoms deep, in which ships could anchor. Secondly it had, in Seyyid Said's opinion, the sweetest water to be found on the east coast. Its third advantage was a central situation, for the island, although nearly twenty miles from the mainland, is just over a hundred miles south of Mombasa and thus in a central position for trade with the mainland. Fourthly, its climate and fertile soil have the comparatively rare qualities needed for the cultivation of spices. These are shared also by the small neighbouring island of Pemba.

Introduction of cloves. With these advantages Seyyid Said considered that he could make his new capital the chief port on the western shores of the Indian Ocean, and thus increase his own and his country's wealth. In this way he would gain power, prestige and security. Soon after his arrival in Zanzibar he took the important step of introducing the cultivation of cloves. Until the end of the eighteenth century, cloves had only been known to grow in the East Indies. Yet they were eagerly sought after both as a preservative and as a medicine. This meant that they were, and are still, a very valuable crop. The idea of planting them probably came to Seyyid Said when, on a visit to Zanzibar, he saw a few cloves growing there and realized that the island's fertile soil might prove to have the rare qualities needed for their cultivation on a large scale. Having decided that clove culture should be the primary industry of his islands, Said set an example by sowing forty-five of his own plantations with the crop. He also put strong pressure on the other landowners on the island to do the same. When a coconut palm died, or was cut down, three clove trees had to be planted in its place. Disobedience resulted in the confiscation of land. As a result, at the end of Said's reign the value of the cloves exported from Zanzibar ranked next to that of the ivory and slaves on which the island had long depended, and today Zanzibar and Pemba produce nearly 90 per cent of the world's supply of cloves.

Exports of slaves and ivory. Nor did the development of cloves lead to a neglect of Zanzibar's primary exports, slaves and ivory. These had to be obtained from the interior of Africa, and during Seyyid Said's reign more and bigger caravans were sent out further inland, so much so that Burton, an explorer who is discussed in chapter IV, tells us that Ujiji was not visited by the Arabs until 1840, yet by 1858 it was already a regular trading post. Speke is another explorer who commented on the extension of the caravan routes which, by Livingstone's time, had reached the three great lakes. As these caravans all went on foot, an increase in the routes meant the establishment of outposts such as Ujiji, for it was impossible to return to a base in Zanzibar during a single dry season.

Said's commercial outlook. These small Arab settlements, however, did not mean that Said was building an empire on the mainland. His interests were commercial, not imperial. 'I am nothing but a merchant', he once told a visitor. He was indeed largely dependent upon customs duties and taxes on the slave trade; his wealth and power increased when trade expanded. This explains why he did not seek to found settlements other than the outposts that were needed to feed the new trade routes, despite the fact that all the Arab caravans that set off from Zanzibar carried the Sultan's red flag and that most of the European explorers who used Said's capital as a base carried a letter of recommendation from him. Yet by the end of his reign men were saying that: 'When they whistle in Zanzibar, the people dance on the shores of the great lakes.' Seyyid Said's part in this had not only been to introduce the profitable clove and to encourage the caravans; he also provided a background of security and peace without which trade seldom flourishes. In addition to this he had seen the need to develop new markets for the products of the African mainland.

Foreign trade. In order to do this he encouraged foreign traders. Already at Muscat he had done all he could to attract the Indian merchants or Banyans who had long been familiar with the East African coast (see chapter I). These men were not only allowed complete liberty of worship, and freedom from taxes beyond the 5 per cent customs duty which was levied on all goods; they were also employed to deal with Zanzibar's finance. Even the important post of collector of customs was usually given to a Hindu. The result was that a large Indian colony grew up in the capital and helped to change it from a fishing village to a town which numbered 60,000 in 1859. This population was larger than that of Mombasa, which had suffered from the long struggle between the Mazrui and Zanzibar, and nearly ten times the size of Mozambique, the capital of Portuguese East Africa. Every Arab coast town soon had its growing group of Indian traders and customs officials and the number and size of caravans increased. This was the beginning of foreign diplomatic relations with East Africa.

The Indian traders whom he encouraged provided the credits which made lengthy expeditions into the interior possible, and it was he who systematically explored the possibility of trade with the interior. Seyyid Said also made arrangements with the Nyamwezi for the security of his caravans and the non-payment of dues by the Arabs of Unyanyembe to the local chief. During his reign a number of settlements were founded from which Arab traders set out in the cool season to collect slaves and ivory. Unyanyembe was the chief of these. Burton wrote, 'The Arab houses though single storied, are large, substantial and capable of defence . . . rich men have ridden asses from Zanzibar, and even the poorest kept flocks and herds.' Arab traders might be away from the coast for years. Tippoo Tip, for instance, returned to Zanzibar after being away twelve years with 2000 porters each carrying a trunk and guarded by 1000 askaris. By 1870 Arab traders were facing attack by the Nyamwezi under their able chief Mirambo, who was determined that they should pay for protection in passing through the Nyamwezi kingdom.

Consulates established. Yet Seyyid Said was too clever a man to give the Indians a monopoly of his increasing trade. He realized that the best markets for his ivory and cloves were to be found in America and Britain. He therefore anxiously sought to develop trade links with these countries. The end of the American War of Independence had given the ex-colonists the chance to share in the trade with the East from which they had previously been shut out by the mercantile system under which the British East India Company had claimed a monopoly over all British and colonial trade in the Indian Ocean. The Americans seized this chance, and the number of their ships in this region steadily increased, until finally an American mission arrived at Muscat. The delighted Seyyid Said was thus able to sign a commercial treaty with the United States in 1833. Four years later the Americans were given the right to open a consulate in Zanzibar town. A similar treaty was signed with France in 1844, and in the same year the French also opened a consulate. Seyyid Said knew, however, that these treaties were not sufficient to safeguard Zanzibar, and it was to Britain that he looked for support. The commercial treaty that he signed with her in 1839 was to be the beginning of a close link between the two countries. Indeed, the British consulate, which opened in 1841, had a powerful influence on Zanzibar policy. This favour with which the Sultan regarded Britain went back to the beginning of his reign in Oman when, as a young man, he had joined forces with the British governor-general of India against the Jawasmi pirates who were attacking British shipping. Seyyid Said was aware, moreover, of the dangers from other European countries, especially France, and was prepared to pay a high price for British friendship.

The Zanzibar slave trade. The price Britain asked was his support in putting down slavery in East Africa. For centuries slaves had been captured in the land behind the east coast of Africa and used to transport the valuable ivory down to the coast, where Zanzibar was the chief slave market. As the Arabs penetrated further inland the number of slaves increased, until at the beginning of the nineteenth century about fifteen thousand were obtained annually. Many of these were shipped from Zanzibar to Arabia, Persia, Egypt, etc.

Britain's attitude to the slave trade. Britain, having played the chief part in stopping the transatlantic slave trade, was now anxious to check the Arab slave trade. Seyyid Said's support in this aim was the price that Britain asked for her friendship and her permission to trade freely with the ports of British India. She realized, however, that suppression of the slave trade would mean a big drop in revenue for Seyyid Said, who would also have to face the indignation of his Arab subjects. Britain, therefore, decided to work in stages. In 1822 pressure was successfully put on the Sultan to sign the Moresby Treaty. Details of this are given in chapter III, in which it is shown that a loophole existed whereby the terms of the treaty could be evaded. In 1845, therefore, Britain forced the Sultan to take further steps to suppress the slave trade; by the time Seyyid Said died in 1856, the slave trade had been very much restricted, although slavery itself was still unchecked.

Benefits of association with Britain. In the opinion of many of the leading Arabs, Seyyid had had to pay a heavy price for British friendship, but he had secured British support against the French, whose interest in East Africa was becoming dangerously active at this time;

his kingdom gained so much materially from his connection with the greatest merchant nation in the world that by 1856 Seyyid Said had transformed his backward East African lands. This was shown by the great increase in the volume of trade which passed through Zanzibar and brought the Sultan a very satisfactory revenue through the only tax he imposed, the 5 per cent tax on all imports. It also meant wealth for the merchants of Zanzibar. The value of the trade between Zanzibar and India in 1859, for instance, was over £333,000, and that between the United States of America and Zanzibar was £245,000.

Extent of Seyyid Said's power. When Seyyid Said died in 1856 his business ability was acknowledged by all who were in touch with East Africa. These men would, however, have found it harder to define the lands over which he ruled. This vagueness was largely due to the fact that Seyyid Said was interested in securing the sole right to levy taxes and develop trade in as much of Africa as possible; he was much less interested in political boundaries, and the phrase 'effective occupation', which was to be discussed so often in the future of Zanzibar, was meaningless to him.

On the coast, although the Sultan's authority was theoretically acknowledged from Rovuma in the south to Warsheik in the north, yet the governors whom he placed in the chief coastal towns were often almost independent rulers. So long as they paid a large part of the customs duties to Seyyid Said he seldom interfered with them. For the rest, his system of government was not complicated by departments or ministers or courts of justice, nor even by the actual collection of taxes. The Sultan himself judged all serious criminal offences, and this was typical of the way in which he himself was the government. But he kept in touch with the people by means of *baraza*, and held such audiences two or three times a day. This form of government was characteristic of Seyyid Said's liking for simplicity. European visitors who had heard of him as one of the most famous princes of the Arab world were often surprised at his lack of outward show. He dressed in a plain Arab robe and coloured turban and wore no jewels. In Zanzibar town he lived in a palace which was 'a kind of double-storied whitewashed barrack, about 140 feet long, roofed with dingy green-red tiles'. Yet visitors were deeply impressed by his personality and appreciated his natural courtesy and generous hospitality.

The Canning award. On Seyyid Said's death his unwieldy lands were divided as he wished. His eldest son inherited Oman, while Zanzibar went to the second son, Seyyid Majid. After a brief struggle this arrangement was confirmed by the award of Lord Canning, Governor-General of India, who intervened in 1861 to enforce the peace which England's interests needed in East Africa and India. The Canning award set out the details of the division, and the two kingdoms have had separate rulers ever since.

CHAPTER III

THE EAST AFRICAN SLAVE TRADE AND THE ABOLITION MOVEMENT

Slavery. Slavery is the absolute possession of one person by another, and it is as old as history itself. The ancient civilizations of China, India, Persia, Mesopotamia, Egypt, Greece, and Rome all accepted it as a necessary part of their society, and there is probably no race on earth which at some time has not participated in slavery, either as one of the enslaved or as the possessor of slaves. But although slavery has been universal, no continent has been so widely and consistently ravaged by it as Africa, from whose interior slaves have been drawn for at least two thousand years, and where slavery still existed when our fathers were born.

The responsibility for the African slave trade. The responsibility for slavery and the slave trade in Africa rests mainly upon the Africans themselves, the Arabs and the countries of Europe.

Slavery was a normal feature of African life before any slave raider set foot on the continent. Sometimes slaves were obtained as a result of tribal wars, in which case the conquering tribe would enslave the women and children of the conquered tribe, and possibly the men as well if they had not been killed. Sometimes too an offence which was regarded as serious, but which did not deserve death, was punished by enslavement. Again, a man might voluntarily offer himself as a slave to another, in order to obtain food or protection. Usually slaves would be employed in cultivation, or in watching cattle and sheep. Sometimes, as with the Baganda and Ashanti, they were used as human sacrifices. It is impossible to estimate with any accuracy the number of slaves in the continent before the demand from other countries developed, but certainly there were fewer in Africa than Asia. Nevertheless it was from these beginnings that the slave trade with outside countries began. It was not usual for slave traders themselves to capture the slaves. On the western coast they often never even landed on the shore. They relied instead on the African chiefs to supply them with the slaves they wanted, either by selling slaves from their own village, or by attacking a neighbouring village and selling the people in it who were caught. Tempted by presents of guns, alcohol, clothing, and trinkets, the chiefs strove to enslave increasing numbers of people, with the result that tribal wars and raids on neighbouring villages increased also.

Motives for the Arab slave trade. By far the most important outside traders who promoted the slave trade in East Africa were the Arabs. They were Muslims, and the Koran, although it did not explicitly forbid slavery, laid down strict rules for the treatment of slaves and positively forbade any Muslim to enslave another. It was therefore necessary for the Arabs to look outside their own country for slaves, and East Africa became their source of supply. From the ninth century a stream of slaves left the East African ports for the markets of Turkey, Arabia, India, and Persia.

Ivory and slaves were the commodities on which the wealth of the Arab settlements in East Africa was based. Unfortunately for the Arabs they were also the most difficult commodities to obtain. Gum-copal, coconuts, copra, and palm oil were easily obtainable from the coastal belt, but the revenue from these was comparatively small. The main wealth came from the caravans which penetrated further and further into the interior, searching for the long elephant tusks and the men, women, and children to carry them to the coast. There, both the black and white ivory could be sold at a very handsome profit.

Area and routes of the Arab slave trade. The main hunting grounds of the caravans moved further into the interior during the first half of the nineteenth century, and especially from the time when Seyyid Said made his capital at Zanzibar, which became the chief market. Although some slaves were taken from the interior north-westwards across the desert, and still more were taken northwards along the Nile to Khartoum, the main slave routes lay across what is now Tanganyika. One of these main routes started from Bagamoyo (or from Saadani or Pangani) on the mainland opposite Zanzibar island,

and climbed from the coastal plain inland to Tabora. This was for the interior what Zanzibar was for the coast: the main centre of communications and trade. Tabora was probably founded about 1830 and by the time Speke and Burton arrived (1857–8) it consisted of about twenty-five Arabs and a few Indians living 'comfortably and even splendidly' in separate little groups of huts and houses.

The houses, though single-storied, are large, substantial, and capable of defence. Their gardens are extensive and well planted; they receive regular supplies of merchandise, comforts and luxuries from the coast; they are surrounded by troops of concubines and slaves whom they train to divers crafts and callings (Burton).

From Tabora one route continued westwards towards Lake Tanganyika and another struck northwards through Karagwe. The westward route in 1842 ended at Usenge, but when Burton and Speke made their expedition it stretched to Ujiji on the shore of the lake itself, which by then had become a regular outpost of the Arab slave-trading route. In 1876 Stanley found the market prices of slaves there quoted as follows:

> A girl aged 13–18 worth 80–200 cloths.
> A woman aged 18–20 worth 80–130 cloths.
> A boy aged 13–18 worth 16–50 cloths.
> A man aged 18–50 worth 10–50 cloths.

From Ujiji the Arab caravans explored southwards and westwards across the lake, and in 1852 one caravan reached Benguela on the western coast, having crossed the continent from Bagamoyo.

The northward route passed through Karagwe to the northern end of Lake Victoria, where it forked north to Bunyoro and north-eastwards to Buganda. As early as 1852 the wealthy Arab trader, Snay bin Amir, had reached Kampala from Tabora, but it was not until the 1870's that the route came into general use. By that time the slave traders pushing southwards from Khartoum had almost reached the Victoria Nile, and but for the European intervention they might well have come into sharp collision with the traders from Zanzibar, as the distance between them was very small.

Map 4. Slave routes.

As well as the routes through Tabora there was to the south another route from Kilwa towards Lake Nyasa, which was extremely important. To the north there was yet another route, of rather less importance, which started from Tanga and struck inland past Kilimanjaro towards Lake Victoria. To the north of this the route from the coast to Lake Victoria was made dangerous by the warlike Masai, whose reputation kept most of what is now Kenya comparatively free from the curse of slave raiding. The route from Mombasa (probably via Kilimanjaro and along the Rift Valley) was attempted by a considerable number of caravans, but many which made the attempt disappeared, so that the prudent Arab slave dealer considered the southward diversion well worth while.

Methods and effects of the Arab slave trade. The size of the caravans varied. On the shorter trade routes a caravan might consist of only fifty men, but for long, dangerous journeys inland, parties might join together, making a total of a thousand or more. With the native guide in front carrying his tattered blood-red flag, the sign of Seyyid Said's protection, the file would set off westwards in search of its prey, through the coastal forest, the hated thorn-scrub, and the long grassland, watching for hostile tribes and wild animals by day, and camping by night beside the watch-fires which kept off the marauding hyenas, jackals and lions. Progress was slow. The journey from Tabora to Ujiji, for example, though only about one hundred miles, usually took over three weeks. When the rainy season started, movement became almost impossible, so most of the caravans started in the dry period of April or May after the long rains, and sometimes they remained away from the coast for two years or more. In the interior slaves would either be purchased from chiefs or Arab merchants, or the caravan might raid a village itself. These raids, whether carried out by hostile tribes or by the Arabs themselves, were devastating and merciless. A shot in the night would be followed by a bonfire of blazing huts while the screaming inhabitants rushed into the bush. Those who were fit would be enslaved, and those who were useless would be massacred. Then the raiders would depart leaving the village a smouldering graveyard. Such was the picture Livingstone saw. Apart from the human misery involved, the unrest and de-population caused by these raids were enormous. When the explorer Speke visited the east side of Lake Tanganyika in 1858 he wrote:

How the shores should be so desolate strikes one with much surprise. Unless in former times this beautiful country has been harassed by neighbouring tribes and despoiled of its men and cattle to satisfy the spoilers and be sold to distant markets, its present state appears quite incomprehensible. In hazarding this conjecture it might be thought that I am taking an extreme view of this case; but when we see every-where in Africa what one slave-hunt or cattle-lifting party can effect, it is not unreasonable to imagine that this was most probably the cause of such utter desolation here. These war-parties lay waste the land for endless time.

On the return journey of the caravan the guide would be followed by the long line of slaves yoked together and carrying on their heads elephant tusks, and bundles of cloth, beads and grain. At the rear of the file came the most important of the Arab merchants. When the caravan reached the coast the ivory and the slaves might be sold on the spot or else shipped to the main market at Zanzibar. For this journey they were heaped in tiers on top of one another and many never reached their destination. By the middle of the nineteenth century about 15,000 slaves a year passed through the squalid, sandy square of the Zanzibar slave market, where men and merchants in every variety of costume from mere rags to the brilliant gold and vermilion raiment of the Arab aristocracy gathered each afternoon from five until sundown to purchase the slaves who were ornamented and arrayed for their inspection. Some of their purchases were kept for the merchants' own use, but most were exported under appalling conditions to Arabia and the Persian Gulf. For every five captured in the interior only one reached his or her destination. Most died before they even reached the coast.

Upon the great expansion of the slave trade which took place during his reign Seyyid Said smiled with satisfaction, as well he might considering the increased prosperity of his dominions which it brought. But the effects of the trade upon the African interior were catastrophic. Tribe attacked tribe to obtain profit from those they captured and enslaved; whole villages were destroyed and their inhabitants removed or massacred, while the slave routes themselves were strewn with the skeletons of those who perished. Constant internal war and depopulation on a vast scale were the price of the East African slave trade.

A comparison of East and West African slave trades. While slaving managed by the Arabs was in full swing in East Africa, on the other side of the continent slaving managed by European countries was on the decline, and we must now turn to the abolition movement which looked first to the West African coast and then turned its attention to the East.

The slave trade from West Africa had grown in order to supply the labour for the development of the American and West Indian plantation colonies. The demand grew particularly rapidly in the later seventeenth century when it was realized that sugar could be grown in the West Indian islands and that it brought tremendous profits; but slave gangs were also needed for the tobacco and cotton plantations on the mainland. By 1770 half the slave trade of the Atlantic was carried by the British, who had nearly 200 ships with cargo space for nearly 50,000 slaves. The French came next with 30,000 and the Portuguese third with 10,000. So great were the profits that if only one ship in three made a successful voyage the enterprise was considered well worthwhile.

There are interesting similarities and contrasts between the slave trade in East and West Africa. The volume of each was enormous, but while we can make some sort of guess at the number of slaves taken from West Africa it is extremely difficult to make an estimate for East Africa, because the volume varied and figures can only be obtained for the comparatively few final years. But we do know that the European slave trade across the Atlantic did not begin until the sixteenth century, that it did not reach its maximum until the eighteenth century, and that at the start of the nineteenth century it was abolished. But the Arab slave trade across the Indian Ocean began before the Christian era and did not stop until the end of the nineteenth century, so that although its volume in any one year did not reach the highest figures of the European slave trade, the total number of Africans exported during two thousand years may well have exceeded fifteen million. The treatment of slaves by those who transported them was dreadful in both cases, but whereas about half those captured as slaves in West Africa reached their destination, we have seen that only about one-fifth of those captured in East Africa survived. Yet those deported from East Africa who reached their destination in the Middle East were usually treated with comparative kindness and were used as domestic slaves, while those who were deported from West Africa to the American or West Indian colonies were used in gangs on plantations.

The abolition movement in England. In view of the profits made by the European slavers, the plantation owners, and the West African chiefs, how did the movement to abolish the slave trade ever manage to achieve success?

The answer has many contributory streams. One was economic, for in 1776 Adam Smith, the Scottish professor, published his *The Wealth of Nations*, which upset the economic beliefs of at least two centuries by arguing, among other things, that slaves were not a profitable form of labour. 'It appears', he wrote, 'that from the experience of all ages and nations the work done by free men comes cheaper in the end than that performed by slaves.'

Even more important than this economic argument was the growth of the evangelical movement which drew its inspiration from the Christian gospel and created a new awareness of Christian obligations. One result was an upsurge of Protestant missions; the Baptist Missionary Society was started in 1792, the London Missionary Society in 1799, the British and Foreign Bible Society in 1804, and the Methodist Missionary Society in 1813. Yet the most spectacular success of the evangelical movement was the abolition within the British Empire of the slave trade in 1807 (and later, of slavery itself).

Granville Sharp and the abolition of slavery in England. The first step in the abolition movement might be dated from 1772, when slavery was abolished in England. The credit for this belongs chiefly to Granville Sharp, who started life as a linen-draper's apprentice and later settled down as a junior civil servant. His position was humble but his heart was great. When he saw, in his own town, an African slave who had been beaten and thrown into the street as useless he took him under his care and found him a job. However, as the man was still officially a slave he was also still officially the property of his owner, so Sharp promptly began to study the law in order to compel the Lord Chief Justice to declare that slavery should not exist in England. As there were about 14,000 African slaves in the country at the time, mostly belonging to West Indian planters, this was certain to arouse a storm of protest with dismal suggestions that it would create a serious unemployment problem. Nevertheless, as a result of Granville Sharp's persistence, on 22 June 1772 slavery in England was legally ended through the case of the African slave James Somerset.

Abolition in the British Empire. The next steps were to attempt the abolition of the slave trade and slavery in the British Empire. When the chief minister of George III heard of the idea he shook his head at the apparent absurdity of it and said, 'It will be found impossible to abolish the slave trade for it has in some measure become necessary to almost every nation in Europe.' Granville Sharp thought otherwise. He became chairman of a Quaker committee dedicated to the abolition cause, and to this was attracted the scholar Thomas Clarkson who had convinced himself, by writing a prize-winning essay in Latin, that slavery was wrong. Clarkson was to provide the solid facts about the slave trade on which the committee based its arguments.

William Wilberforce. The greatest name in the abolition movement was that of William Wilberforce, because he alone had the power and ability to drive the cause through Parliament. In his early days Wilberforce was a gay young man with a gift for talking wittily and continuously, and among the fashionable upper class in which he moved he was extremely popular. He came from a wealthy Yorkshire business family, and finished his education at Cambridge. Well supplied with money, he then lived a leisurely life in London, where he made friends with Pitt, his contemporary at Cambridge. In 1780 both Pitt and Wilberforce were elected to Parliament, and when Pitt became Prime Minister in 1783 Wilberforce was his most loyal supporter. It was at this time that the gay young man of leisure suddenly had his career turned into an unexpected channel. Between 1784 and 1785 Wilberforce was touched by the influence of the evangelical revival, and partly through the influence of John Newton —the fierce old slaver turned clergyman—he was converted. For the rest of his life he was guided by a sense of the nearness and goodness of God. His old interests faded, and clubs, parties, and theatres saw him no more. In this new spirit he became interested in the slave trade, until he was convinced that it should be stopped. The final push came from Pitt, who during a country walk one summer's day persuaded Wilberforce to take up in Parliament the abolition of the slave trade.

His influence there depended on three things. First, he had Pitt as Prime Minister and his best friend; secondly, he possessed a quite extraordinary power of speech, and his exceptionally pleasant voice gained him the title of 'the nightingale of the House'; and finally he belonged to no political party and thus could gain support from both Whigs and Tories. These assets, in addition to his high ability and character, gave him the influence in Parliament without which the abolitionist cause might have failed, and would certainly have been delayed. Yet such was his power that not only were the slave trade and slavery abolished but also their abolition took a surprisingly high priority. Factories and mines in Great Britain still depended on the extreme exploitation of child labour, when slavery no longer existed in the British Empire. Wilberforce made the victory of the abolitionists certain; he also hastened its arrival.

The Parliamentary campaign. Wilberforce began his campaign to get Parliament to abolish the slave trade in 1788, but the struggle was long and hard, and it was not until 1807 that the bill prohibiting 'all manner of dealing and trading in slaves' was passed, and it did not become operative until 1808. Even then slavery itself continued until a further bill was passed in 1833 by which the legal status of slavery was to cease within a year, while £20,000,000 was to be paid as compensation to the slave owners. It was fitting that Wilberforce should have lived until the passing of this bill was certain. He died a month before it was actually passed. 'Thank God', he said, 'that I should witness a day in which England is willing to give £20 million for the abolition of slavery.'

The abolition movement and East Africa. Although the abolition bills of 1807 and 1833 only applied within the British Empire, their implications were far-reaching. For one thing, there was the economic consideration that having forbidden British ships to participate in the trade the government was not anxious to see the ships of other countries take over and profit in their place. Therefore a series of agreements, which were not very effective, were made with Portugal, Spain, and France. But in addition to this economic argument there was also in Britain a widespread desire to see the slave trade ended throughout the world, because people had sincerely come to believe that it was an evil thing.

The scope and conditions of the slave trade on the East African coast had been realized in Britain as a result of British interests in India and the Indian Ocean, yet it was one thing to observe the trade and quite another to know how to stop it, for Seyyid Said was a completely independent ruler. Slaves were his most valuable export and the British were not anxious to antagonize him by high-handed demands that he should abolish slaving altogether. Therefore they first of all attempted to persuade him, not to abolish the trade, but to limit it to certain areas.

The Moresby Treaty, 1822. The first definite move in this direction was the Moresby Treaty of 1822. For centuries slaves had been shipped from East Africa to India, and they were also sent to the sugar plantation island of Mauritius which had come under British control after the Napoleonic Wars. Captain Moresby, on behalf of the Indian and Mauritius governments, managed to persuade Seyyid Said to forbid his slaving ships to approach these two areas or to sell slaves to any Christians, but the treaty did not in any way interfere with the trade between Zanzibar and the Sultan's dominions in Oman, which were the main market. Moreover, it depended for its enforcement upon the British naval patrols, and as the Indian Ocean was too large to patrol effectively not many smugglers were caught and the Moresby Treaty had very little effect.

The Owen Protectorate, 1823–6. It so happened that the very year after the Moresby Treaty had been signed it looked as though the British intended to take a short cut to abolition in one region of the coast when Captain Owen established his protectorate over Mombasa. Seyyid Said was understandably taken aback by what appeared to be a hostile act by the British Government, but in fact, as we have seen already, the protectorate was entirely unofficial. Owen did achieve his object of temporarily ending the slave trade through the town, but, as the British Government could hardly support him against the Sultan and he could not continue alone, in 1826 he withdrew—much to Seyyid Said's relief.

The Hamerton Treaty, 1845. More than twenty years went by before the British made another move to persuade Said to restrict the slave trade in his dominions. Again the policy was one of restriction, not abolition, and Captain Hamerton, as British Consul, officially requested that all exports of slaves from Zanzibar to Oman should end. This restriction was a much greater one than the Moresby Treaty, as Oman had been the chief purchaser, and if it had been effective the Hamerton Treaty would have ended all slave trading except between Zanzibar and the east coast towns. However, despite the Sultan's agreement in 1845 (and officially from 1847) the treaty could not be properly enforced and slaving continued.

Difficulties of the policy of restriction. It took nearly another thirty years to convince the British Government that attempts to restrict the East African slave trade instead of abolishing it completely could never be more than partially successful. Nevertheless, during that time the restrictions imposed by the Hamerton Treaty were made as strict as possible, and Seyyid Majid, who succeeded Seyyid Said, forbade any dhows to sail from Zanzibar during the time of the southwest monsoon, and imposed heavy punishment upon anyone selling slaves to the northern Arabs. In theory it was impossible to smuggle slaves from Zanzibar to the north. But in fact the whole system met with such universal opposition from the Sultan's subjects that the laws depended for their enforcement upon the Sultan's untrustworthy Baluchi garrison at Zanzibar, whom the slavers openly defied, and on

Map 5. Slave-trade treaties.

the British naval patrol in the Indian Ocean. This patrol normally consisted of seven or eight small cruisers stationed along the African coast to watch the area of export, and between the mouths of the Red Sea and the Persian Gulf to watch the area of import. From these cruisers smaller boats, carrying about twenty men, were launched, and these made explorations of several days, or even weeks, up the inlets along the coast. It was an extremely unhealthy, dangerous, and heartbreaking business. Malaria took a heavy toll of life, and the Arab slavers fought desperately when caught and often outnumbered and killed their attackers. But perhaps the main difficulty was in distinguishing between a dhow carrying slaves, and a dhow carrying legal goods, for the Arabs usually claimed that their slaves were crew. Out of 400 dhows examined, for example, in the early part of 1870, only eleven were condemned as slavers, and it was reckoned that while over 2500 slaves were caught by the patrol between 1867 and 1869, 37,000 were successfully smuggled overseas. In brief, the British naval patrol, despite all its heroic efforts, was a failure, for the main flow of the East African slave trade still went on.

Decision for complete prohibition. Meanwhile, Livingstone had seen the slave trade in action in the African interior, and his vivid descriptions gave a new impetus to the abolitionists' efforts in East Africa. As a result, in 1871 Parliament appointed a select committee to inquire into the question. The conclusion they reached was that so long as the slave trade was still permitted between Zanzibar and the coast towns the work of the naval patrols was made unnecessarily difficult, and smuggling was sure to continue on a large scale. Unanimously they agreed that the only answer was to prohibit the East African slave trade completely. A special mission led by Sir Bartle Frere, the ex-Governor of Bombay, was sent to Zanzibar to gain the Sultan's agreement to this proposal.

The Frere mission and treaty of 1873. In January 1873 the mission arrived at Zanzibar and was met with great ceremony and friendliness by the Sultan Barghash. Three months later it left with less ceremony, less friendliness, and an absolute refusal by the Sultan to accept complete abolition. The reason was obvious, for the abolition of the slave trade would certainly mean, within a fairly short time, the abolition of slavery itself, because the birth-rate among slaves was far below the death-rate. As the economy of Zanzibar was based upon slave labour Barghash's refusal is easily understandable. However, the British Government was not to be put off, and when Frere had made his report methods of peaceful persuasion were replaced by methods of force. Sir John Kirk, the British consul at Zanzibar, was

ordered to inform Barghash that unless he agreed to complete abolition Zanzibar itself would be blockaded by the British navy. Barghash
had no longer any choice. On 5 June 1873 he duly signed the treaty
making the slave trade illegal between all his ports, and at once
messengers were sent to close the gates of the Zanzibar slave market
for ever. Upon its site the Universities Mission built its Cathedral
Church with the altar standing where the whipping-post once
stood.

Methods of enforcement. The 1873 treaty was the death blow to the
Arab slave trade in East Africa, but the trade took some time to die.
The Arabs could no longer transport slaves by sea, but they could—
and they did—march them from Kilwa northwards along the coast,
secretly selling them as they went. Once more Kirk, who was the
greatest influence in the suppression of the east coast slave trade,
pressed Barghash to take action. Barghash had visited England in
1875 and stayed with Queen Victoria. He was vastly impressed by
the wealth and power, which far exceeded his expectations. When he
returned to Zanzibar in 1876 he was very ready to put Kirk's suggestions into practice by making two proclamations: one forbade slaves
to be moved by land; the other forbade slave caravans to approach
the coast from the interior. In order that these proclamations should
be effective the Sultan also raised a new armed force which was
trained and commanded by Lt. Lloyd Mathews. This force was on
the watch for slavers by land in the same way as the naval patrols
were on the watch by sea, and Lloyd Mathews proved himself to be
not only a soldier of reckless courage but also one of the most trusted
advisers of the sultans for nearly thirty years, until his death in 1901.

These measures, and the determination of Kirk and the Sultan to
enforce them, had a decisive effect, especially in Kilwa, which was the
greatest of the slave-collecting ports. There the population made
£120,000 a year from slaving and had no intention of giving it up, but
when a small army from Zanzibar and a British warship were sent
against them there was no more room for argument. When Kilwa
still tried to evade the proclamations in 1877, the governor himself
was thrown into the common prison in irons, which settled the

matter. So Kilwa gave up slaving and quickly developed a trade in rubber instead.

Meanwhile, further north in Mombasa, a crowd of low-class Swahili slavers rioted and threatened to attack the Church Missionary Society's station of Freretown, where freed slaves were kept and trained for employment. Here the Arabs supported the governor, and the riot was rapidly dispersed.

Thus, from 1877 the East African slave trade became a trickle compared to the former flood, and legitimate trade gradually took its place. Yet Livingstone's lesson was nevertheless true; it was only by opening up and occupying the interior that the slave trade was finally and completely extinguished, for it was only at the very end of the century that the last slave caravan was caught on the shores of Lake Nyasa.

The effects of abolition. The end of the slave trade was the beginning of a new age for East Africa. It changed the country within a generation from a land of wars and insecurity, into a land of comparative peace where development was possible. For this the British abolition movement, stretching through the century from Granville Sharp to Sir John Kirk, was fundamentally responsible. One testimony among many is that of Joseph Thomson: 'If the Anti-Slavery Society', he wrote, 'require an argument for continuing their good work they have it here [the present Tanganyika], for undoubtedly the stoppage of the slave traffic formed the turning point in the great moral and social revolution which has taken place.'

The abolition of slavery in East Africa. With the end of the slave trade slavery itself was doomed for, as we have seen, the death-rate of slaves far exceeded their birth-rate. However, slavery was not merely allowed to die a natural death. It was hustled on its way by a series of decrees. The first was an agreement made between the British Government and the Sultan in 1889, by which it was agreed that all persons entering the Sultan's dominions after 1 November of that year should be free, and added that children born after 1 January 1890 should be free also. This decree was followed by further instructions giving slaves the right to complain against their masters. The most

47

important step came in 1897 when a decree abolishing the legal status of slavery on Zanzibar and Pemba was signed by the Sultan on 5 April. By this decree slaves were able to obtain their freedom by application to the District Courts, and compensation was to be paid to the owners. Many slaves were slow in claiming this freedom, and the 1897 decree was heavily criticized by the missions as inadequate. Its moderation was due to the fear that too strict and rapid a declaration might lead to the ruin of the clove plantations, and it came as a surprise to every-one when, in fact, the production of cloves rose after 1897 instead of declining.

So far as the mainland was concerned abolition was less rapid. The legal status of slavery was not abolished in the British area until 1907. In 1910 Compensation Courts were set up in Mombasa, Lamu, and other coastal towns, and, in Zanzibar and Pemba, compensation could not be claimed after 1 December 1911. In the German area the pace was slower still. The Germans had indeed taken steps to improve the conditions of slavery and had proclaimed the freedom of all children born in, or after, 1905, but it was not until Tanganyika became a British protectorate that the legal status of slavery was finally abolished.

CHAPTER IV

EUROPE HEARS OF AFRICA

Geographical obstacles. Until modern times, deserts have been as serious an obstacle in the way of men's movements as the oceans over which they learnt to sail, the mountains they climbed, and the forests through which they pushed their way. That is why the Sahara divided Africa into two: a northern Muslim portion linked with Mediterranean Europe, consisting of Egypt, Libya, Tripoli, Tunis and Morocco; the grasslands and forests of tropical Africa, which in their turn are linked with the sub-tropical countries of South Africa and Rhodesia.

The inaccessible interior. The second of these areas was further isolated because travel from the sea was hindered by the scarp edge of the plateau which forms the interior of Africa and causes the rivers flowing down to the coast to be broken by waterfalls and rapids. Men were unable, therefore, to reach the interior of Africa in the way they were able to reach the interior of North America; for not only was the way guarded by these obstacles, it was further blocked by forests and mangrove swamps.

Limits of early exploration. Of the four main obstacles to men's movements in the southern part of Africa which have been listed in the first paragraph, only one had been overcome by the end of the eighteenth century; and Swift's well-known verse

> So Geographers, in Afric maps,
> With savage pictures fill their gaps,
> And o'er uninhabitable downs,
> Place elephants for want of towns

still rang true, despite the great discoveries of the sixteenth and seventeenth centuries. These had merely revealed the coast of Africa to the people of Europe. The eastern side of this had, of course, long been known to the peoples of Asia. These, however, had been halted by the lack of navigable rivers which is shown in the map on page 50.

Nor had men found easy the long march up from the coast through the waterless land which stretched inland for many miles behind most of the coast. The early traders, therefore, stayed on the coastal plain, where men died from fever.

Map 6. The navigable stretches of waterways in Africa.

First contacts with Africans. Some knowledge of the interior was possessed by the Arab slavers, and the Portuguese had had considerable knowledge of parts of it; but there was no real contact between the Africans and the peoples of either the East or the West until the nineteenth century. It was then that the first vague outline of the features of the interior became known to the peoples of Europe. They had been known for centuries to the Africans who lived there, but travel for these was still a slow matter, and very few had knowledge of any large area. The coming of European explorers was to bring Africa into touch with the peoples of the West. This was important for it brought the stimulus of new ideas to East Africa. It was also important for the people of Europe, who were finding out about a continent that was to play a big part in world affairs in the twentieth century.

Everywhere the explorers went they came across trade with its tolls, market-places, tracks and people who enjoyed singing, story-telling, dancing and drinking. The degree of organization varied from that of nomad tribes to the well run kingdom of Kimweri described on page 130. Those for whom the explorers wrote were usually more interested in Africa itself than its peoples till Livingstone wrote and made his fellow-Europeans realize that Africans were human beings with all their faults and virtues, just like themselves. Europeans had for a very long time been fascinated by two mysteries in Africa: one the source of the Nile and the other the course of the Niger. Old charts show that Africa was one of the three continents which were known in ancient days. Yet, on closer examination it will be seen that the Nile is drawn as rising in very queer places, and it flows in impossible directions. It even sometimes joins the Niger.

Exploration of the Niger. The course of the Niger was the first of the two mysteries to be solved. In 1788 the African Association was founded to provide the money for expeditions to find out where the Niger went. The Association was to choose the leaders, and eight years later they had their first real success when they employed a young man called Mungo Park. At the time there were considered to be two possible approaches, from the north and from the Gambia.

On his first journey (1795–8) Mungo Park tried the second way, and wrote that he was successful in seeing at Segu 'the great object of my mission, the long-sought-for, majestic Niger, glittering to the evening sun, as broad as the Thames at Westminster, and flowing slowly to the eastward '. Park went back to Scotland and married, but his thoughts kept turning to the mystery of where the Niger flowed to the sea. In 1805 he returned to Africa at the head of an expedition three-quarters of whom died. This did not check Park, who was determined to push on, even if the others died too. He wrote: 'I would at least die on the Niger.' And such was his end, reported a later explorer, Clapperton, when in 1825 he reached the spot where Park was drowned.

Five years later the mystery of the Niger was solved by Clapperton's companion, Richard Lander, who sailed down the Niger to its wide delta, and found out that it had long been familiar to men under the name of the Oil Rivers.

The problem of the Nile. In the second century A.D. there was a great Greek geographer called Ptolemy. In his time men knew that there were both a Blue and a White Nile, and it was Ptolemy's opinion that both the Niles had their source in lakes. The Blue Nile, he considered, rose in a lake in the east. The White Nile, on the other hand, he thought, rose in large lakes which were fed by the Mountains of the Moon. This was the sort of information that some times trickled through from traders with the east coast of Africa; but for over sixteen hundred years the peoples of Europe knew no more about the source of the White Nile. It was a fascinating problem; and the first step to its solution was taken when, in 1770, the British explorer Bruce reached the source of the Blue Nile at Gheesh in Abyssinia, south of Lake Tana.

Krapf and Rebmann. In the middle of the nineteenth century, European interest was greatly increased by the discoveries of two German missionaries, Krapf and Rebmann. They were both members of the Church Missionary Society, and when Krapf arrived in Mombasa in 1844 he had already worked for some time as a missionary in Abyssinia. In 1846 he was joined by Rebmann and together they established a mission station at Rabai. Malaria had already killed Krapf's wife and child; and throughout their work in East Africa both had to struggle with unknown diseases, master new languages, and explore the land sufficiently to establish the chain of mission posts of which Krapf dreamt as the bases from which Christianity could be spread throughout the interior.

In 1847 Rebmann became the first European of whom we have record to go into the interior of East Africa. In that year he went into the Taita hills, about a hundred miles from Mombasa. It was in these hills that a pygmy people had probably lived, some 500 years earlier, before they were poisoned by later invaders, in whose history Rebmann was interested.

Discovery of Mounts Kilimanjaro and Kenya. As, by 1847, many of the Taita tribe had spread to Taveta and to the slopes of Kilimanjaro, where they mingled with the Chagga, Rebmann decided in the following year to follow up what he had heard about the Chagga people and the mountainous country in which they lived, and on 11 May had his first glimpse of Kilimanjaro. This was the first of four journeys which he made to and from the Chagga country. At the end of this he was convinced of the existence of a great snow-covered mountain, a fact which Krapf later confirmed. Their reports were not however believed at first; one man even wrote a book to prove that Kilimanjaro could not exist. He had not realized the passionate interest which Krapf and Rebmann had in scientific accuracy. In the former's book, *Travels, Researches and Missionary Labours*, the care with which all reports about the mountain had been checked is clearly shown. On 3 December 1849 Krapf had a glimpse of East Africa's other great mountain, Kenya, which he was shown by Chief Kivoi when staying with the Kamba at Kitui. This chief was an important trader, as well as being a typical Kamba in that he was a great traveller, and had been therefore to both mountains. On hearing that Krapf wanted to go beyond the river Tana to the country in which the mountain was to be found, he offered to accompany him there; and the trip was finally arranged in 1850. On the way the party was attacked by robbers, Kivoi was killed and his followers scattered: Krapf struggled on in the direction of the Tana, longing only for water. As soon as his thirst was satisfied, he began to explore the river, which he estimated as 150 feet wide and from six to seven feet deep.

Burton and Speke. These discoveries interested the Royal Geographical Society so much that they commissioned Richard Burton to investigate reports that there existed a lake of sweet water, 800 miles long by 300 miles broad. It seemed very unlikely; but the idea interested Burton, an Indian Army officer who was a fine Arabic scholar and had already made a daring journey to Mecca in disguise. In 1856 he set out with Lt. John H. Speke, also of the Indian Army. As they drew nearer to Lake Tanganyika, they found, by conversation with the Arabs, that the great lake they were seeking was really three lakes, great distances apart, and that the tales Krapf and Rebmann had heard referred to Lakes Tanganyika, Nyasa, and the largest of all, later named Victoria. Despite the help they had received from the Arabs in the way of transport, supplies and information, the journey had proved a great strain and both men were ill. Speke had a form of temporary blindness and could not even see Lake Tanganyika clearly when it lay in the distance; while Burton was so broken down in health that, on their return to headquarters, the Arab centre of Tabora, he let Speke go on alone in the direction of Victoria Nyanza. On this journey he was lucky and, on 3 August 1858, he was able to write:

The pale blue waters of the Nyanza burst suddenly upon my gaze. It was early morning. The distant sea-line of the north horizon was defined in the calm atmosphere, between the north and west points of the compass, but even this did not afford me any idea of the breadth of the lake. . . . I no longer felt any doubt that the lake at my feet gave birth to that interesting river [Nile] the source of which has been the source of so much speculation and the object of so many explorers.

When Speke told this news to Burton the latter admitted that there might be a lake there, but denied the possibility that it was the source of the Nile. Speke's guess later proved right.

Speke and Grant. On coming back to England, Speke was commissioned by the Royal Geographical Society to return to Africa to check the details of his discovery and to trace the link between the lake and the Nile. This time he took as his companion an old friend called Grant; they left Zanzibar in 1860.

Speke and the Nile. On the earlier expedition Burton and Speke had been forced to return to Tabora, partly because of illness, and partly because they ran out of calico, which they needed to purchase supplies on their journey. Burton said bitterly that on this kind of journey baggage was life. The truth of this statement was to be shown in the journeys of many other explorers, among them Livingstone and Stanley. Speke, too, continued to have endless trouble with porters and baggage. At one time he complained that more than half his property had been stolen; and it was not until he reached Karagwe, which is to the west of the Victoria, that he and Grant were able to rest and enjoy the generous hospitality of the local chief, King Rumanika. When they went north from here Grant became so ill that he had to be left behind, leaving Speke, in 1862, to become the first European to enter Buganda and to be received with ceremony at the court of the Kabaka, of which Speke wrote,

At each gate as we passed, officers on duty opened and shut it for us, jingling the big bells which are hung upon them, as they sometimes are at shop-doors to prevent a silent, stealthy entrance. The first court passed, I was even more surprised to find the unusual ceremonies that awaited me. There courtiers of high dignity stepped forward to greet me, dressed in the most scrupulously neat fashion.

Here, on the north shore of Lake Victoria, he reached what proved to be the Nile and told his men to bathe in the holy river for, as he wrote, he saw that 'Old Father Nile without any doubt rises in the Victoria Nyanza, and, as I had foretold, that lake is the great source of the river'. A tablet was later placed where Speke declared that the Nile had its origin. Today a growing industrial centre, Jinja, is developing there.

Return journey. Presently Grant recovered sufficiently to join Speke and they went to the kingdom of Bunyoro. Part of the journey had to be carried out in boats made of planks and tied together with rags; and at the end of it they found a kingdom which was less developed than Buganda. Here they were detained for a time by the king, who was on bad terms with the Kabaka of Buganda, so they were pleased when they were free to continue their journey northwards to Cairo.

This took longer than they had expected and, when they finally reached Gondokoro, 'Speke was excessively lean; he had walked the whole way from Zanzibar, never having ridden once during that wearying march. Grant was in rags, his bare knees projecting through the remnants of trousers.'

The Bakers. This description of them was given by Samuel Baker. He was at Gondokoro with his determined wife, who had insisted on sharing her husband's dangers. The Bakers were personal friends of Speke and had set out from the mouth of the Nile to follow it up to its source. In doing this they hoped to meet Speke and Grant and bring them stores which they would be certain to need. The latter had meanwhile been coming down from Victoria Nyanza by the course which the Bakers had proposed to follow south, and the two parties met at Gondokoro. Baker's idea of following the Nile from its mouth, and so finding its source, seems an obvious one. But the country along the Sudd portion of the Nile was a formidable obstacle which he was fortunate to have passed, and there were further difficulties ahead.

The meeting in Gondokoro was, therefore, sensational. Baker wrote: 'All my men perfectly mad with excitement; firing salutes as usual with ball cartridges, they shot one of my donkeys, a melancholy sacrifice as an offering at the completion of this geographical discovery.'

Discovery of Lake Albert. At first Baker was convinced that his friends had really solved the mystery of the sources of the Nile. But when Speke told him of a rumoured lake to the south-west of the Victoria, and when the four explorers had discussed the lie of the land, it became clear that in Baker's own words 'one leaf of the laurel remained' for him to pick. Armed with Speke's own map, the Bakers set off across country in the direction of the kingdom of Bunyoro, and reached the southern tip of the lake in March 1864. They named it Lake Albert.

Samuel Baker had meant to celebrate this by all the men giving three cheers in English style; but the knowledge that he had found a great inland sea, one of the twin sources of the Nile which men had sought for centuries, overwhelmed him. Instead he thanked God for having guided and supported the party through all dangers, with this magnificent result.

Murchison Falls. Sailing in canoes up the eastern shore of Lake Albert, the Bakers reached the point where it was entered by the Victoria Nile; and they completed their exploration by going up this river for some eighteen miles. Suddenly there was a roar of water and they came to a great waterfall of the Nile, which they named the Murchison Falls in honour of the President of the Royal Geographical Society. The christening ceremony was an exciting one. Baker shot at the crocodiles, a boatman was so frightened that he collapsed on the bottom of the canoe, a paddle was lost, a hippo rammed the boat and the African women with the party screamed. Finally it all became calm again and the boat was held steady while Baker sketched the Murchison Falls.

The Nile system. The exploration was now almost complete. It was clear that the Nile was fed by at least two lakes, Victoria and Albert (see map on page 111). Another map (on page 63) will also show one reason why men were so long confused by the Nile, the Congo and the Zambezi. This reason is that the watersheds of these great rivers all come near together. The whole Nile system, indeed, was not accurately mapped until another explorer, Stanley, paid a visit to this area years later. Before this a very great explorer, Livingstone, had puzzled over the problem for years.

Livingstone. Mungo Park, Speke, Burton, Grant and Baker were all geographers and naturalists whose interests were in scientific exploration; but Krapf and Rebmann had shown the close link that could exist between the spreading of Christianity and the discovering of more about the unknown continent; and the greatest explorer of all was a medical missionary, David Livingstone.

Youth. By the time he was ten David Livingstone had shown great determination. As there was no money to educate him, he went to work for fourteen hours a day in a cotton mill, but that did not mean that he gave up hopes of learning. When he was ten he bought a Latin Grammar with his first week's wages and studied after working hours. In this way he qualified himself to be accepted by the London

Map 7. Explorers of East Africa.

Missionary Society; and while waiting to be posted abroad he studied medicine and became a doctor.

First post. He went to his first post in Bechuanaland in 1841, and from there he crossed the Kalahari Desert and got into touch with the Africans living round Lake Ngami. Pushing further north still in search of sites for missions he met the Makololo, who were to give him his most faithful followers; and it was through his good relations with this tribe that in 1851 he found the mighty River Zambezi. He also learnt that the Makololo had recently combined with another tribe to raid for slaves with which to buy guns from the Arabs. This helped to convince him that it was essential to adopt a positive policy in regard to this evil, if it was to be stopped. To do this he thought it was necessary to establish a mission station which should also be a centre for farmers and traders; for in his opinion the greatest obstacle to the spread of Christianity among the Africans was the poverty and ignorance which surrounded them with fear. If they were to be freed from this, they would have to be introduced to a higher standard of living and shown that it was possible for the different tribes to work together, thus increasing their power to resist violence.

First expedition. In those days a settlement of the nature Livingstone had in mind depended on climate and communications. He considered that he had already found a healthy area in the Bakota uplands: the problem was to link it with the civilization of the coast. In searching for this, Livingstone set out on the first of his three great journeys. This lasted from 1853 to 1856 and took him right across Africa, from Barotseland to the Atlantic Ocean at Loanda, and then back to reach the sea on the east coast at Quelimane. For a large part of this journey he had followed the course of the Zambezi, and in doing so he had in 1855 discovered the Victoria Falls. Now he wondered whether this river would not be a better means of communication than any land route.

Appeal to Cambridge. On his return to England he found himself famous through the publication of his book *Missionary Travels and Researches*; and he used his fame to appeal to Cambridge University for help in carrying on the work he had begun in opening the way for commerce and Christianity in Africa. The result was the foundation of the Universities Mission to Central Africa, whose work is described in chapter v. He also secured government support for his second important expedition, the object of which was to explore the Zambezi valley up from the mouth of the river in the hope that it might prove a good means of communication.

Second expedition. This second expedition lasted from 1858 to 1864; and was different from the first in that Livingstone travelled on a steam launch, the *Ma Robert*, and took with him European companions, with whom, however, he did not get on so well as with Africans. The first difficulty was the discovery that the Zambezi was not as easily navigable as Livingstone had hoped, and when he had surveyed its mouth, therefore, he turned to the Shiré River. This flows into the Zambezi not far from its mouth and led Livingstone to the Murchison Falls (not to be confused with those on the Nile). At this point he left the steamer and set out on foot for a great lake which he was told was nearby. It took a month to reach and proved to be Lake Shirwa. The highlands around seemed to be a possible site for the kind of missionary colony Livingstone had in mind, and after he had returned to Tete he marched off again to find out more about the land. Information, however, was not easily obtained. This was country where the slave trade had turned fertile land into a wilderness, and the results were to be seen in starving people and corpses. In these circumstances the Africans were afraid of the explorers; however, Livingstone persisted, and in 1859 he reached the southern end of Lake Nyasa. The size of this lake convinced him that it could prove a valuable waterway and strike a blow at the slave trade, which he was more determined than ever to uproot. He reasoned that if a steamer were placed on the lake, ivory could be bought for European goods and transported by water all the way to England, except for one stretch above the Murchison Falls. If ivory were carried in this way, the slave trade would be cut out, for it would never pay to drive slaves all the way to the coast by land, unless they could pay for their keep by carrying ivory. His letters home telling of his ideas persuaded several missionaries to come out, but the area proved too unhealthy, and the mission was abandoned.

It was later that Livingstone's discovery of Lake Nyasa led to mission stations, followed by traders, and eventually to the establishment of the Protectorate of Nyasaland. At the time the importance of his new discoveries was not realized; and he had also to face great personal distress through the death of his wife, who had come out to join him.

Object of third expedition. Undaunted by the disappointments at the end of his second expedition, Livingstone set out on his third important journey in 1866. This was to be his last. Its object was geographical: Speke and Baker had reported their discoveries, but Burton and some others maintained that their theories of the source of the Nile were incorrect, or at least incomplete. Besides, no one yet knew where the central watershed lay. The President of the Royal Geographical Society suggested that Livingstone might be able to settle the question by going from the Upper Rovuma to Lake Tanganyika and then exploring westwards. This would give him a chance to see if the Nile not only flowed out of Lakes Victoria and Albert in the north, as Speke and Baker had shown, but first flowed into the southern end of these lakes. If this idea should prove correct, the true source might be Lake Tanganyika. Livingstone was far from convinced that Speke and Baker were right and was delighted at the opportunity of exploring these possibilities. He at once agreed, provided he was allowed also to use every opportunity to fight against the slave trade and to spread Christianity.

Results. In view of these plans, Livingstone decided to operate from two bases. In the first, Zanzibar, he planned to recruit porters, obtain supplies and arrange for reinforcements. The second was to be Ujiji on Lake Tanganyika. From here Livingstone meant to explore the land around, looking for the Nile and endeavouring to identify the central watershed. Although far to the south of his goal, the true Nile sources, Livingstone's last journey was not unproductive of results. He discovered Lake Bangweulu in 1868 and was exploring the Lualaba, or upper reaches of the Congo, when he died.

Difficulties. Throughout this last expedition Livingstone had great difficulties to overcome. He hated the atmosphere which he thought slavery created in Zanzibar, and could not recruit sufficient reliable porters. Nor was he popular with the Arabs, or the Banyans of the coast, who knew of his ceaseless efforts to get slavery stopped. This made it difficult for his friend Kirk to send further supplies to his second base at Ujiji, near Lake Tanganyika, especially as few were willing to carry the explorer's letters back to Kirk for fear of what they might reveal about the slavery in the district.

Lack of supplies. Yet Livingstone was in great need of further supplies, for a porter had deserted with his medicine chest, and without drugs he was soon dangerously weakened by fever. Despite this he carried on to Lake Tanganyika, undaunted by the desertion of most of his porters. From here he discovered Lake Bangweulu in 1868, then returned to Lake Tanganyika, where he found that the supplies which he had arranged to have sent on from Zanzibar had nearly all been stolen. After resting awhile, he set out again looking for the Nile and found the Congo, or Lualaba River as he called it, in 1871. He then returned to Ujiji, where in 1871 he was met by Stanley, whose commission to find out what was happening to Livingstone will be described later.

Death. Stanley failed to persuade him to return. He was determined to solve the problem of the Nile while he still had the strength to do so; but his once magnificent body was fast failing, and on 30 April 1873 he died near Lake Bangweulu.

Achievements. It is not easy to sum up Livingstone's achievements: he carried on Wilberforce's work for the abolition of slavery, enlisting the sympathy of the British for the Africans by making Africa real to them through his letters and books. As an explorer he changed the map of Africa. Lastly, it was through his work that Nyasaland eventually became a part of the British Commonwealth. Today his reputation still stands high as an utterly fearless man, serving the highest ideals, and marked by a real understanding of the Africans, which may have come from his great affection for them. This was returned in full measure by the faithful Susi and Chummah who had followed him in all his travels, and on his death carried his journals and his body for hundreds of miles to the coast.

Map 8. The watersheds of Central Africa.

Stanley. Among those bearing Livingstone's coffin at the state funeral in Westminster Abbey was Henry Morton Stanley (1841–1904), who in his turn was to rank as a great African explorer. All his life he was to be a great admirer of the man to whom he had brought supplies and news when he was cut off from the world at Ujiji. It is more doubtful whether Livingstone would have continued to feel a similar admiration for Stanley if he could have known how bitterly the latter was to attack Kirk, Livingstone's faithful ally and friend in the fight against slavery. Stanley even made a speech in Edinburgh, where Kirk had been a student, in which he spoke of the indifference of the 'gentleman [Kirk] who had got his fame and position as the friend of Dr Livingstone', and 'left him in Africa, silent, alone, deserted and almost at death's door'. In saying this he referred to the fact that Kirk had not been able to get supplies to Livingstone when he had been stranded in Tanganyika and that Livingstone was eventually relieved by Stanley himself. This failure, however, was not due to indifference on Kirk's part, but to the fact that the caravans had not been able to get through.

Character. This readiness to attack others, regardless of the damage he could do to their careers, was typical of Stanley, who troubled very little about other people's feelings. It is for this reason that before Stanley's character is condemned, and his achievements praised, his early life must be described. Its hardships exceeded by far the difficulties that faced Livingstone, so that by the time Stanley had won success in life, he had become a self-confident man who was convinced that those who could not overcome difficulties were weaklings. He thought he knew by then the rough ways of the world and was prepared to give as good as he received, with the result that people found it difficult to accept his successes.

Youth. John Rowlands, later to be called Henry Morton Stanley, lost his father soon after his birth at Denbigh in 1841, and his mother left him to be brought up by his grandfather and two uncles. When he was four his grandfather also died and the two uncles sent him to live with a couple to whom they paid half a crown a week. Later, on being asked to increase this sum, they refused and John was sent to the workhouse. This shock was made even worse because he was told that he was going to live with his aunt Mary who lived in a big house. When he got inside it proved to be the workhouse. Here food was scarce and beatings frequent; but through it all John grew in strength and intelligence and eventually he became head boy in the workhouse school. At fifteen, being no longer prepared to be beaten by the cruel head of the workhouse for something he had not done, he turned on his master and gave him the thrashing instead. He then ran away to his other grandfather, who refused to do anything for him and told him to get out of the house. Fortunately John had worked success-fully at his lessons, and in the end was accepted as a pupil teacher by a schoolmaster cousin. He was not really welcome, however, and eventually he ran away to sea. Here he lived again in a world of blows and kicks. On landing in America fortune was kind to him and he was adopted by a Mr Stanley, who gave him his own name. Mr Stanley, however, did not live long enough to make provision for his adopted son. So Henry Stanley, as he must now be called, was caught up in the American Civil War, out of which he was finally invalided. He then worked his way back to England and in his journal wrote later:

Like a bride arraying herself in her best for her lover, I had arranged my story to please one who would, at last, I hoped prove an affectionate mother! But I found no affection, and I never again sought for, or expected, what I discovered had never existed.

I was told that 'I was a disgrace to them in the eyes of their neigh-bours, and they desired me to leave as speedily as possible'.

'*How I found Livingstone.*' Eventually a gift of vivid description and aptitude for a life of adventure gave Stanley the chance to become a press correspondent; and a brilliant piece of reporting won for him the commission to go wherever dramatic events were taking place. In this way Stanley became the first explorer to be financed by a news-paper when he was commissioned, in 1871, by the *New York Herald* to find David Livingstone. This mission was not likely to be popular with the more conservative Englishmen, who rightly said that although Livingstone might be cut off his whereabouts were perfectly well known to the well-informed, and who did not care for the idea of the

British national hero being rescued by an American newspaperman. Nor was Stanley's account conciliatory. His book, however, *How I found Livingstone*, was a best-seller. In 1874 the British *Daily Telegraph* and the American *New York Herald* fitted out an expedition under Stanley's leadership which was to complete the work of Speke, Grant, Baker and Livingstone.

'*Through the Dark Continent.*' This was geographically a most successful expedition and was later described by Stanley in *Through the Dark Continent*. It began with a long march towards Lake Victoria. As soon as the column entered Ituru it was clear that they were not welcome. Stanley, however, fought his way through, pursuing the defeated Africans from village to village and setting fire to each as soon as captured. From Ituru he entered friendly and hospitable land and travelled safely to Lake Victoria, which he circumnavigated, and so finally settled the question of its size and nature. This stage of the journey revealed the two sides of Stanley's character. On the one hand it brought him into touch with Mutesa, the Kabaka of Buganda. Their relations were friendly, and he wrote afterwards of the Kabaka's desire to imitate the ways of the Europeans which gave an opportunity to talk to him of Christianity. Later Stanley followed this up by appealing to the C.M.S. to send missionaries to Buganda. The other side of his nature was shown, however, to those who lived on Bumbireh Island in the Nyanza. The inhabitants had made it very clear that they violently resented Stanley's landing on the island to buy food on his journey to Uganda. He and his followers had indeed with difficulty escaped with their lives from the place. After further considerable trouble, Stanley maintained that the hostility of Bumbireh was blocking his route to Uganda. In his opinion, the only action he could take to clear the route was to attack the islanders with guns, having tempted them to show themselves in the open. The uselessness of spears against guns in these circumstances was shown. Forty-two Africans were killed and over a hundred were seen to retire wounded. Against this only two of Stanley's followers were injured, and those were by stones which had been thrown. This incident resulted in very strong protests from England condemning

Stanley's savage behaviour. It should be noted that his judges had not themselves lived through the terrifying moments when Stanley's first landing on Bumbireh was met with treacherous violence.

The source of the Nile. Next came the exploration of the land between Lakes Edward and Victoria. So began the final stage in solving the mystery of the Nile; for it was now clear that it had its principal source in Victoria Nyanza, which is higher than the secondary source in the Lakes Albert and Edward which are linked by the Semliki River. Some people, however, consider that the real source of the Nile is to be found in the Ruchuru, which the map on page 111 shows as the largest river flowing into Lake Edward.

The Congo. After this, Stanley carried out an equally thorough survey of Lake Tanganyika and then turned his attention to the river which Livingstone had called the Lualaba, but which is known today as the Congo. He reached this at Nyangwe. From here he had to force his way through land from which Livingstone had been forced to turn back by the unfriendly attitude of its people. Stanley partly solved the problem by coming to an arrangement to travel in the same party with Tippoo Tip, a well-known Arab slave dealer, and for a fortnight he marched through a forest so dense that it shut out the daylight and left the men to stumble in the half-light through streams and over fallen trees. At the end of this he was able to launch on the waters of the Congo the boat which his party had carried. Nor was the passage an easy one. The Stanley Falls, for one thing, blocked the way further down; and the boats had to be dragged past these in the face of ceaseless attacks from cannibals, shouting for human meat. But at last Stanley reached the great pool named after him, and in 1877, after losing his last European companion, struggled to a point which had already been surveyed on the lower Congo. For the rest of his career in Africa he was closely connected with the Congo. This was an area rich in commercial possibilities. Stanley, who had seen the pioneers in their wagons developing the west of the United States, was quick to appreciate these possibilities and to urge that England should take control of the Congo, a task which she refused. Leopold of the Belgians, however, was eager to undertake it and he eventually persuaded Stanley to return to Africa to open up the Congo for trade under Leopold's control.

Communications and trade. From 1879 Stanley spent five years developing communications and trading stations on the Congo, and signing treaties with over 450 independent African chiefs, who gave their rights of sovereignty and ownership to Leopold's Association. These were the years when Stanley was nicknamed Bula Mutari, or the Breaker of Rocks, by the Africans, who watched him working 2352 miles backwards and forwards to carve out only fifty-two miles of road.

Emin Pasha. Stanley returned to Africa a fourth time in 1887, on an expedition to rescue Emin Pasha, the governor of the equatorial province of the Sudan. Many felt that he was in danger of being over-whelmed by the forces of the Muslim prophet (the 'Mahdi') who had defeated the English General Gordon; for when Emin Pasha sent out an appeal for help a number of people not only wished to rescue him but also hoped that the rescue might result in his province of equatorial Africa being added either to the Congo State or to the Imperial British East Africa Company. Stanley was now so famous that he could make his own terms. He refused to lead the expedition unless it followed the short, but hazardous, route up the Congo. From his point of view this had two advantages. First of all, it gave him the chance of dealing with Tippoo Tip, who was threatening to get control of the new state of the Congo which was largely Stanley's creation. Tippoo Tip was now appointed governor of the Stanley Falls station, in which position he was to put down slavery below the Falls. Secondly, it offered the chance of further exploration.

The impenetrable forest. Stanley seized this opportunity when he set off from the Congo through the unknown forest to meet Emin Pasha. The horrors of this jungle were so great that only one-third of those who went into it with Stanley came out alive. Giant trees 150 feet high were so interlaced with thick creeper that there was no space between them, and all the time the men were attacked ceaselessly by painful insects and snakes, while in the undergrowth the pygmies lurked with their poisoned arrows and skewers. Over all there often hung a thick white mist, and food was so scarce that the expedition was threatened by starvation.

An unwelcome rescue. Five months later the survivors came out on a plateau leading to Lake Albert. Emin Pasha came to greet them, and to rescue his rescuers with gifts of supplies.

They did not receive the welcome they expected. Emin did not even wish to be rescued, if it meant leaving Equatoria, and it was with difficulty that Stanley persuaded him and his followers to come with him to Bagamoyo. (Before that was achieved Stanley had crossed the Great Congo Forest three times.) On this return journey Stanley saw the Mountains of the Moon for the first time. Later he was able to tell Europe of this important discovery in the book *In Darkest Africa* which he published on his return.

The last part of Stanley's life. This last journey was really the end of Stanley's work as an explorer. The rest of his life can be summarized very shortly; he married, was elected to Parliament in England, was knighted, and in 1904 died.

Joseph Thomson. One major task remained for those who sought to establish links between Europe and East and Central Africa. This was to find a quicker route from the coast to Uganda than the old track from Zanzibar via Bagamoyo, Tabora and Ujiji. It was known that a better way probably existed, for in 1882 Dr Fischer had reached Lake Naivasha from Kilimanjaro; but this route meant passing through Masailand, and travellers did not dare face the powerful tribe who lived there. However, the Royal Geographical Society was aware that a shorter path was badly needed if the slave trade was to be suppressed and trade encouraged. In 1883, then, Joseph Thomson was chosen to lead an expedition, 'To find whether a useful direct route for European travellers exists through the Masai country from any one of the East African ports to the Victoria Nyanza, and to examine Mount Kenya; to make a preliminary survey and to make observations regarding the peoples, rocks, animals and plants of the regions traversed'. Thomson's qualifications for this post were, first the success with which he had taken over the lead of an earlier Tanganyika expedition when he was only twenty, and secondly his qualifications as a scientist. His first attempt was, however, a failure and he was forced to retreat, because the numbers of his caravan proved too small to face the Masai, who were threatening to fight.

Across Masailand. His second attempt was luckier. The El Moran 'Masai Warriors' were away on a raid, so that he was able to reach Kikuyuland. Here the dense forests sheltered the Kikuyu, who attacked the expedition with poisoned arrows and stole all they could. From there he pushed on, past Lake Naivasha to El Menteita. He then took the great risk of leading a small party to Mount Kenya, through the Masai of Laikipia. That he got through, and was the first European to see the Aberdares and Thomson's Falls, was largely due to the skill with which he acted the part of a great Laibon (medicine man), who was able to cure a disease which was killing the cattle. After rejoining the main party, Thomson travelled on to Victoria Nyanza, being thus the first European to cross Masailand and find a quick route from Victoria Nyanza to the coast. He was also able to return with information about Mount Elgon, which he had included in his return journey.

Views on Kenya's prospects. Thomson's remarks about the prospects of the country that was soon to be crossed by the Uganda railway show that he had grasped its relative poverty:

Many people have proved with most convincing logical power that a railway is the proper means to open up the country. They have sketched with a daring hand a few thousand miles of the iron road, connecting the coast with the various great lakes: bringing untold wealth to Britain, and taking unlimited quantities of its Brummagem [industrial] wares and flimsy adulterated cottons instead. To make the picture complete, they have told us to expect, as an important result, the stoppage of wars and of the slave trade—industrious and contented tribes taking to civilized ways, and shouting unanimously for missionaries to come over and help them. The utter absurdity of such brilliant schemes will require no further proof than the remarks I have made upon the hopeless prospect of developing any trade in the interior for several generations to come.

The agricultural potentialities of part of this area were seen by a later explorer, Count Teleki, who was the first European to travel to

Lakes Rudolf and Stephanie. He wrote, 'In the light grey volcanic soil of Kikuyuland grow nearly all the cereals native to East Africa, and it is, in fact, the granary of a very extended district'; adding that 'The Wakikuyu are not only zealous agriculturists, they also keep bees and breed cattle, sheep, poultry and goats . . .'. His comments on the organization of the area are also interesting. 'There is no one ruler of the whole of Kikuyuland nor, indeed, of separate districts. Each valley is independent of every other, and has four elders of its own.'

CHAPTER V

MISSIONARY SOCIETIES AND THE DEVELOPMENT OF EAST AFRICA

African beliefs: Kamba. When the Christian missionaries came to East Africa they found that the inhabitants were used to the idea of one God (Mungu), but, unlike the Christians, they did not think of him as bothering about what happened among men. The practical Kamba, for instance, thought it was wasteful to give sacrifices to the creator of all things, or Mumbi as they called him, because he lived in the skies and was too far away to be influenced by men. They made their sacrifices to a man's 'aiimu' (spirits) who go and live in a wild fig tree when he dies. That is why small huts were often built close to fig trees.

Kikuyu. The Kikuyu also worshipped a god 'Ngai' who lived on Mount Kenya and was a god of love. He concerned himself with men in so far as he punished those who disobeyed him by sending famine, disease and death; but the Kikuyu considered that more ordinary troubles were due to the spirits of the dead. If assistance was needed the spirits of the ancestors would first be approached. If no help was given, it was assumed that they were offended and an approach might then be made to Ngai. His assistance would always be sought by a family group; no individual might ask for this on his own. Ngai was also called on in birth, death, marriage and initiation.

Baganda. The Baganda had rather different ideas. They believed in Lubare who lived in certain places. These Lubare had special power over some objects. The most important Lubare, for instance, was called Mukasa, and lived in the Victoria Nyanza. He not only controlled the waters of the lake but also had a fair amount of power over the whole of Buganda.

Masai. In Mr Richards's manuscript, 'History of the C.M.S. in the Highlands', he quotes an early missionary who wrote about the Masai beliefs that: 'Beyond their word for God, "Engai", I cannot find that they have any word for soul or spirit, not even for the spirits of the departed; in fact they seem to have no idea of a future existence. To them a man is like the beasts that perish.' He was worried also about their morals because they had no word for good that did not also have a bad sense.

These few examples serve as an indication of the kind of religions existing in East Africa before the coming of the Muslims and Christian Missionaries.

Spread of Islam. Most of the Muslims on the coast today are Shafite Sunnis, and it is reasonable to assume that the conversion of the coast people began some time after A.D. 813 when Muhammad bin Idris es Shafi, the founder of the Shafite school, started his teaching. After Seyyid Said's transfer of his capital to Zanzibar, the Arab traders carried their religion inland as far as the great lakes and later Uganda. At this stage Islam took root in several places and secured some African followers. However, converting people was solely the work of isolated Arabs, Swahili and Somali traders, and their African converts. It was not directed by any missionary organization and lacked plan, money and literature. Despite this, the period of European occupation from 1885 onwards was one in which the Muslim faith spread to parts of central and western Tanganyika, southern Uganda and a number of townships in Kenya; for European penetration of the interior meant that the Swahili population, who were Muslim, found openings as troops, traders, skilled craftsmen, interpreters, domestic servants etc., and could thus help to spread Islam.

Today, in British East Africa, there are thought to be over two million Muslims, that is, one-tenth of the total population, and among the African converts there are several hundred former Christians.

The first Muslim Mission to East Africa was opened in 1935 in Tabora, Tanganyika, by the Ahmadiyya Mission, and is now active in all three territories. The first task of its head in 1954, Sheikh Mubarah Ahmed, was to prepare a Swahili translation of the holy Koran with a commentary. Other Islamic literature is being produced;

but, apart from this, the Muslims have mostly conducted village Koranic schools, where the standard of religious and secular learning is low. As many Muslims are afraid of religious pressure if they send their children to Christian schools, the African and Arab communities are apt to be backward and economically handicapped. Nor has the Ahmadiyya mission yet undertaken hospital work of the type undertaken by the Christian missionaries. The Muslims who follow H.H. the Aga Khan, on the other hand, established schools, hospitals, dispensaries and libraries after the end of the First World War. They do not, however, support missionaries, for they believe that conversion should result from the activity of the individual.

Hinduism. From very early days, the Hindu religion has been practised along the coast by traders who visited East Africa from India and settled there. Hindus do not, however, regard it as part of their religion to make converts, for they recognize that their vegetarian and teetotal habits make it difficult to absorb those who were not born Hindu. This lack of missionary work accounts for the lack of further allusion being made to Hindus in this chapter.

Christian missionaries: Krapf. The first Christian missionaries belonged to the Church Missionary Society, which had been founded for work in Africa and the East. The pioneer in this society was Dr Krapf, whose large part in exploring a new country has been described in the previous chapter. In 1844 he set out from Zanzibar, armed with a letter of introduction from Seyyid Said which told the Arab governors of the coast that 'This letter is written on behalf of Dr Krapf, a good man who wishes to convert the world to God. Behave well to him, and be everywhere serviceable to him.' Two years later he was joined by the Rev. John Rebmann, and together they opened a mission station at Rabai, some fifteen miles inland from the present Mombasa. From here Rebmann moved to Kilimanjaro, home of the Chagga people, whence he startled Europe in 1848 by announcing that a snow-capped mountain was to be found near the Equator. But it was at Rabai that East Africa's first school was started a little later by Krapf, who realized that his converts must be taught to read the Bible, which in future was to be their guide.

The study of Swahili. These early missionaries were quick, too, to realize the importance of studying the languages of the people among whom they worked; and Krapf gave much time to this, with the result that he was able to publish the first Swahili dictionary, together with a translation of part of the Bible. He was followed in this work by Dr Steere of the Universities Mission to Central Africa, who gave a great deal of his time to studying Swahili. He was determined that this knowledge should be spread, and trained some of the young men at his first mission as printers; in 1865 the first copies of his book *A Handbook of the Swahili Language as spoken in Zanzibar* were produced in Zanzibar. Today his *Swahili Exercises* are regarded as the standard grammar of the language and studied by those who have to pass examinations in the subject. Steere, however, like Krapf, regarded his studies as a means to an end, which was to make the Bible available to those who knew the widely spoken language of Swahili; and to this end he translated the Bible and a good deal of the Church service into Swahili. While he was doing this work, Dr Steere became interested in some of the tales he heard, and made an interesting collection of them in Swahili.

Livingstone. As an early missionary, explorer, linguist and teacher, Krapf laid the foundations for a line of missionary stations which he thought of as a chain of Christian 'forts' linking up eastern and western Africa, but few would have noticed the foundations when he left. It was Livingstone who was to introduce East Africa to a wider public. His travels caught men's imaginations; and his attacks on the slave trade filled them with sympathy for the African, whom they now saw as suffering from a poverty which limited his ambitions to satisfying his immediate material needs, and haunted by fears: fears of the slavers, and the fears that arise from ignorance.

The Universities Mission to Central Africa. In 1857 Livingstone appealed to Cambridge for help to destroy these handicaps from which the Africans suffered. The result was the foundation of the Universities Mission to Central Africa. This aimed at raising the African's standard of life and at the same time bringing him into the Christian fold. Unfortunately the first expedition started in the Shiré River district, where so many of the party died that Bishop Tozer, who came out to take over its leadership in 1863, decided that the difficulties of carrying on in Nyasaland were too great and moved the mission's headquarters to Zanzibar. Here he began to train young African boys for the Christian ministry: and here his assistant Dr Steere began the study of Swahili. After the slave market was closed in 1873, Dr Steere, then Bishop Steere, also took over the building of a stone church on the site. It took four years to complete; and the bishop himself supervised the mixing of the mortar and showed his trainees how to place the stones, as well as doing all the really skilled work himself.

The freed slaves. The work of the Universities Mission to Central Africa soon began to spread out from Zanzibar town; and a new responsibility was taken on when Mbweni was started a few miles south. This village was to be a centre for freed slaves, for the missionaries who were coming to work in Africa were drawing increasing attention to the evils of the slave trade. This meant that the Government was having more and more pressure put on it to check the East African slave trade. At the same time it was not much good to free a slave and then leave him hundreds of miles away from his tribal lands. It was necessary, therefore, to cater for the freed slaves before more could be rescued. The Universities Mission played their part in this work; and in 1867 they started their first station on the mainland at Magila, in the hilly country behind Tanga. From this centre they opened up a number of mission posts with schools and hospitals; and in 1875 they went further afield and explored the area round the Rovuma River. Here Dr Steere selected a place called Masasi and led there a number of Africans from Mbweni.

The Society of the Holy Ghost. The third mission society to rank among the pioneers in East Africa was that of the Fathers of the Society of the Holy Ghost, together with the Sisters of the Sacred Heart. They also landed at Zanzibar, where Catholics had already opened two hospitals, one for European sailors, and the other for Africans, together with an elementary and an industrial school. The Holy Ghost Mission, however, intended to use Zanzibar only as a depot, the headquarters of the Society being established in 1868 on the mainland, at Bagamoyo. This village concentrated on the care of freed slaves, the majority of whom were bought from slave traders and helped to pay for their keep and training by their work. Père Horner, who was in charge, reckoned that £5 would pay for the training that would make a man self-supporting. After this he would be married off before going to settle in one of the Christian villages that had been planted inland to act as Christian oases. In this way hundreds of people were rescued from slavery, taught Christianity and given a chance to live a successful agricultural life. Bagamoyo was like a torch on a dark night. The Africans who lived there learnt to use the plough instead of the digging stick, saw the first coffee bushes, and cast away many of their superstitious fears as they entered the fold of the Church.

Freretown. This concern of the Universities Mission, and that of the Holy Ghost, for the freed slaves was shared by the C.M.S., who deliberately placed their settlement of Freretown near to Mombasa. It was such a disturbing influence among the domestic slaves and their owners that the Mombasa Arabs took a vow to make soup of the missionaries' livers. Concern for the slaves also caused the Society of Friends to start their mission on Pemba, just before slavery was finally abolished in Zanzibar.

Two other pioneer missionary societies. Two other mission societies belong to the pioneer group who settled on or near the coast. They are the United Methodists, who came out to Ribe in 1876, and the society which Livingstone had joined as a young man, the London Missionary Society. A year later this society accepted the offer of £5000 made towards the purchase of a steamer for work on Lake Tanganyika. This mission was very unlucky in the number of deaths it suffered, and eventually it moved down to Northern Rhodesia. Its decision to undertake work on Lake Tanganyika is interesting for three reasons. First it was typical of a change which was coming over mission work in East Africa, which was moving inland; secondly, it led to the making of a link between Lake Nyasa and Lake Tanganyika, and this helped in influencing Rhodes to occupy Northern Rhodesia. This connection between missionary work and politics was also typical of East African history in the last part of the nineteenth century. Thirdly, there is an odd coincidence between the offer of £5000 made to the London Missionary Society and another offer of the same sum which was made to the C.M.S. on condition that they undertook missionary work in Uganda. This was made three days after the explorer Stanley had written a letter describing the opportunities in the country for Christian missionaries. On the strength of this offer, a small party of C.M.S. missionaries set out on the long tramp to Uganda, where they were at once followed by Catholic missionaries, members of a new order, the White Fathers, which had been founded by Cardinal Lavigerie. The Catholic Church owed the rapid development of their work in East Africa to the Cardinal, for he was deeply moved by the needs of this continent. His ambitions for the Church were also limitless, and acute friction soon developed in Uganda between the Catholic and the Protestant missions, both of whom were faced with the rivalry of the Mohammedans, who were also keenly seeking converts. Finally a 'religious war' developed between their converts, further details of which will be found in chapter VII.

The position of the missions at the end of the pioneer period. The close of the pioneer period saw the C.M.S. established at the coast and with their work beginning in Uganda; the Universities Mission with their bases in Zanzibar, the hilly country behind Tanga and the area round the Rovuma River; the United Methodists at Ribe, and the London Missionary Society at their temporary base on Lake Tanganyika. All these were Protestant missions with their headquarters in Britain. The Catholic Missions were drawn from France and consisted of the Holy Ghost Fathers and the White Fathers. These had established centres at Zanzibar, Bagamoyo and Tabora, and on Lake Tanganyika and in Uganda.

The social achievements of the missions. The missions were now playing an important part in East Africa, of which Dr Oliver has summed up one aspect in his book *The Missionary Factor in East Africa*. He wrote of the Africans' new mission settlements:

All acquired some new tool which made life easier. Digging sticks were replaced by iron hoes, sometimes even by the plough. Saws came

Map 9. Missionary occupation of East Africa to 1885.

to the aid of axes, metal cooking pots to the aid of earthenware. With settled agriculture houses became more permanent and more comfortable. Doors and windows made their first appearance, together with the simplest kind of furniture. Clothing became more plentiful and more hygienic, if not more becoming, and soap made its debut in East African life.

The influence of the missionaries. Judged by the European standards the missionaries were poor men living simple lives, but they were all employers of workers whom they paid in trade goods, and the wages they paid made it possible for the chiefs to enjoy the calico and other goods for which they had once exchanged slaves. It is no wonder that in one slave-centre the price of cloth fell by more than 50 per cent in the first ten years that the missionaries were there. Nor were they without political influence, for well-informed chiefs were interested in securing the friendship of those who were in touch with the influential British consul at Zanzibar. Indeed, much of England's information about the interior of East Africa came from missionaries at this time, and reference has already been made to their work as explorers. Apart from the sensational discoveries made by men like Krapf and Rebmann, there was the work done by such men as the members of the U.M.C.A. who were the first Europeans to find their way about the Rovuma district; and this was supported by the work of many who travelled on new routes and methodically recorded their findings. Finally the missionaries of this period were the first students of the African languages, of which they drew up dictionaries and grammars.

Bishop Hannington. The work did not proceed without opposition. In Uganda, for instance, when Mutesa died and was succeeded as Kabaka by Mwanga, the persecution of the Christians was begun which is described on page 122 in chapter VII. It was to aid the Christian missionaries that Bishop Hannington hurried to Uganda in 1885. Dawson's biography of Bishop Hannington shows the courage that was possessed by the best of Christians. On one occasion, for instance, Hannington killed a lion cub, which was quickly scented out by the enraged parents. When he heard them approaching, Hannington turned round and faced them. They suddenly checked and stood glaring a few paces away. He then fixed his eyes on them, slowly increasing his distance until he could walk away. Later Hannington went back to get the skin of the cub. When he got near he heard low growls and saw the lion and lioness licking its body. Hannington, however, was more interested in a rare flower growing nearby. He picked it carefully and inspected it, and only then did he fling up his arms and shout at the lions. They looked up, turned tail and ran away.

Such a man naturally took the shortest route to the place where he was needed; but it was unfortunate in 1885 that this was Thomson's route across Masailand, by way of Kavirondo to the north-eastern shores of Victoria Nyanza, for this was the path by which ancient prophecies declared that the conquerors of Buganda would one day come. The Kabaka feared that the Bishop might be coming to take his country away by the same means which the Germans had used further south. He therefore ordered his death.

I.B.E.A.'s decision to retire from Uganda. Events like this had political results. In 1888, eleven years after the arrival of the first C.M.S. missionary in Uganda, the Imperial British East Africa Company had been founded to spread British influence in East Africa. In doing this it had been led to dispatch caravans to Uganda. During the reign of the weak Kabaka, Mwanga, the Company found that England looked to it also to keep order in Uganda, a task which was complicated by the bad terms on which the different religious bodies in Kampala were living. Details of this are given in chapter VII. Here it is sufficient to say that the French Catholics, who had arrived in the country soon after the C.M.S., feared that if the Kabaka supported the Company it would result in giving the Protestant C.M.S., with its headquarters in Protestant England, a monopoly in Christian converts. The Catholics, therefore, favoured the German efforts to secure control of the country, hoping that Germany would be more friendly to Catholic missionaries than England. The third, or Arab party, was that of the Muslim missionaries. In 1891 the Imperial British East Africa Company, feeling that they could no longer afford to stay on in Uganda, announced their intention of retiring. This greatly dismayed the C.M.S., who feared for the safety of their followers. The outcome of this is described in chapter VIII, pages 140–2.

Trouble round Lake Tanganyika. Nor was Uganda the only area in which the position of the missions was challenged. There was trouble round Lake Tanganyika, where the Arabs had come to realize that their power was being undermined by the European missionaries, whom they suspected of being in league with the Europeans at Zanzibar, with the object of undermining their influence in Africa. This suspicion was increased by the activities of the Germans who, led by the German East Africa Company, were actively seeking influence and power for their country. In these circumstances some of the missionaries believed that the Arabs had been 'commissioned by the sultan of Zanzibar to take possession of all countries round the Lakes'. The years 1884–8 were troubled ones in this area for the missions, which were threatened with violence.

The arrival of new missionary societies. At the same time the European occupation of East Africa, which will be described in chapter VI, resulted in the coming of new missionary societies to this area: in 1891 the Church of Scotland Mission, in 1895 the Africa Inland Mission and the Mill Hill Fathers; those societies also which were already established received considerable reinforcements.

This spread of missionary activity was followed by another increase after British East Africa had been linked by the railway to the coast: the Society of Friends settled on the Uganda border in 1902 and the African Institute of God began its work, while in 1907 the Consolata Fathers opened a mission at Nyeri.

Proposed federation of the missions. This was the period when the influence of the European missionary was at its greatest; it was soon followed by a development of African Christianity, marked by steady recruiting of African clergy. These developments led to the calling of a conference at Nairobi to discuss proposals for a federation of missions as the first step towards the establishment of a United African Church. These proposals were not accepted in the end, although the Kenya Missionary Alliance, the parent of the Christian Council of Kenya, was an important result of the movement.

The missions and education. As time went on there was an increasing demand on the missions for educational and medical work. Reading and writing had begun to be looked on as a means of obtaining well-paid work. It was felt, too, that the Africans were faced with new problems: they needed medical care and education, and the European missionaries were therefore called on to devote a larger proportion of their time to supplying these services. Indeed, up till 1911 all education for Africans in East Africa was in the hands of missionaries, who often met with a good deal of opposition. The Kamba, for instance, considered that they ought to be paid for attending school; and at Kabare, according to Richards's (unpublished) 'History of the C.M.S. in the Highlands', rumours were spread that 'schoolboys, if they continued to read, would never be allowed to eat cold food or to marry, would be given the nickname of Mwalimu (teacher) and eventually would suffer much harm'. Despite this, education spread like a fire; and in 1911 the government of British East Africa laid down rules whereby they gave grants-in-aid to mission schools. At first a few isolated grants only were given. But by 1926 sufficient Africans had secured a primary education for it to be possible to start secondary education, and in this year the Alliance High School was opened in Kenya.

Buganda had already led the way by the founding of secondary schools some twenty years earlier. Before that, primary education had begun with the start of a school in 1895–8; and in 1898 when the first educational missionary arrived there were ninety-eight boys and twenty-eight girls at school. Later schools were supported by the chiefs, but they received no financial help from the government. Despite the increasing interest taken by the government in education, in 1952 it could still be said of Uganda that its system of African education was based almost entirely upon schools supplied, staffed and managed by Christian missions. In 1925 a Department of Education had been set up and the first grants-in-aid were made to Indian schools. Two years later the active Muslim community in Uganda founded a training college called the Uganda Muslim Association.

Education in Tanganyika. When German East Africa was taken over by England as a mandated territory under the League of Nations, many of her administrators were impressed by the relatively high educational standard prevailing, and declared that it was the best in East Africa. The change in administration involved, however, a change in policy. In the period 1920–37 the foundation was laid of the present government school and aided Indian school system. In 1925 a special conference was held in Dar es Salaam which drafted a Bill to give effect to a state scheme of African education. Regulations governing a system of grants-in-aid for mission schools were included. This system was severely hit, first by the depression of the 1930's, and then by the Second World War. Through all these difficult years the Christian missions continued to take an active part in education, and in 1952 it was still true that the majority of African children who received primary education went to a mission school.

Medical missionaries. The Christian missions realized, too, that European medicine had a big part to play if the witch doctor's hold was to be weakened. The medicine men also were quick to see the threat to their position in this, and Mr G. C. Richards, in his (unpublished) 'History of the C.M.S. in the Highlands', writes that they were disturbed when the services of Dr Crawford, a medical missionary, were sought by such numbers of men that half of them had to sleep on the earthen floors of the reception huts, while another 250 called at his dispensary: all within a few months. This, the witch doctors thought, must stop, and they tried to poison some of the patients so that Dr Crawford should not seem so successful. It was not long before the position changed, so that by 1936 it was generally agreed that European medicine had considerable value. The efforts of the missionaries were now substantially supplemented by those of the government, which maintained a number of hospitals.

The government and mission hospitals. In Kenya, for instance, the government in 1936 had three principal hospitals for Europeans, together with six for Asians and Africans in the towns, supplemented by twenty-three in the Native Reserves and six small hospitals in the northern part of the Colony. An active government policy, however, did not mean that the missions could now dissociate themselves from medical work—they realized the great need that still remained. This can be illustrated by Tanganyika, where in 1936 the government maintained a number of hospitals, and at the same time the missions had a staff of about eighteen qualified doctors, with whom they ran a number of hospitals, while also undertaking maternity work of high quality and the training of African orderlies and nurses. In Uganda the C.M.S. mission hospital of Mengo stood to remind men of the pioneer work of Sir Albert and Lady Cook who had built it.

The missions and Christianity. In stressing the part played by the missions in supplying vital social services to East Africa the growth of the Church itself must not be ignored; for the primary purpose of all Christian missions is to spread Christianity. In doing this it is doubtful if they were really helped by the vague belief in one God which lay in the background of most tribal religions in East Africa. In fact Dr Oliver suggests, in *The Missionary Factor in East Africa*, that this belief was so overlaid by the cult of tribal ancestors that the African who came into contact with a religion stretching beyond the bounds of any one tribe had his own tribal faith shaken.

African clergy. In spreading the knowledge of Christianity, the missionaries relied a great deal on the services of the African lay catechists whom they taught. These were the men who started the Bush school and through whom many consider that virtually every convert to Christianity is still being made. The catechists, who were 'pupils of a few years' standing able perhaps to read the gospel or recite the catechism', could not build up the Church by teaching the Bible and administering the sacraments. The number of ordained European missionaries therefore imposed limits on the growth of the Church. Once Africans were ordained those limits could be extended, but time was needed before this could happen.

In 1893 seven Africans of mature age who had shown their sincerity by long years as lay-readers and catechists were ordained deacons, and three years later three of them became priests. By 1938 in all six of the Anglican dioceses African clergy outnumbered the ordained European missionaries, and by 1950 they were about four to one. A similar position existed in other branches of the Protestant Church. As the Roman Catholics aspired from the first to a celibate African clergy having roughly eighteen years' education, their numbers grew more slowly, and by 1948 they had 208 African Catholic priests. Considering the Christian Church as a whole, by the middle of the twentieth century the growth of the African clergy has reached the point where the European missionary is required chiefly for specialized aid.

Church government. Church government is closely linked with the position of African clergy. To the Catholic this was an international concern: Africans who were ordained priests would not only gradually replace the missionaries, they would be eligible for service anywhere in the world, in any office of the Catholic Church. This has come about, and there is today an African Cardinal in East Africa. The Protestant organization was more local in outlook, and they developed Church government and councils with Europeans and Africans working together. The number of African bishops working in the area, as well as an African Presbyterian chief executive, are clear signs that the balance of authority has now shifted. The indigenous people are providing their own leaders; and the Church can claim to have set the pattern for much that has followed in the field of secular government. The role of the European missionary has also altered and he is devoting more of his time to medicine and education, in which he has long given valuable service. Of late, missionary effort has also concentrated on the under-privileged urban areas.

That the foundation of the Christian Church in Kenya was well laid was demonstrated by the courage shown by many African Christians in defence of their faith during the State of Emergency.

CHAPTER VI

THE SCRAMBLE FOR
AFRICA AND THE FIRST PARTITION OF
EAST AFRICA

I. THE SCRAMBLE FOR AFRICA

Colonies before 1880. Before the 1880's European rule in Africa south of the Sahara was confined to coastal patches and the Cape region. On the western side the British had colonies at Gambia, Sierra Leone, Lagos and the Gold Coast, but of these only the Gold Coast was of considerable size. The main colony of the French was at Senegal, although they also had a calling place at Gaboon. On the western and eastern side the Portuguese had colonies at Angola and Mozambique, but their rule in these regions, as in the tiny area of Portuguese Guinea, was neither strong nor extensive. Trade, not government, was the great purpose of these colonies, and responsibility for them had been taken, almost with reluctance, by the governments concerned. Trade they wanted, but the expenses and responsibilities of government they would have liked to do without.

Motives for imperial expansion. Why was it then that scrambling for African territory took place at all, and why should so many countries have pursued the same purpose at the same time? We may trace the growth of competition through several stages. First came the explorers. They brought news of conditions and resources in the regions they explored. Their reports further aroused the interest of missionaries, geographers, and manufacturers. To the missionary there was a new kingdom to be won for Christ; to the geographer there was a new field of information; and to the manufacturer came the realization that the new areas might be extremely useful as a new source of raw materials and as a new market for his products. But however the newly discovered areas were regarded, missionaries, geographers, and traders all desired the same thing—that the new regions should be opened to peaceful trade without delay. Fortunately the development of the

87

steamboat and railway engine during the nineteenth century made this possible for the first time.

Bismarck and Germany. The various German states had united under the leadership of Prussia in 1862, had defeated Austria and then France, and in 1871 proclaimed the formation of the German Empire with the King of Prussia as Emperor, or Kaiser, and Bismarck as his chancellor. The confidence and excitement of the Germans was tremendous, and many of them urged that Germany should gain further prestige and wealth by acquiring colonies. But the man who had been responsible for Germany's development, and who still guided her policy, was Chancellor Bismarck, and at first he firmly opposed overseas possessions. In 1884, however, he changed his mind. There were several reasons for this. Partly it was due to his annoyance over the British Government's ambiguous policy in South West Africa, as we shall see; partly it was due to a hope that it might help to increase French antagonism towards Britain while reducing it towards Germany; and partly it was due to the knowledge that it would be a popular move in Germany and increase his support in the Reichstag. Therefore Bismarck, while still believing that Europe was the most important field of politics, nevertheless decided that colonization in Africa would be a useful move in the game.

This put Britain in an embarrassing position, because in 1882 she had taken over the administration of Egypt in order to restore order there. The occupation, originally intended to be temporary, proved to be permanent, and it was agreed that there should be international control of Egyptian finances. Such an arrangement made German support a necessity and made an important contribution to Britain's remarkably docile attitude to German annexations in Africa.

Leopold and the International African Association. Leopold, whose splendid waistcoats and vast ambitions caught the eye of those who met him, became King of the Belgians in 1865 and it was he who started the scramble in earnest, when he looked from his little neutral kingdom in Europe to the vast unclaimed stretches of tropical Africa, and decided that he would be the leader of the movement to open up the interior. In 1876 he called a meeting of all who were interested and this developed into the International African Association, presided over by Leopold himself, and having as its aims the abolition of the slave trade and the civilization of Africa. At first Leopold hoped to reach the interior of Africa from the east coast, but finding this approach unsatisfactory he sent Stanley to explore the approach from the west, by way of the Congo, in 1879. The French had also sent an expedition there under De Brazza, and both explorers laid claim to the area. Portugal also revived her ancient claims to the Congo mouth, and in order to gain Portuguese support in abolishing the slave trade in that area Britain recognized her claims in 1884. Both Leopold and the French objected.

The Berlin conference, 1884–5. It was at this point that Germany, in the person of Bismarck, intervened by inviting all the European countries concerned to a conference in Berlin to discuss the future of the Congo in particular, and the partition of African territories in general. This Berlin conference (November 1884–February 1885) was willingly attended, and its decisions were stated in the Berlin Act of 1885. The particular importance of this was to state that the 'conventional Congo basin' was to be an area under international protection, whose trade was open to all. At the same time all the powers recognized Leopold as sovereign of the new Congo Independent State. The general importance of the conference was to assert that protectorates should not be claimed and would not be recognized, unless evidence could be shown that they were, or could be, effectively managed. At the same time all the powers agreed that the slave trade should be destroyed wherever it still existed.

Rivalry in West Africa. In the Niger area, as well as in the Congo, rivalry was keen. The French and British had both been interested in the West African Coast since the seventeenth century, and both had started to extend their influence inland in the nineteenth. But Sir George Taubman Goldie had bought out his French rivals in 1884, so that the British claim to Niger was recognized at the Berlin Conference, and the delta region became the Oil Rivers Protectorate. At this stage the Germans also competed for the region. They had traded along the west coast since about 1850, but it came as a surprise to the other European countries when Dr Nachtigal visited the region in June and July of 1884 to 'report on German commerce', and in fact made treaties with the chiefs of Togoland and the Cameroons and claimed them as German protectorates. Rather than quarrel with Germany the British recognized these claims.

Rivalry in South West Africa. Further rivalry took place in the south. German missionaries and settlers had established themselves in Damaraland and Namaqualand in South West Africa from the mid-nineteenth century. They complained that the British gave them no protection against native attacks, which the British countered by asserting that, apart from Walfish Bay, the Cape Government had no responsibilities north-west of the Orange River. Therefore, when Herr Luderitz took a German expedition to Angra Pequena Bay, 150 miles north of the Orange, in 1883, and purchased part of the hinterland from the Hottentots, the British Government should not have been surprised. But in fact they were surprised and attempted to claim the whole region from the Orange to the Portuguese Congo, although in June 1884 these belated claims were withdrawn and the German Protectorate over South West Africa was officially recognized. Yet the Germans did not have things all their own way, for at this same time Cecil Rhodes was dreaming of an Africa which he hoped would be British from the Cape to Cairo. With his millions from the diamond mines of Kimberley and the goldfields of Johannesburg he made at least part of his dreams come true. In 1885 he was instrumental in annexing Bechuanaland in order to secure the 'missionaries' road' into the interior and prevent the Boers from the Transvaal joining up with the Germans in South West Africa. This was the essential preliminary to the much greater expansion which took place into what became Southern and Northern Rhodesia, after he had formed his British South Africa Company in 1889.

Rivalry in North and East Africa. Meanwhile in North Africa the French pushed south from Algiers and westwards from Senegal, thus encircling the British west coast possessions, and established a huge area of influence across the Sudan which joined with their area north of the Congo. From there an attempt was made in 1898 to extend the area right across to the east coast, but this was halted at Fashoda on the Upper Nile, and in 1898 the French withdrew and recognized the British status in the eastern Sudan. In East Africa France occupied Madagascar in 1886, and the Portuguese claim to the whole interior of Africa between Mozambique and Angola—which cut across the region of Nyasaland and the ambitions of Rhodes—was happily settled by the Anglo-Portuguese Treaty of 1890, which fixed the boundaries which still exist. The areas of what are now Kenya, Uganda, and Tanganyika, were divided between Britain and Germany by the treaties of 1886 and 1890; they are considered more fully later at pages 108 and 129. Meanwhile the Italians, despite their defeat at Adua, had maintained their hold on Eritrea, and by the end of 1889 had established a protectorate over all the Somali coast.

The effects of partition on the European powers. Thus was Africa partitioned. France had gained in prestige from her African colonies what she had lost by her defeat in Europe in 1870. Leopold of the Belgians soon gained a virtual monopoly of the Congo trade, but his reputation as a philanthropist was ruined when his unprincipled exploitation of the native population was revealed. Bismarck was left with colonies whose political value he strongly doubted. Britain had acquired new protectorates to prevent them falling into the hands of her European rivals, but was unwilling to develop them. Their development was therefore left at first to chartered companies. In the west coast region Goldie's Royal Niger Company was chartered in 1886; on the east coast Sir William Mackinnon's Imperial British East Africa Company was chartered in 1888; and in South Africa Rhodes obtained a charter for his British South Africa Company in 1889.

The effects of partition on Africa. It would be quite wrong to think of the partition of Africa as a struggle for profit alone. Some people did see it as this, but that was only part of a very large picture. There were also the missionaries and abolitionists who in many cases gave their lives and received no tangible reward. In East Africa they dominated the early picture.

It would be equally wrong to assume that there always was a profit from the colonies acquired. In fact nearly all of them proved very expensive additions.

Map 10. The partition of Africa, 1879–99.

Another striking point is the general lack of interest by the governments in the spheres of influence which had been acquired. The acquisitions had been made largely as part of European political rivalries and, once the claims had been made and agreed, the actual task of administration and development was left at first to private companies. Nevertheless, it was clear that certain obligations rested on the European powers, and the main result of the scramble was to speed up the pace of development.

The Brussels Conference, 1889–90. Of the meetings which were held between the countries concerned in the colonization of Africa, one at least shows that the interests of the African peoples were not ignored. The Brussels Conference (1889–90) had three aims, all of which were humanitarian: first, to destroy the African slave trade completely and finally; second, to protect the African population; and third, to ensure for Africa 'the benefits of peace and civilization'. The conclusions of the conference are dealt with in chapter x, but it is mentioned in connection with partition as evidence of the genuine good will of the countries concerned.

II. THE FIRST PARTITION OF EAST AFRICA

The extent of the Sultan's dominions in 1875. In 1875 the coast and the interior of East Africa between Warsheik in the north and the Rovuma River in the south were, in theory, the dominion of the Sultan of Zanzibar. In fact his lack of resources and the difficulties of communication over so large an area prevented him from keeping a tight hold over the whole of the region, so that his main interest was confined to the area nearest to Zanzibar and the main trade routes to Lake Tanganyika from which he drew so large a proportion of his profits. Over this central region his rule was effective though not always secure against revolts. To the south and to the north it was less effective, but garrisons with governors or sub-governors were stationed in most of the coastal towns.

The Sultan warned by the Egyptian invasion, 1875. Before the Germans staked their claim to East Africa in 1884, the Sultan had been well aware that he was in no position to defend his dominions from any invasion from without. In 1875 he had watched with some apprehension the Egyptian occupation of Barawa and Kismayu in the north. In fact this occupation, which had aimed at establishing a route from the Indian Ocean to the Great Lakes to help General Gordon exterminate the Nile slave trade, only lasted two months, but it showed the Sultan that East Africa had a strategic importance. The journeys of the explorers had shown what might be the value of East Africa as an entrance to the heart of Africa. The Sultan, therefore, rightly feared that the Egyptian invasion would be the prelude to others which might lead to permanent occupation, and not being strong enough himself to prevent an attack he decided that his safest course would be to invite Britain to safeguard and develop his dominions for him.

The Mackinnon concession, 1877–8. In 1876 Sultan Barghash first requested that British 'capitalists' should help him in 'the development and civilization of Africa, and the opening up of trade on the coast and in the interior'. The request was taken up by Sir William Mackinnon. This energetic little Scottish businessman had already done much for East Africa. It was he who had started the first steamship and mail service, and he had also helped in providing a telegraph cable to Zanzibar. In the same year that Barghash made his request Mackinnon was busy on plans for opening up the interior by means of a road from Dar es Salaam to the northern end of Lake Nyasa. By 1881 this road was over seventy miles long and carrying considerable traffic. But the request which the Sultan had made was for much more than a road. It was virtually a request for a British company to colonize his East African dominions. At first Mackinnon took up the idea with enthusiasm and in 1877 negotiations between his representatives and the Sultan began. Both parties were assisted by Sir John Kirk, who gave whole-hearted encouragement to the scheme, and for a year negotiations continued on excellent terms. But by May 1878 the atmosphere had changed; the next month negotiations finished and the proposed 'Mackinnon concession' was dead. The reason for the failure, Kirk said, was not the attitude of the British Government but the delay of the company in taking over the area, and the tactlessness of one of Mackinnon's negotiators, Badger, who 'made an ass of himself' by trying to bully the Sultan. But whatever the causes of failure, there can be no doubt that when the proposed concession failed both Britain and the Sultan lost a golden opportunity for the peaceful development of East Africa. The time of the scramble was approaching and competitors were coming into the area in increasing numbers.

The work of the explorers has been described already in chapter IV. They included missionaries, geographers, naturalists and patriots. In this chapter we shall only be able to mention briefly those on an official national basis.

The Belgian expeditions to East Africa, 1877–84. Well to the fore among the competitors for East Africa was Leopold of the Belgians. The Africa International Association which he had started in 1876 to promote the exploration and civilization of Central Africa decided that the easiest approach to the centre of the continent would be from Zanzibar. At the end of 1877 the first expedition arrived, but as three of its four leaders were Belgians, and as it was organized by the Belgian National Committee of the International Association, it was virtually King Leopold's expedition rather than an international one. Within six weeks of their arrival two of the four leaders of this expedition were dead and one had deserted, but Lt. Cambier, who survived, started with a caravan to the interior, and despite many difficulties succeeded in establishing posts at Tabora and at Karema on Lake Tanganyika, which he reached in August 1879. In the same month another expedition started inland from Bagamoyo, led by the Belgian Captain Popelin and the Englishman Carter. The most important members of this expedition were four elephants which Carter had brought to see if they could survive the climate, in which case they would have provided a useful means of transport. By the time Tabora was reached in October two of the elephants had died, but a triumphal entry was made into the settlement on the two that remained, to the huge delight of the inhabitants. By the end of the year when the caravan entered Karema only one elephant remained and in a few months that too was dead. But Leopold was not content with the footholds which his expeditions had gained at Tabora and the small marshy settlement at Karema. A foothold on the coast was also needed, and in the June of 1880 he sent M. Emile de Ville as consul to Zanzibar to request a part of the coast near Malindi as a training ground for elephants, with the intention that it should in fact become a Belgian colony. This request was refused by the Sultan and Leopold did not press his claims. Nevertheless, Belgian interest in East Africa continued, and between 1880 and 1884 three more expeditions were sent and another post was established on the western shore of Lake Tanganyika at Mpala. The last expedition, however, never went beyond the East Africa coast, for in 1884 Leopold had realized, as a result of Stanley's efforts, that the Congo was his most profitable approach to Africa, and from that time his interest in East Africa ceased.

The French expeditions to East Africa, 1878–81. Meanwhile the French had also made a series of attempts to open up the East African coast. Their connection with Muscat was about as old as that of Britain, although their influence in Zanzibar during the time of Barghash was nothing like so great. In 1878 they equipped one of the most interesting and pathetic expeditions that ever penetrated into the Sultan's dominions. Its leader was the Abbé Michel-Alexandre Debaize, a young French priest, who felt that both God and his country were calling him to help in the exploration of Africa. The French Government gave him permission to blaze a trail for the French National Committee of the International Association, which was still being formed. In 1878 Debaize landed at Zanzibar. By October he had reached Tabora with his 800 porters and his amazing collection of supplies, which included two suits of armour, two dozen umbrellas, and a barrel organ. In May of 1879 he was in Ujiji with a caravan much decreased by desertion, but still full of enthusiasm. 'The thought', he said, 'that I am working for the glory of God and the glory of France will sustain me in all my trials.' Not content with having reached the lakes, he planned to press on to the Congo, but in November fever caught him and on 12 December he died. In the next year the French were ready to make another and more serious attempt to open up East Africa; a French business firm asked Barghash for a concession to build a quay and docks at Bagamoyo and a railway along the main route from Bagamoyo to Ujiji. For a while the Sultan looked favourably upon this proposal, but in 1881, as a result of Kirk's influence, he finally decided to reject it. With the collapse of this scheme the French Government virtually abandoned official interest in the Sultan's dominions and turned their eyes southwards. By 1883 they had succeeded in establishing protectorates over part of the Comoro Islands and had gained a foothold on Madagascar.

So far as Britain was concerned these were wasted years.

Britain's wasted opportunity. While European interests in Africa increased, and as one expedition after another plunged into the interior from East Africa, the British Government deliberately rejected opportunity after opportunity for helping the Sultan to develop his territory. So far from trying to 'grab' colonies, the Gladstone government did its best to avoid having colonies forced upon them. Yet, for several reasons, the British had by far the best claim of all the nations to govern and develop the East African dominions. In the first place the opening up of the interior was the work of British explorers, and of the few Europeans who had already settled there by 1880 the great majority were British missionaries. In addition to this there were, at Zanzibar and all along the coast, Indian traders who had been in East Africa as long as the Arabs, but whose numbers had much increased since the British consul had been established at Zanzibar. These people managed almost all the business and provided nearly all the revenue, and they felt that they were entitled to British protection. But the chief claim of Britain lay in the abolition of the slave trade in 1873, for without British aid the slave trade would have turned the interior of East Africa into a despoiled and depopulated waste. Yet, despite these reasons, and despite the forceful suggestions of Sir John Kirk, the British Government refused to accept any sort of commitment in East Africa. The last chance came in 1882 when the Sultan asked the British Government to be responsible for seeing that his son succeeded him, and to act as regent in case of a minority. This request might well have involved the Government in establishing the equivalent of a protectorate over Zanzibar, a responsibility which Sir John

Kirk would have welcomed, for he believed that the ideal way of developing East Africa was through the rule of the Sultan supported by British commercial and military power. But the Gladstone government would have none of it, and the request was politely refused.

Map 11. Anglo-German agreements of 1886 and 1890.

This was Britain's last chance, for at the end of 1884 a party of four Germans led by Carl Peters landed at Zanzibar and staked out a claim to Usagara which they maintained for over thirty years.

Early German expeditions to East Africa. They were not the first Germans to take an interest in East Africa, for the German National Committee of the International Association had, like those of Belgium and France, sent expeditions into the interior in 1880 and 1881 with the purpose of starting trading bases. Moreover, the Denhardt brothers, who were Germans, had been interesting themselves in scientific expeditions along the Tana river since the 1870's, and were about to appear on the scene again. At the same time the Germans had decided to obtain a more official position at Zanzibar by sending Rohlfs there as consul. He arrived in the January of 1885 and looked forward to obtaining a substantial area of the interior for Germany.

Carl Peters's expedition, 1884. Such was the position when Carl Peters and his expedition made their claim upon East Africa. Peters himself was then a young man of twenty-eight who had started the Society for German Colonization early in 1884 with the purpose of acquiring part of the East African coast and interior. Supported by funds from the society he and his companions sailed in disguise to Aden and then re-embarked for Zanzibar, where they arrived on 4 November 1884. Within a week they had crossed to the mainland and were journeying up the Wami river to Usagara, where they made twelve treaties with different chiefs by which the chiefs signed agreements giving up their territories to the German company. The treaty made with the Sultan of Msovero is a typical example:

Treaty of eternal friendship: Mangungo, Sultan of Msovero in Usagara, offers all his territory with all its civil and public appurtenances to Dr Carl Peters as the representative of the Society for German Colonisation, for exclusive and universal utilization for German colonization.

By December the expedition was over and Peters was back at Zanzibar, and by February 1885 he was in Berlin.

The importance of Peters's treaties. For two reasons the treaties he had collected did not deserve to be treated seriously. In the first place it was extremely unlikely that the chiefs who signed them understood what they were about, and in the second place the areas concerned were part of the dominions of the Sultan of Zanzibar. But for an equally clear reason the treaties were very important indeed—they were recognized and supported by Bismarck. This support, and this support alone, gave the expedition and the treaties of Peters their importance. The previous expeditions had penetrated deeper and taken much longer, but Bismarck had then maintained that Germany was not interested in colonies; the expeditions, therefore, had come and gone without leaving any appreciable mark on East African history. But Peters's expedition came at the right moment when Bismarck had changed his mind and was seeking colonies wherever they could be found.

The official annexation of Usagara, March 1885. When Peters arrived back in Berlin the conference on Africa was still sitting. Bismarck had already laid claims to regions in West and South Africa, besides annexing the north coast of New Guinea, and he therefore decided not to bring up another claim before the conference. He waited, therefore, until the day after the General Act of the conference was passed before getting the German Emperor to sign a bill officially taking the areas gained by Peters under the protection of the German Government, and he then waited until the day after all the delegates had left before he published it, on 3 March 1885.

The Sultan's protest. It was not until 25 April that Sultan Barghash heard that the government of part of his dominions had been handed over to Peters's company by the German Government. He was very indignant. Not only had the Germans made their expedition to the interior with the utmost secrecy, but the claim which they now made was for the most valuable area of all his mainland possessions; it included the mainland opposite Zanzibar and the first part of the main trade route to the interior leading to Tabora and Ujiji. Barghash sent a vigorous protest to the German Emperor: 'These territories are ours', he wrote, 'and we hold military stations there, and those chiefs who profess to cede sovereign rights to the agents of the Society have no authority to do so.'

So indignant was the Sultan that he considered following the telegram by a personal visit to the Emperor, but Sir John Kirk dissuaded him.

The annexation and significance of Witu, April 1885. Usagara was not the only part of the Sultan's dominions in which Germany was interested. In January of 1885 the younger Denhardt left Zanzibar for the port of Lamu in the north, and started negotiations with Simba, who was sometimes referred to as the Sultan of Witu, but who was, in fact, an old ruffian with a following of over 3000 bandits who were the scourge of the northern coastal area. When Denhardt started negotiations with him Barghash was apprehensive, and with good cause, for in April 1885 Denhardt calmly announced that a 'covenant of friendship' between Simba and Germany had been made giving Germany a protectorate over 'Witu and the neighbouring Swahili lands'. Of course Simba had no right to make such an agreement, and the Sultan Barghash protested. Nevertheless the German Emperor confirmed the agreement. The possession of Witu was of considerable strategic significance, for it meant that now Germany controlled an area to the north as well as to the south of the British region. If only these northern and southern regions could be joined by the acquisition of the area to the west of the British sphere then the British possessions would be encircled by those of Germany. As we shall see, this was precisely the plan which the Germans pursued, first by trying to expand their northern possessions, and secondly by the expedition which Peters made to Uganda.

The attitude of the Sultan, Kirk, and the British Government. The Sultan Barghash had good cause for indignation, but it was quite useless. Without British support he could do nothing but protest, and British help was not forthcoming. To both Kirk and the Sultan this was a bitter disappointment, and both felt that they had been let down. Yet the British Government had reason enough to hesitate about picking a quarrel with Germany at this time, for when 1885 opened East Africa was a comparatively small worry among British overseas possessions. In the Sudan General Gordon was murdered on 26 January by the Mahdists; in Egypt there was serious tension with France which might have led to war; on the Indian frontier a Russian army was threatening Afghanistan. Considering these threats to her position in North Africa and India it is not surprising that the British Government thought it unwise to risk a war with Germany over the ownership of the Usagara area. But however difficult the circumstances were the Sultan had been let down, for he had conformed to British desires even to the extent of abolishing, in 1873, the most profitable trade of his subjects, and he therefore had a right to expect some effective support when his dominions were annexed. Moreover, the Anglo-French declaration of 1862, recognizing the independence of his dominions, implied some willingness to uphold that independence against aggressors. In view of this, one can only suppose that Gladstone did not fully understand the position, or was too much influenced by the retention of Egypt, when in March of 1885 he remarked, 'If Germany becomes a colonizing power, all I can say is "God speed her".' Thus Germany had nothing to fear from Britain, and alone the Sultan could offer no effective opposition.

Germany forces the Sultan to accept the annexations, August 1885. Thus Bismarck settled the question as he chose, and his methods were by no means so gentle as those of the British. Instead of sending a friendly diplomat to negotiate he sent a squadron of battleships and an ultimatum that the Sultan Barghash must withdraw all protests against treaties made by Germany with the Sultans of Usagara, Nguru, Useguha, Ukami, and Witu, or else Zanzibar would be blown to bits. The Sultan, as might be expected, agreed, but he did so under protest.

The Zanzibar Commission, 1885–6. The claims of Germany to the Usagara area raised the question of what exactly were the limits of the Sultan's territories. In this point the British Government did take an active interest and in June 1885 persuaded Bismarck to agree to a commission with representatives of Germany, Britain and France 'to investigate what are the just limits of the Sultan's dominions'. The Zanzibar Commission met at the end of the year and inspected the coast from south to north in three separate voyages. No one disputed the Sultan's claim to the islands of Zanzibar and Pemba, but the distance inland to which the Sultan's authority extended on the mainland was hotly disputed. The German representative, Schmidt, who was anxious to make it appear as small as possible, estimated it at a maximum of ten miles inland, and in parts denied that the Sultan had any authority over the coast at all. The British and French commissioners estimated that the Sultan's rule was effective to a depth of about forty miles inland. In the middle of 1886 the Commission broke up without coming to any clear decisions except that Zanzibar, Pemba, and the chief mainland ports were definitely in the Sultan's dominions.

Kirk advises partition. So far as Britain was concerned the problem of East Africa had resolved itself into the question of whether Germany was to be allowed to take over the whole region, or whether Britain should claim a part of it. Sir John Kirk made this very clear in his dispatches.

The question to be decided [he wrote] is practically this: whether we are prepared to see Germany paramount over all the Zanzibar coast, using the trading capacities of our Indian subjects to advance and develop her commerce, or whether some compromise cannot be come to whereby our influence is upheld and admitted as legitimately paramount over a certain district, without necessarily affecting the independence of the Sultan of Zanzibar.

Kirk not only posed the question. He also answered it—Britain's duty was to demand partition. It remained to be seen whether the British Government would act on his advice.

Other factors favouring partition. Besides the fear of German domination of the whole coast, other minor considerations also made partition desirable. Ever since Johnston's expedition to the slopes of Kilimanjaro in 1884, when rights had been acquired over Taveta, there had been serious consideration as to whether the area should be taken over. Now, in 1886, the Taveta concession was made good by a British expedition which established a post there. Moreover, in 1886, H. H. Kitchener, while serving on the Zanzibar Commission, had written a dispatch on the defence of British communications with India and the East. In this he emphasized the need for a British key-point in the northern part of the East African coast to offset the German harbour of Dar es Salaam. The key-point he recommended was Mombasa. Besides its use for protecting communications in the Indian Ocean Kitchener also pointed out that 'Mombasa is the most probable port from which any railway system for the opening up of the interior would start, and its possession would give to England a commercial base, without which it would be impossible to develop the trade of Central Africa'.

The partition treaty of 1886. While the British Government were considering the possibility of partition, Bismarck once more took action, this time because he wished to settle affairs in East Africa before the dispute between Britain and France concerning Egypt was settled. He sent Dr Krauel, a high Foreign Office official, to London to bring the affairs of Zanzibar to a satisfactory conclusion with the suggestion that if Britain would help Germany at Zanzibar Germany would support Britain against France over Egypt. Both Bismarck and Krauel realized that it would be worth making some concessions in order to reach an agreement; the talks in London, therefore, were far more profitable than the Zanzibar Commission had been. By the end of October 1886 the settlement was made. The main points were: (i) Britain and Germany recognized the Sultan's authority over the islands of Zanzibar, Pemba, Mafia, and Lamu, and also over the coast to a depth of ten miles from the River Rovuma in the south to Kipini in the north. North of that the towns of Kismayu, Barawa, Merka, Mogadishu and Warsheik were also recognized as the Sultan's. (ii) The territory between the rivers Rovuma and Tana was to be divided into German and British 'spheres of influence' by the line which now marks the boundary between Kenya and Tanganyika. (iii) Britain agreed to support Germany's claim to establishing a customs house at Dar es Salaam. Dar es Salaam thus became virtually a German possession leased from the Sultan. (iv) Britain agreed to recognize the German possession of Witu and its corridor to the sea at Manda Bay.

The effects of the partition treaty. The only things which were left undefined were the western boundaries of the protectorates. Britain, on the other hand, had succeeded in maintaining her influence over a large part of East Africa, so that the possibility of Germany's taking over the whole region was removed.

There were several regrettable results of the intrusion of Germany into East Africa. One was that as Barghash's authority in the interior decreased slave trading revived, and reports that slave dhows were reappearing on the coast, and that parents were selling their children, reached Zanzibar during these two years. Worst of all was the belief which developed among the Africans that what the white man really wanted was land—the Africans' most treasured possession. They did not realize that the British and Germans were interested in the land as a political possession for strategic reasons and had no intention of dispossessing individual landholders, and there developed a hatred of all white men which had not been felt before. In 1885 missionaries in Uganda reported that this hatred and fear that Europeans wanted 'to eat the country' was felt by Mwanga. In the same year Bishop Hannington was murdered. Had he come two years before he would have been safe.

The Imperial British East Africa Company. The development of the German and British spheres was not undertaken by the governments of those countries but by companies. The British East Africa Association with Sir William Mackinnon as chairman was therefore started in 1887, and in the following year the Sultan gladly conceded all his mainland possessions opposite the British area to the Association. Later in 1888 a royal charter was granted and the Association was re-formed as the Imperial British East Africa Company. The German East Africa Company also started in 1888, and like the British company it received from the Sultan a concession to administer the mainland opposite its sphere of influence.

Difficulties of the Company. The years which followed the partition were not easy either for the Company's administrator, Mackenzie, or for the British consul, Colonel Euan Smith. One of the troubles was the new Sultan Khalifa who succeeded Barghash in 1888. He was mentally unbalanced as a result of long imprisonment, and he was not respected by his subjects. Moreover he disliked Colonel Euan Smith and put his faith in two worthless favourites. His death in 1890 was regretted by none. Another trouble was the attempt of the Italian consul at Zanzibar to claim the province of Kismayu on the pretext that the Sultan had insulted the King of Italy. This annoyed not only the Sultan but also the British and German consuls, who protested to the Italian consulate. Italian claims to the Zanzibar dominions were then withdrawn. A third difficulty arose over the question of runaway slaves who had taken refuge in the mission stations near Mombasa. Many slaves from the Arab coast at plantations had escaped and taken refuge in the mission stations of Rabai (C.M.S.) and Ribe (Methodist), and while the missions were naturally reluctant to give them back to their masters, the Arabs were equally reluctant to accept this refusal to return what they considered to be their rightful property. A state of great tension developed and war between the Arabs and missions seemed imminent until the tact of Mackenzie, the Company administrator, solved the problem by a promise to pay the Arabs £3500 as compensation if they would agree to give up their claims to the runaway slaves. The offer was accepted and on 1 January 1889 nearly 1500 slaves were freed amid great rejoicing and with good feeling on all sides. Apart from this episode the relations between the British company and the inhabitants of the area which it administered were good, largely because very few changes were made. Mombasa became the Company's headquarters and an advance post was set up at Machakos. At the same time treaties were made with the Nyika, Kamba and Taita tribes and preparations were made for the occupation of the interior.

The British and German companies. By far the greatest trouble came from the German company. Almost at once a rebellion broke out in the German-administered area as a direct result of their harsh and arrogant methods of colonization. The leader of the rebellion was a fiery bearded Arab, Bushiri bin Salim. Bismarck reproved the company for its inefficiency and appointed a new imperial commissioner, Captain Wissman, who arrived with a force of 600 Sudanese troops early in 1889 to restore order. Throughout the year the rebels were steadily harassed until the end came in December, when Bagamoyo was stormed and Bushiri was hanged. Meanwhile Bismarck had suggested that Britain and Germany should carry out a combined naval blockade of the coast to prevent the export of slaves and the importation of arms and ammunition. To this Lord Salisbury agreed, chiefly because he feared the results of allowing a purely German naval force to patrol the area. The suppression of the rebellion in the German sphere and the blockade caused great anti-European feeling, and for a while a general attack was expected on all Europeans in Zanzibar; but it did not materialize.

Another serious problem in these early years came from German claims in the north. We have seen already that by the 1886 agreement the British recognized the possession of Witu by the Germans. As Witu itself had little value it was regarded by the Germans simply as the first step towards gaining control of the northern part of the coast, and in 1887 the Witu Company was formed to promote this expansion. This company promptly claimed the island of Lamu, which was a useful port, but in August 1889 the claim was rejected by a special international committee set up to investigate it. Two months later the Witu Company made a still more extravagant claim. This time it was for all the territory between Juba and Witu, and later the islands of Manda and Patta (north of Lamu) also, which were already occupied by the British. Once more an international committee was appointed to investigate the claims and once more it rejected them (1890). The third German attempt to gain profit from their region was more subtle. No official claims were made this time. Instead, a force of men from Witu simply established a customs house on the Belesoni Canal and demanded that all who used it should pay. The purpose of this canal was to provide an outlet for the considerable trade of the Tana River. As the Tana is unnavigable at its mouth, the coastal tribes had built the Belesoni Canal to join it with the Ozi eight miles from the sea, at a point where the rivers were only two miles apart. Thus goods from the interior could reach the sea by sailing down the Tana, through the Belesoni Canal, and finally down the Ozi to the coast. It was this trade which the Witu detachment started to tax. The British immediately protested that the region was not in the German sphere, and this time the trespass was so plain that the German Government itself ordered the detachment to withdraw.

The expedition of Peters to Buganda, 1889–90. It was from Witu also that Peters made his bid to extend German East Africa by gaining the area to the west of the British sphere. This had not been defined by the 1886 treaty, and Peters hoped that he might be able to form a continuous belt of German territory from Witu to Tanganyika via Uganda, thus encircling the British area and cutting the British off from the headwaters of the Nile. He landed at Witu in June

1889, and led an expedition up the Tana, over the Kenya highlands into Uganda. His excuse was that he was going to relieve Emin Pasha, but this was merely an excuse, because two other expeditions had already set out for that purpose, one from the Congo led by Stanley, and one from Zanzibar led by Sir Frederick Jackson on behalf of the I.B.E.A. Company. Sir Frederick Jackson, as it happened, reached the border of Uganda before Peters, but despite the Kabaka's request for help, Jackson, who had strict orders from the Company not to enter Uganda, refused to commit himself. Instead, hearing that Emin Pasha had already been found by Stanley, Jackson set off to the Mount Elgon district to shoot elephants, hoping that the ivory might pay for the expenses of his expedition. While he was away Peters arrived and without scruple made a treaty with the Kabaka by which the kingdom of Buganda was placed under German protection. He then moved off southwards before Jackson returned, and reached Bagamoyo in July. There, this unscrupulous treaty-maker had a salutary lesson, for he learned that the territory which he thought he had just obtained for Germany had already been recognized as a British sphere of influence. In his book *New Light on Darkest Africa*, Peters wrote that his feelings on hearing this news were so strong that he had to withdraw to a private room for two hours to regain his composure.

The Heligoland Treaty, 1890. The chief reason for the 1890 agreement between Britain and Germany, which settled the western boundaries of their East African possessions over the head of Peters, was Bismarck's desire to secure Germany's position in Europe. His great fear of French or Russian attack caused him to become increasingly anxious for the friendship of Britain. To gain this he was quite prepared to make concessions in East Africa.

From the British point of view three things were desirable: (i) That a British protectorate should be recognized over Zanzibar, where German influence had grown at such an alarming rate since Wissman had made it the headquarters of the German company that the German residents there outnumbered other European residents by six to one. This protectorate the Sultan was very ready to accept, for he feared that the Germans would soon overshadow his own authority there. (ii) That the western frontiers of the German and British spheres should be continued westwards to Lake Victoria and across it to the boundary of the Congo Free State so that Uganda should be included in the British area. (iii) That the Germans should abandon all claims to regions north of the British sphere, which would mean the end of the Witu protectorate.

The Germans on their side were willing to agree to this in return for two main concessions: (i) That the British should help to persuade the Sultan to cede absolutely to Germany the ten-mile coastal strip of the mainland which had been held on lease since the 1886 agreement. The Sultan, with some reluctance, agreed to this in return for a compensation equivalent to £200,000. (ii) That the island of Heligoland in the North Sea should be given to Germany by Britain. The Germans believed that this would be a valuable naval base, although the future was to show that it was not.

Such was the 1890 agreement which ended the scramble so far as East Africa was concerned. There were some who criticized it, especially the French who maintained that the 1862 declaration had been ignored. By way of compensation Britain therefore agreed to recognize French claims to a protectorate over Madagascar. The indignant Peters criticized it and remarked bitterly that two kingdoms in Africa (Witu and Uganda) had been sacrificed for 'a bath-tub in the North Sea [Heligoland]'. But on the whole the agreement was a good one, for it achieved its main purpose, which was to end the dangerous rivalry in East Africa between Britain and Germany. It also confirmed Sir John Kirk's belief that British economic and strategic interests could not be maintained without some fairly clear political control. Nor was it a mere land-grabbing bargain, for if Britain had not taken over the area Germany certainly would have done so. In view of the German company's methods in Tanganyika this might not have been entirely beneficial to the inhabitants.

CHAPTER VII

THE HISTORY OF UGANDA UP TO 1890

The history of Uganda before the nineteenth century is a shadowy affair depending partly upon fact and partly upon speculation. The difficulty is not so much that the African people of Uganda took no interest in their past. They did, and the story passed on by word of mouth from one generation to the next included the names and clans of hundreds of royal wives and children which were carefully memorized. But unfortunately the stories told in different parts of Uganda have only a few points in common, and each clan and tribe usually magnified its own part in the story to such an extent that the story of Uganda's early development varies from place to place.

The peoples and kingdoms of Uganda. Despite these differences there are some facts about which we may be reasonably certain. In the first place it is generally accepted that the population of the areas which now comprise Uganda is composed of Bantu, Nilotes, and Half-Hamites. These races are mixtures in varying proportions of the original negroes who may have come from Asia five or ten thousand years ago, and groups of Hamites of Caucasian stock who probably entered Africa at a very much later date from the north-east. The purpose of the Hamitic emigrations was to find new grazing grounds for their long-horned cattle. The last group of them to arrive in Central Africa probably travelled via Abyssinia and reached the highlands between Lakes Edward and Tanganyika in the late sixteenth century. From this centre these later Hamites, or Bahima as they are often called, spread out still searching for new pastures. As they spread, their organization and knowledge gave them superiority over the existing agricultural groups, and the kingdoms of Ruanda, Urundi, Karagwe, and Ankole came into existence. Further to the north the traditional kingdom of Kitara was started, of which Bunyoro claims to be the successor, and it was probably from Bunyoro–Kitara that

Map 12. Uganda, showing tribal areas.

outposts were pushed eastwards into what became Buganda, although tradition also suggests that Hamites had arrived in the Buganda area earlier from the region around Mount Elgon. It is at this time, in the latter part of the sixteenth century, that we also get the first names in the Buganda list of kings, which included Kintu, who is said to have entered with his people from the Mount Elgon area and eventually to have disappeared with his companion Nambi, the mother of the race, because he was so distressed at the behaviour of his people. Another of the kings was Kimera, who is said to have conquered Buganda from Bunyoro.

The growth of Buganda. During the seventeenth century these various kingdoms which now comprise Uganda began to develop each its own way of life and to achieve some sort of unity. At first Bunyoro seems to have been the most powerful and her warriors raided southwards into Ankole and Ruanda, and eastwards into Buganda and Busoga. During the eighteenth century Buganda became preeminent and in the reign of Mawanda raids began into Busoga. In the reign of Kyabagu, who died about 1780, Busoga was completely overrun. It was also during Kyabagu's reign that the first contact with the outside world was made, when cups and plates were brought in by way of Karagwe. Before the end of the century further articles, including cotton cloth, copper wire, and cowrie shells also arrived by the same route. In the last quarter of the eighteenth century the attack by Buganda upon Bunyoro began, and Kyabagu's son Junju drove the Banyoro from Buddu, which has since been part of Buganda. He was also accepted as overlord of Koki and Kiziba. At about the end of the eighteenth century Junju was killed by his brother, Semakokiro, whose son, Kamanya, continued the attack on Bunyoro by conquering Buwekula. Kamanya was succeeded by his son, Suna, who ruled from about 1831 to 1856. He was a bloodthirsty old tyrant whose corpse the funeral bearers threw upon the ground in contempt, but nevertheless by the end of his reign Buganda had built up the most advanced society in Central Africa and was the strongest power north and west of Lake Victoria. However, new powers, of whom the Arabs were the forerunners, were about to enter upon the Central African scene. But let us first look at the condition of Buganda before they appeared.

The political and social organization of Buganda. The political organization of Buganda before any Arab or European arrived was very similar to the feudal system on which European society was based during the Middle Ages. At the head was the king (Kabaka), who was elected by an assembly of the great chiefs and court officials. Usually the candidates from whom the new Kabaka was elected were the sons of the previous king, who would have had at least one wife from each clan (or kika), and it was the usual practice for each chief to vote for the son of the wife from his own clan. When the election to the throne had been decided the unsuccessful candidates were either imprisoned or executed. Apart from the Kabaka, the queen-mother (namasole), and the queen-sister (lubuga), who was chosen from the princesses, also occupied positions of great influence. In addition to the queen-mother and queen-sister the king would have several hundred wives. They were of less importance, however, although the chief wife (kadulubare) often exercised considerable influence.

The great chiefs (bakungu). To assist the king there was a council (lukiko) composed of the great chiefs (bakungu) who were non-hereditary officials appointed by the king. The most important of these great chiefs were those who ruled the four main districts other than Buganda proper. These districts were Kyagwe to the east ruled by Sekibobo, chief of Kyagwe; Bulemezi to the north-west ruled by Kangao, chief of Bulemezi; Buddu to the west ruled by Pokino, chief of Buddu; and Singo to the north ruled by Mukwenda, chief of Singo. In addition to these and other less important great chiefs, there were also officials in the royal household who were considered to rank as chiefs. Among these were the chief butler (musenero) and the chief baker (mufumbiro). All great chiefs had to spend several months each year at the king's capital (Kibuga), where each would have some honorary office. The rest of their time would be spent in their own province, where they acted as petty kings, each having his own body of officials, including a second in command, a head of slaves, a head of the upholsterers, and a chief of the gate-keepers. In addition each had a large number of wives, pages and slaves. From their subjects the chiefs were entitled to collect taxes, and in time of war it was the chief's duty to lead the army. When a chief died he would be wound in strips of bark-cloth and buried in one of his houses.

The sub-chiefs (bataka). Besides the great chiefs there were the heads of clans (bataka). As clan elders they were guardians of clan

113

lands, and formed an important class in Buganda, their position being an hereditary one and not depending on royal appointment like that of the great chiefs. Like the great chiefs, however, they kept large households of wives and slaves.

The peasants (bakopi). Far below them came the great peasant class (bakopi). They attached themselves to chiefs and in theory were allowed to change their service from one master to another if they wished; in fact such a change would usually be followed by severe punishment from the deserted chief. The main duty of the peasant was to follow his chief to war, which was for him an affair of tremendous suffering: smallpox took a very large toll of soldiers, and almost as many lives were lost in obtaining slaves as there were slaves obtained. At home the peasants' work consisted of cultivation and building houses. In return for his services the peasant would be given one, or possibly two wives, by the chief, but these were loaned rather than given permanently, and might be taken away by the chief at any time.

The slaves (badu). The lowest class were the slaves (badu). These were mostly drawn from the raids on the neighbouring countries of Bunyoro to the north-west, and Busoga to the east. Each would be worth an average of 15,000 cowrie shells (about £5). They had no rights, and Mackay mentions an instance when a chief with whom he was dining killed his slave for upsetting a gourd of cider. In general the slaves were used for cultivation and for service in the houses of the king and the chiefs.

Occupations, clothing, and housing. The Baganda were essentially a fighting people, but nevertheless a considerable standard had been reached in peaceful occupations. One of their chief staples of wealth was bark-cloth made from the bark of a type of fig tree; and bead work, which was exclusively a woman's occupation, had reached a remarkable standard of skilfulness. The two most usual articles of clothing were the bead necklet worn by both men and women, and a girdle made of grass and worked over with very small beads into beautiful patterns, worn by women only. Other clothing consisted of cow, goat, and antelope skins. The leopard was considered to be the royal animal, and for anyone other than royalty to wear a leopard skin was high treason. The houses in which the Baganda lived were simply beehive-shaped structures of grass supported by wooden poles, and the importance of the person to whom the house belonged could be estimated from its size.

Religion. The religion of Buganda was chiefly a mixture of witch-craft and ancestor worship known as Lubareism. Underlying this was the vague idea of a sublime creator, 'Katonda', of whom nothing was known and from whom nothing was expected. Next came Lubare, the upper air and waters, including the gods who inhabited them. The chief of these gods who inhabited the upper air and waters was Mukasa, the god of Lake Victoria, who was responsible for the lives of sailors, all of whom tried to win his favour by throwing offerings of bananas into the lake before starting a voyage. Lubare was also the giver of wealth and the giver of children. Among the many demigods Kintu, the traditional hero king, was outstanding. Others were Budo and Kibuka, and of these Budo may be taken as a typical example of how these demigods were worshipped. Budo was the mummified corpse of a very large man who was kept in a sitting position behind the curtains of his temple; he was guarded by a virgin who was honoured as his wife, and whose sacred person no one dared approach. On certain days drums were beaten and Budo was brought from behind his curtains to hold a reception attended by the neighbouring chiefs and important people, who knelt in his presence. Unfortunately, however, Lubareism did not stop at such harmless practices, for on important occasions such as the accession of a king a vast human sacrifice known as 'kiwendo' was necessary. On the accession of Mutesa in 1856, for example, many hundreds of slaves had their throats cut as a sacrifice.

An estimate of Buganda in the mid-nineteenth century. Because early explorers were surprised to find a society such as we have described in Africa they sometimes tended to represent Buganda as better than it really was. Indeed, there was little resemblance to Paradise in the kingdom over which Kings Mutesa and Mwanga ruled. Each was a despot with no regard for human life. When Speke first showed Mutesa his gun the king immediately ordered a page to go outside and test its efficiency by shooting at the first man he saw, and he was delighted to hear that the man had been killed. On a picnic to the lake one of Mutesa's wives playfully offered him a fruit, and he immediately ordered that she should be executed because, he said, it was the first time a woman had ever had the impudence to offer him anything. For more serious offenders a permanent set of executioners were ready who mutilated and killed their victims in the most horrible ways they could devise, the standard method of finally killing a man being slow fire. Nor were the activities of the king confined to his court and to those who offended him. His chief interests were war and slave raiding, which necessitated a permanent army and kept the route through which the army passed and the areas which it raided in desolation, while peasants perished, slaves were captured, and children were killed by the thousand. In West Africa at the same time the same despotic rule by chiefs with absolutely no regard for human life was found. Perhaps it reached its most hideous depths at Benin, where the King and Juju priests, and most of the population, practised wholesale human sacrifice, torture, and mutilation on such a scale that the smell of blood was overpowering and the roads were lined with crucified corpses, skulls, and skeletons. Few now living in West Africa or on the sunny lands of the central African plateau would choose to step back a century in time.

The arrival of the first Arabs, 1848–52. Such was Buganda when it was first visited by Arabs and Europeans. The first outside influence of modern times to penetrate into Buganda was Arabian. Somewhere about 1848, in the reign of Suna, an Arab half-breed named Saim entered the country and was followed a few years later by Isa bin Hussein, a Baluchi deserter from the Sultan of Zanzibar's forces, who became one of Suna's advisers and was found at the capital when the great Tabora trader, Snay bin Amir, visited it in 1852. From these beginnings grew the substantial Arab population which the first missionaries found in Buganda when they arrived in 1877. The chief interests of the Arabs were—as usual—slaves and ivory, and this, together with the guns they brought, gave a disastrous impetus to slave raiding. The result was that the kings of Buganda rapidly became the greatest slave-hunters in the world. Mutesa kept a permanent army of 6000 men continually devastating the neighbouring tribes merely for the sake of slaves who were sold to the Arabs at the rate of one musket for two slaves, or one red cloth for one slave, or one hundred bullets for a female slave. The effect of the Arabs on the court was to increase luxury and immorality; although they preached the Koran and gained a considerable number of converts, they were mainly interested in trade, and Mohammedanism never established a hold comparable to that of Christianity. In one way it actually helped the Christian missions by its effects in undermining the old beliefs in Lubareism, which was already in decline when the C.M.S. arrived. By the 1870's the Arab traders in Buganda were some of the most influential people in Mutesa's court. They brought him guns and ammunition for his raids; they brought him cottons, silks, and bracelets for his clothing; and they brought him news of an outside world which he could not understand, but whose power he grew to fear.

The arrival of Speke, 1862. Before the Arabs had become influential in Buganda the first European had appeared on the scene. This was Speke, who arrived in 1862 and provided Mutesa and his court with a great deal to laugh at and a great deal to think about. His hat and his umbrella were regarded with tremendous admiration, and his rifle and pistol created a great impression. Speke was also impressed by Mutesa:

The king was a good-looking, well-figured, tall young man of twenty-five. He sat on a red blanket spread upon a square platform of royal grass and was scrupulously well dressed in a new raiment of bark-cloth. The hair of his head was cut short, except on top, where it was combed into a high ridge. On his neck was a large ring of beautifully worked small beads. On one arm was another bead ornament, prettily devised, and on the other a wooden charm, tied by a string covered with snake skin. On every finger and every toe he had alternate brass and copper rings, and above the ankles a stocking of pretty beads. Everything was light, neat, and elegant.

From February until July Speke was detained at Mutesa's court, where Grant joined him in May; thence he marched first eastwards, looking for the Nile, and then northwards to Gondokoro, where he met Sir Samuel Baker and his wife and encouraged them in their southward exploration of the Nile, which resulted in the discovery of Lake Albert. After Speke's departure from Mutesa, twelve years passed before the next white man, Colonel Long, entered Buganda.

The Egyptian invasion. During these twelve years two things of great importance occurred. First, in the southerly part of what is now Uganda, and especially in Mutesa's court in Buganda, the Arabs greatly increased their influence. Secondly, in the north an invasion came from the Sudan. The root cause of this invasion lay again in the zeal of the British anti-slavery movement. As the British had requested the Sultan of Zanzibar to abolish the east coast slave trade, so they had also requested the Egyptian rulers to end the trade in slaves and ivory which came down the Nile to Khartoum from areas including what is now the Acholi area of Uganda; but despite British protests Egyptian rulers had in fact encouraged and profited from the Nile slave trade, until in 1863 Ismail became the ruler, or khedive, of Egypt. Ismail was by no means the perfect ruler—he was reckless with finance and brought Egypt to bankruptcy—but at least he did make a sincere effort to stop the Nile slave trade which his predecessors had encouraged. His method was to occupy the southern Sudan, from which most of the slaves were drawn, and which became known as Equatoria. Since Mehemet Ali's invasion of the Sudan in 1819 the Egyptians had maintained a loose occupation of the country as far south as Gondokoro. Now, in 1869, Ismail extended this southwards to include the whole of the equatorial Nile region, and as governor-general of this province of Equatoria he appointed Sir Samuel Baker. No doubt Ismail was interested in exploiting the resources of Equatoria, but had he not sincerely desired the abolition of the slave trade also, he would not have appointed men like Baker and Gordon as its governors.

Baker's work for Equatoria, 1872–3. Equatoria included the northern part of what is now Uganda, and the first act of Baker after his arrival at Gondokoro to assume his office as governor-general was to advance southwards into Acholi and Bunyoro. He arrived in Bunyoro in 1872 and formally announced its annexation to Egypt. Naturally enough King Kabarega of Bunyoro resented this, and attacked Baker at the battle of Masindi, forcing him to withdraw northwards again. On his northward march Baker fortified Foweira and Fatiko and then proceeded down the Nile to Gondokoro. When he resigned in 1873 he had gained a great reputation amongst Africans and Europeans alike, but the Nile slave trade had not been seriously checked and the posts of Foweira and Fatiko, which had been intended to stop the trade, became themselves centres of oppression to the local population.

Gordon's work for Equatoria, 1874–6. Mutesa of Buganda had observed this activity with considerable alarm, and when General Gordon took over from Baker as governor-general of Equatoria in 1874, Mutesa hastened to send him presents and messages for the khedive. In return Gordon sent his American lieutenant, Colonel Chaille-Long, to Mutesa and obtained from him an acknowledgement of Egyptian sovereignty. In the following year, 1875, Gordon sent his second envoy to Mutesa. This time it was a Frenchman, Ernest Linant de Bellefonds, and his purpose was to obtain Mutesa's promise to forbid the buying and selling of slaves in his country. Again Mutesa was alarmed, but gave immediate consent, for, although he had no intention of keeping the promise, he had no desire to gain the enmity of the governor-general of Equatoria. Meanwhile Gordon was struggling with his tremendous task of bringing Equatoria into some sort of order and ending the slave trade by establishing a network of forts to safeguard the route from the Sudan up the Nile into Lake Albert, and then via Lake Kyoga to Lake Victoria. In January 1876 he was constructing a fort at Mruli on the western end of Lake Kyoga and from there he sent to Mutesa his third mission, this time under an Egyptian, Nuehr Aga, and supported with troops, to ask permission to establish a fort at the place where Speke had first encountered the Nile. In July yet a fourth mission was sent to Mutesa, this time led by the German Emin Pasha, with presents for the king and to support Nuehr Aga. Fortunately, however, for Mutesa in the next month Gordon finally decided to abandon any attempt to occupy Buganda; he had become convinced it was impossible to control the area with soldiers of such poor quality and with a line of communications 2500 miles long constantly interrupted by the jealous governors of the Sudan. Much to Mutesa's relief, Emin and Nuehr Aga were accordingly withdrawn from Buganda and rejoined Gordon at Mruli in September. But although Gordon had abandoned his scheme for occupying Buganda he had no intention of abandoning interest in Bunyoro, and from Mruli he marched across Kabarega's kingdom and arranged for a greater degree of control over it, which resulted in the establishment of forts at Masindi, Kisuga, and Londu. Then he turned northwards to return to England, and resigned his post. The resignation was only temporary, however, for in the next year, 1877, Gordon returned to Egyptian service, this time as governor not only of Equatoria but also of the northern Sudan; in this capacity he appointed Emin Pasha as governor of Equatoria under his supervision. Emin was an efficient governor, and although the Bunyoro forts were withdrawn in 1879 the presence of Emin's troops so near his frontier kept Mutesa uneasy.

The arrival of the C.M.S., 1876–7. By this time another invasion had taken place which was primarily neither political nor concerned with the abolition of the slave trade. It was simply concerned with bringing Christianity to Buganda, and it was the direct result of Stanley's visit to Mutesa's kingdom in 1875. During that visit Stanley—the rough, tough journalist of African exploration who had looked upon the face of Dr Livingstone at Ujiji and never forgotten it—had taken the opportunity of introducing the precepts of Christianity to Mutesa, who listened so attentively that Stanley sent a letter to the *Daily Telegraph* appealing for missionaries. De Bellefonds, who was at Mutesa's court at the same time, took this letter back to Gordon, who forwarded it to England. In fact Mutesa saw in Christianity not a new spiritual inspiration but the possibility of a new political power which might prove a useful weapon against the Egyptian advance from the north and the Arab influx from the east. At the time this was not realized and when Stanley's letter appeared in the *Daily Telegraph* in November 1875 an anonymous offer of £5000 was received by the C.M.S. within three days, and others followed rapidly. From the missions' point of view it was a wild idea: for the route to Buganda along the old Arab route from Zanzibar through

Tabora and then north to Lake Victoria, which was the only route yet explored, took at least six months; moreover, even when the mission had been established it would be completely isolated from any others. Despite these disadvantages eight missionaries volunteered to go to Buganda, and the expedition, under the leadership of Lt. Shergold Smith, landed at Bagamoyo in July 1876. Within a year only half of them were still alive, two having died of fever, and two, including Shergold Smith, having been killed in a skirmish on Ukerewe Island. By the end of 1877 only Wilson was in Buganda. Next year he was joined by the greatest of all the early Buganda missionaries, Alexander Mackay, who had been struggling through from the coast for over two years. Mackay was a professional engineer, and from the outset Mutesa had a very genuine respect both for his personal character and for his technical ability. In 1879 three more Anglican missionaries, Litchfield, Pearson and Felkin, arrived, having travelled up the Nile; like Mackay and Wilson they were warmly welcomed by Mutesa.

The arrival of the White Fathers, 1876. The Anglican missionaries were not the only invaders of Buganda on behalf of the Christian faith. The Roman Catholic White Fathers, governed by Cardinal Lavigerie, were also interested, and a week after the arrival of the three Anglican missionaries Father Lourdel and Brother Amans reached Mutesa's capital, soon to be followed by three more White Fathers.

Mutesa and the missions. Buganda was not the only region of Africa where both Roman Catholic and Protestant missionaries worked, but it was the only place where they were brought into close contact with one another, both sets of missionaries being obliged to stay at Mutesa's court. The results were unfortunate. Mackay and Lourdel, the Protestant and Roman Catholic leaders, were not men who were fond of compromise, and from the outset both misunderstood and opposed the teaching of the other, so that fierce rivalry grew up between the two missions. To increase the difficulties the Mohammedan Arabs were a still greater enemy to both Protestants and Roman Catholics, and they took every opportunity to discredit the Christians before Mutesa, who became increasingly confused and hostile. To him religions represented political powers. Behind Mackay he saw Queen Victoria; behind Lourdel he saw the power of France; and because he believed England and France to be more powerful than the Sultan of Zanzibar, he at first favoured the Christian missions in preference to the Mohammedanism of the Arabs. Before long he realized that the rival missions could not provide him with armies, and his favours to them ceased. By the end of 1879 both Mohammedanism and Christianity were out of favour and Lubareism, accompanied by its human sacrifices, temporarily revived.

The work of the missions, 1879–82. Meanwhile the missions proceeded with their work. In 1880 Lourdel baptized the first of his converts into the Roman Catholic Church, and in 1881 Mackay received a request for baptism from one of his most trusted pupils, Sembera, who was received into the Church with four others in 1882. At the same time Mackay's little printing press produced the first translations of parts of the New Testament in Luganda. The next step was to teach the people to read, and soon both missions had more 'readers' than they could easily manage. Protestant and Catholic rivalry did not prevent Christianity from gaining in Buganda one of its most rapid conquests.

The years of persecution, 1882–5. But the path was far from easy. By November 1882 the king had become so unfriendly that the Roman Catholic Fathers withdrew their mission altogether from Buganda to the south of Lake Victoria, although Mackay and O'Flaherty remained. The worst years, however, were 1884 and 1885. Several circumstances made these the worst from the missions' point of view. Mutesa died in October 1884. He died a pagan and at first the missions had high hopes that his son Mwanga, who was elected Kabaka and had been one of Mackay's 'readers', would be a great improvement. He was, indeed, the first Buganda king whose accession was not accompanied by vast human sacrifices to Lubare. But hopes were soon disappointed, for Mwanga proved extremely unreliable. Almost at once he supported the Arab party and became a Mohammedan. At the same time he started persecuting the Christian mission, partly because the Christian pages opposed the immorality of

his court, and in January 1885 he seized, mutilated, and then burnt
to death three young boys who were helpers of Mackay and Ashe.
Behind this persecution there lay also the political fear that the
Europeans would take his kingdom. Several incidents had suggested
this to him. In December 1883 Joseph Thomson had reached the
northern end of Lake Victoria by the direct route from Mombasa
through Masailand. No one had taken this route to the lake previously, and as the Baganda tradition was that Buganda would be
conquered by people approaching from that direction Mwanga was
particularly alarmed. His alarm was greatly increased when, early in
1885, news reached him of Carl Peters's annexations on the mainland
opposite Zanzibar, and the Arabs did all in their power to persuade
him that Thomson's journey and Peters's treaties were all part of a
determined plan by the Europeans to conquer Buganda. The missionaries, they said, were secretly assisting this plan. Mwanga believed them.

The murder of Bishop Hannington, 1885. It was therefore a particularly unfortunate moment for the newly appointed Bishop of
Eastern Equatorial Africa, James Hannington, to attempt to take up
his work in Uganda, at the earliest possible moment, by taking
Thomson's route. He took the direct route because he was enthu-
siastic and brave, and because General Mathews and Kirk had both
sanctioned it, but he took it in direct opposition to the advice of his
missionaries in Buganda and of the only man who had taken it before
—Joseph Thomson. He left Rabai on 3 July 1885. On 1 January 1886
the following telegram was sent from Zanzibar:

Bishop Hannington, who left Mombasa in June last, in order to find
if possible a new road to the Victoria, which will obviate the long
detour by Unyanyembe, has been seized by order of the king within
two days march of Buganda. The latest report is that the king has given
secret orders to have the Bishop executed.

And such was the unfortunate truth. In October, as Hannington
entered Luba's in Busoga he was imprisoned, and eight days afterwards, on Mwanga's orders, he was killed.

The martyrs of 1886. Having taken such a decisive step, Mwanga now considered murdering the European missionaries at his capital, and for a while their lives were in extreme danger. Then, in May 1886, he decided to get rid of the pages in his court who opposed his immorality, and he demanded which of them were 'readers'. Of those who stepped forward twelve Protestants were done to death and thirteen Roman Catholics, while in a general persecution of Christian converts in and around the capital 200 victims were martyred. As a proof of the sincerity of the Baganda Christians the persecution was a lasting inspiration, but as an attempt to wipe out Christianity it was an utter failure. In fact it left the Church in Buganda and the neighbouring areas stronger than ever, for even when persecution was at its height converts came to the missions by night asking for baptism, while converts who fled spread their faith to the friends who sheltered them. By August 1886 persecution had died out, but in the next year Mackay was exiled to Usambiro on the southern shore of the lake for his persistent criticism of Mwanga's behaviour. In 1887 his place was taken by another missionary, Cyril Gordon.

The revolution of September 1888. In September of 1888 a revolution took place in Buganda. The occasion was a childish plot of Mwanga's to get rid of all the Mohammedan and Christian supporters, whose growth he found alarmingly rapid, by marooning them on an island in the lake. Then he planned to revert to Lubareism and rule in absolute power unhindered by the rival parties whom he found so difficult. His plot was discovered; the Protestants, Catholics and Mohammedans refused to embark for the island, and the Baganda of all three parties combined to depose Mwanga, who fled to the south of the lake. His elder brother, Kiwewa, was made Kabaka in his place; freedom of worship was declared, and the most important official positions were shared among the three parties.

The importance of the revolution and the growth of parties. This revolution was a turning point in Buganda history, for Mwanga, by his exceptional incompetence and cruelty, destroyed his own prestige and some of the enormous traditional respect of the Baganda for their Kabaka. The loyalty of the chiefs, which had once been wholly his, was now divided into factions. Under a strong Kabaka this division would have been most unlikely, but Mwanga was not strong, and the chiefs who crowded his capital were in many cases 'readers' and had developed a certain loyalty to one or other of the missions. As Mwanga's conduct made loyalty to him increasingly difficult, so were the chiefs thrown more towards the missions in their loyalty, and began to divide into parties centred on the new religions. But it would not be accurate to describe these parties as only religious in their origin. Many of the chiefs simply saw in Mwanga's weakness and the development of rival parties a chance to increase their own power, and joined what they considered to be the strongest party in the hope that when war came they would share in the spoils. Politics was also a major factor, for the Mohammedans corresponded to the Arab party, the Roman Catholics to the French party, and the Protestants to the English party. How deeply politics entered into the question varied, but with the scramble for Africa in full swing suspicion was rife. The Protestant missionaries hoped that Buganda would become a British protectorate and not come under the power of the Arabs, French, or Germans. The Catholic mission also had some slight hopes that Buganda might become French, but they were especially anxious to prevent its becoming a British sphere of influence; fearful of losing their own influential position, they did everything possible to discourage Mwanga from accepting a British protectorate. Above all, the Arabs, no longer content with no more than their trading profits, were quite clearly aiming at the domination of Buganda instead.

The Arab conquest of Buganda, October 1888. It is not surprising, therefore, to find that the month after Mwanga had been deposed and Kiwewa had been installed as Kabaka it was the Arabs who attempted to dominate him and drive out the Christian missions. For a time their method was most effective. They simply persuaded Kiwewa that the Christians intended to depose him, and then secretly filled the royal enclosure with armed men and forced the Christian chiefs to leave the capital. The European missionaries also, both Roman Catholic and Protestant, were obliged to escape to the south of the lake, the Protestants to Usambiro and the Roman Catholics to Bukumbi. Thus the Arab, or Mohammedan party, was left in complete control with Kiwewa as their figurehead. When he refused to submit to the Mohammedan rite of circumcision he was deposed by the Arabs, and his younger brother Kalema was proclaimed Kabaka. Buganda became in fact an Arab state.

The Arabs expelled, October 1889. It did not remain Arab for long. The Christian chiefs and their supporters who had fled from the capital in October 1888 had taken refuge in Ankole to the west, where their numbers steadily increased, for the Mohammedan rule was intolerant and unpopular. At the same time an unexpected event had suggested a plan to the exiled missions on the south of the lake. In December 1888 Mwanga had paddled up in a canoe to the White Fathers' base at Bukumbi; he had appeared to be penitent and had been given refuge. The idea was now put forward by the White Fathers that the Christians at Ankole, assisted by the Protestant and Roman Catholic missions, should combine to drive out the Arab party from Buganda and restore Mwanga to his throne. Mackay refused to help, having had quite enough experience of Mwanga already, but the Christians of Ankole readily agreed and Charles Stokes, who had come to Buganda in 1879 as a C.M.S. missionary, but was now a trader, offered to lend his boat to help in the restoration. In April 1889 Stokes took Mwanga across the lake to Buddu. From there he advanced towards the Buganda capital, but his forces were poorly organized and were at first defeated by Kalema's troops. The defeat was not decisive, however, and Mwanga and his supporters were able to withdraw from the mainland and establish a new base first on the Sese Islands opposite the Buddu shore, and then, in June, on Bulingugwe Island in Murchison Gulf, only eight miles from the capital. Here he was joined by Lourdel and Denoit of the White Fathers, and Walker and Gordon of the C.M.S. Meanwhile the Christian refugees in Ankole, led by the Protestant chief Apolo Kagwa, started their advance towards Buganda in September; aided by Mwanga's troops from Bulingugwe they defeated Kalema and the Arab party, and re-took the capital. On 11 October Mwanga entered in triumph. Apolo Kagwa was appointed Prime Minister in recognition of his leadership of the victorious Christian army; the chief offices of state were divided equally between the Catholic and Protestant chiefs; and Mwanga built for himself a new capital at Mengo.

The Christian victory was a brief one, however, for after their defeat the Arab party had withdrawn north-westwards into Bunyoro and made an alliance with King Kabarega. Thus reinforced, they returned to Buganda in November 1889, and reoccupied the capital, Mwanga and the Christians being forced to withdraw again to the islands. For three months Kalema and the Arab party remained in power; then once more the Christians rallied, and in February 1890 they decisively defeated the Arab–Muslim troops at Bulwanyi. Once more Kalema and the remains of his army withdrew to Bunyoro, and Mwanga re-entered his capital.

Roman Catholic predominance. It was, perhaps, natural that after this triumph Mwanga should rely most for advice upon the Roman Catholic party, who had sheltered him and helped to organize the movement which resulted in his return. Thus, Father Lourdel became firmly established as his exclusive European adviser. This was doubly unfortunate for the Protestants. In the first place it led to the Catholic party's becoming easily the larger of the two, chiefs who had no particular loyalty to either party naturally siding with that which the king favoured. In the second place it caused Mwanga to be prejudiced against the British by Lourdel, who realized that as a result of the 1886 treaty Buganda and the country surrounding it were likely to become a British or German sphere. Of the two he preferred that it should become German, for he feared that a British occupation might mean the triumph of the Protestant mission.

The expeditions of Stanley, Jackson and Peters. While the Muslim–Christian war had been in progress three expeditions had been approaching with the alleged purpose of relieving Emin Pasha, whose province of Equatoria had been cut off from the Northern Sudan by the Mahdist revolt, leaving Emin stranded in Central Africa. The first of these three expeditions was that of Stanley, who took Emin with him to Zanzibar. But he left behind a large number of his Sudanese troops under Selim Bey, who arrived at the collecting base at Kavalli's on the south-west of Lake Albert. In July 1889 Stanley passed through Ankole, where he was asked to help the refugee Christians, but being unprepared for delay he passed on. The second expedition was that of Sir Frederick Jackson, on behalf of the I.B.E.A. Company, which had arrived at Mumia's in November 1889; not wishing to break his orders by entering Buganda Jackson had hesitated to answer Mwanga's appeal for help and had set off towards Mount Elgon in search of ivory. In February, while he was away, the third expedition arrived. This was the German one of Dr Carl Peters, who calmly searched Jackson's base camp at Mumia's, read all his letters there including those of Mwanga requesting help, and then hastened on to the Buganda capital and offered Mwanga a treaty. The Arab party had been defeated at Bulwanyi a fortnight before Peters arrived, but they were still in Bunyoro and a potential danger; Mwanga, on the advice of Lourdel, therefore signed the treaty Peters offered him. In great jubilation Peters then continued his journey to the south of the lake, having heard that Jackson had returned to Mumia's. Jackson had indeed returned to Mumia's in March and had discovered all that had happened. He was not pleased. Bristling with indignation he bore down upon Mengo in the hope of laying his hands upon the incorrigible Peters, but his bird had flown. Then, in place of the German treaty, he offered Mwanga a British one, which even the C.M.S. missionaries considered onerous. Not surprisingly it was rejected, whereupon Jackson returned to the coast for further orders. This comedy of errors played out by Peters and Jackson had one very unfortunate effect. It widened the division between the Catholic and Protestant parties. Even before either expedition arrived the Protestants had resented the way in which Father Lourdel monopolized Mwanga. When he pushed Mwanga into accepting Peters's treaty without consulting the Protestant party the friction was greatly increased, and although the Protestant, as well as the Catholic, chiefs signed the agreement they did so with great reluctance.

The Heligoland Treaty. So far as political results were concerned Jackson and Peters might just as well have stayed at home, for the whole question of Buganda's future had been decided over their heads by the Heligoland Treaty which definitely assigned Buganda and its neighbouring territories to Britain. Yet the British Government itself had no more intention of financing the occupation and administration than it had had of financing the area acquired by the 1886 treaty. In Uganda, as well as on the coast, the I.B.E.A. Company was expected to organize and pay for the occupation. It was a task far beyond its financial resources, but it gallantly accepted the challenge, and in the next chapter we shall see the results.

CHAPTER VIII

KINGDOMS AND LEADERS

In this chapter we shall look at three men—Kimweri, Tippoo Tip and Lugard. They have been chosen because each in his different way was important, and because each one will help us to see in a little detail some portions of the very varied picture which East Africa presented as outside influences became increasingly felt. By looking first at the African chief, then at the Arab trader and finally at the European soldier-administrator we may also realize how the pattern of African life was altered first by the Arab traders and then by Europeans.

Kimweri and Usambara. Before we look at our African chief we must remember that all East Africa was not ruled in the same way before outsiders arrived. Political and tribal organization ranged from despotism in some areas to extreme democracy in others. Much depended on the ability of the individual leader; much depended on the traditions of the tribe. Kimweri was strong and he ruled as a dictator—so did the Kabakas of Buganda. But in other areas some tribes, such as the Kikuyu and Wakamba, preferred a more democratic form of government with councils. With this in mind let us see how Kimweri's particular sort of rule worked out.

Tradition has it that in the eighteenth century a man named Bega came to the Usambara Mountains and was accepted by the Sambaa people there as their king. He was a bold warrior with bold descendants, and the greatest of all was Kimweri, known by his subjects as 'Simba wa Muene' or 'Lion of Heaven'. He was born about 1800, and by 1840 he ruled a kingdom which included most of the Pare Mountains and the Usambara Mountains, and reached to the coast itself. Its southern boundary was the Pangani River, beyond which the firearms of the Zigu prevented further advance. All the same, Kimweri's kingdom had half a million people and comprised an area similar to a parallelogram 140 miles long and 60 miles wide.

He ruled it with an iron hand. Taxes, usually in cloth, had to be paid even though hut-owners hastily buried their valuables when the soldiers collecting them appeared. Discipline was swift and strong. Disobedience meant instant selling into slavery. No one was allowed to rival the king in grandeur; it was illegal to ride on a horse or donkey, to wear expensive clothes, or to travel far from home. No one cared to look rich for fear of appearing to rival the king in wealth. Only on the coast, where the people might have turned the Arabs against him, was there some relaxation of the strictness of Kimweri's rule. There the Swahili were exempt from taxation and could ride and wear expensive clothes if they wished. They even called themselves the 'Wangwana' or 'Free People'.

Krapf, who visited Kimweri in 1848 and 1852, was most impressed. He noticed the efficiency and discipline as soon as he crossed the frontier into Usambara because his entry, his route, his timetable and his departure were all organized and fixed. Every movement was laid down. But there were assets as well as restrictions. He was given an official guide, soldiers were detailed to carry his baggage, and free food was provided at every village. True, he was expected to give the king a present; but this was a small price to pay for so many conveniences. Krapf could hardly praise Kimweri enough. 'Never before had a journey been made so easy for me', he wrote; and he went on to say, 'As regards security, I do not believe that one could be safer in any European country than in Usambara.'

In his court at Vuga, Kimweri had two main officials to help him. They were the Mdoe (or vizier) and the Mboki (or military chief). In addition he divided his kingdom into districts and put a governor, usually one of his sons, in charge of each. Every governor had to send a representative, called a Mlau, to Kimweri's court, and it was through the Mlau that the governor would transact his business. Sometimes Kimweri delegated his authority to his daughters also, for Krapf speaks of them as ruling various villages.

Along the coast we have already seen that Kimweri had to handle his kingdom with a less rigid hand, because in this region his authority overlapped with that of the Sultan of Zanzibar, whose commercial activity made its busy way into Usambara, as elsewhere. Tanga remained under the exclusive control of the Sultan through a governor, but along the rest of the northern coastal strip Kimweri asserted his authority by appointing headmen known as Diwanis. Their appointment was confirmed by the Sultan. This solution seemed to please everyone. The Sultan's trade continued, Kimweri's authority was acknowledged, and the Diwanis themselves had the special privileges of being entitled to carry an umbrella of state and walk about accompanied by a band of music.

Kimweri died about 1860. A period of internal strife followed and his kingdom diminished, but its fame was so proudly remembered that when Sir Donald Cameron was reviving tribal authorities in the next century Africans from the mountains to the coast were anxious to be considered descendants of Kimweri's subjects.

Tippoo Tip and the Upper Congo. Kimweri was a strong king ruling over a kingdom into which Arabs came as traders and sometimes, by invitation, as court officials. In the next generation, from the 1860's to the 1880's, Mirambo, the Nyamwezi chief whom we met in chapters I and II, found himself in a rather different position. His domain lay across the main route of the Arab caravans, and as a result of his demand for tribute from them he found himself in competition with the Arab settlements at Tabora and Ujiji, which tried to bring the local chiefs over to the Arab side. Nevertheless, Mirambo remained the paramount power. In some areas, however, where the African people were more primitive and had no powerful rulers, the Arab influence was much greater, and to the west of Lake Tanganyika there was for a while something resembling an Arab empire. Its creator and ruler was Tippoo Tip, the son of an important Arab trader at Tabora.

He was born in the early 1840's and seems to have realized quite early in his career that a greater political control would give him a greater opportunity to collect ivory. With this idea in mind he took an increasing interest in the land to the west of the lake, where elephants and their ivory were found in abundance and where human life was cheap. In 1867 he defeated the chief of Itawa, lying between the south of Lake Tanganyika and Lake Mweru, but his more important period began in the early 1870's when he led an expedition into the area of Utetera, between the Lomami and Luapula tributaries of the Congo, and began to exercise a direct political as well as commercial authority there. He collected taxes, he arbitrated and punished in tribal disputes, he deposed chiefs, he set up regents—and he collected an enormous quantity of ivory and slaves. In the centre of the continent Tippoo, in the 1870's, was a foremost power to be reckoned with. Whoever penetrated to the heart of Africa seemed to meet him at some stage. Livingstone met him near Lake Mweru in 1867, and Tippoo also participated in Stanley's expedition down the Congo in 1877. To both explorers he was always courteous and often gave vital help, although fundamentally their interests were incompatible.

In 1879 the Sultan of Zanzibar's messengers told Tippoo Tip that the Sultan required him to return to the coast and pay his accounts, which were ten years overdue. It then took him one year to settle the widespread spider's web of his Upper Congo empire, but by the end of 1882 he was back at Zanzibar.

There he found a worried Sultan Barghash, for European interest in the Sultan's dominions was becoming alarming. In view of it Sir John Kirk encouraged Barghash to consolidate his authority inland from the coast. This seemed sound advice, and Tippoo Tip seemed clearly the outstanding Arab trader, so Barghash intended to offer him the post of *wali* (or governor) of Tabora. Then came another bid for Tippoo's services, this time from Leopold's International Association, which offered to provide him with the firearms to defend his Upper Congo domain provided that he would share the profits. Barghash, hearing of this, feared that the trade of the continent which had flowed out through Zanzibar might soon begin to flow out through the Congo instead. Determined to resist this, he urged Tippoo to return and take possession of the Congo Basin, making sure that no ivory was shipped westwards down the river.

In 1883, with a caravan miles long and containing 1000 guns, Tippoo hastened back to the Upper Congo. For three years he seems to have attempted to assert the Sultan's authority in some ways, although others considered that his commercial journeys were in the main 'plundering expeditions. . . . Anything else, any introduction of law and order, any spread of civilization, was merely subsidiary and incidental.' In 1886 he was back again in Zanzibar with another enormous caravan. By then both he and Barghash knew that the European countries had allotted the Congo to the Belgians and were partitioning the East African mainland itself. In view of the superior forces confronting them there was little that the Sultan or Tippoo could do. Barghash was a disillusioned man, and although Tippoo Tip himself reluctantly accepted the governorship of Stanley Falls district on behalf of the Congo State in 1887, he was soon back permanently in Zanzibar. There he spent a very wealthy retirement, saying very little about his past.

With the retirement of Tippoo Tip the great age of the Arab slavers ended, and the last hopes of a mainland empire attached to Zanzibar disappeared. It is hard to regret their passing. Even the missionaries who opposed political interference, and those who were inclined to support the Arab cause, did not condone the increasing inhumanity and could hardly fail to realize that effective occupation by Europe provided the most likely method of relief.

Lord Lugard and Uganda. Livingstone had said that his aim was to 'introduce the Negro family into the body corporate of nations'. This aim was shared by others as well as missionaries. For example, the leading businessman, Sir William Mackinnon, was more interested in developing East Africa than in making a profit, and his ideals were shared by a young man named Frederick Dealtry Lugard.

By profession Lugard was a soldier. In 1879, at the age of twenty-one, he was in India fighting against the Afghans; six years later he was in the Sudan campaign, and the year after he was fighting in Burma. This last campaign led to a breakdown in his health, so he asked to be put on half-pay and be temporarily released from regimental duties. Never did anyone choose a more extraordinary convalescence. So far from resting at home Lugard decided to find a change in visiting Africa, where he hoped he might be useful in doing something to prevent the continuance of the Arab slave trade.

Therefore, in 1888, at the age of thirty, and with only £50 in his pocket and his rifle, he took a passage on a boat to Africa.

His first employment was on the northern shores of Lake Nyasa, fighting slavers on behalf of the African Lakes Company, who had accepted his services. Probably they would have accepted anybody. To them this rather short, strange captain with his sharp nose and long moustache was useful because he knew how to fight, but they had no more knowledge of his real worth than anyone else. For the young captain was much more than just a man with a gun. He was a born leader with immense courage and a charmed life. Where he led others would follow, whether it was storming the slavers' stockade at Kopa-Kopa's or breaching the defences at Kano. In his East and West African campaigns he gained the confidence and respect of Europeans and Africans to a quite exceptional extent. His courage was remarkable. In battle he never hesitated to attack overwhelming odds, and in 1903 set off with a force of 732 native troops and 36 British troops to attack the fortresses of Kano and Sokoto, which mustered well over 3000 troops behind their crenellated walls—and he succeeded. While hunting in India he once crawled through a narrow aperture into a dark cave after a wounded man-eating tiger in order to kill it—and kill it he did. In addition to the usual dangers of war there was endless malaria to be faced, and other tropical troubles which brought so many of the early European visitors to East and West Africa to the grave within a few months of arrival. There must have been a particularly vigilant providence over such a man to enable him to survive to the age of eighty-seven. Along with this leadership and courage there went a strong sense of duty and a real kindness and depth of understanding. He believed it was the duty of the white man to assist the African, and it was his desire to help to prevent the continuance of the slave trade that led him to Africa in the first place. Moreover, his ideals had a definite human warmth about them. When his caravan succeeded in freeing some slaves near Tsavo he looked after the freed African children himself, referring to them as his 'nursery' and watching over their health and games with a paternal eye.

Some of these qualities became evident after a year's campaign against the Nyasaland slavers, during which a bullet went through his chest and both his arms were broken. Requests for his services came from several sides. One offer came from Cecil Rhodes, but Lugard decided instead to accept employment with Mackinnon's British East Africa Association.

The Expedition to Uganda. For the first months of 1890 he was occupied in establishing supply bases for the Company's caravans travelling inland. When he started, the only inland base was Machakos, 350 miles from Mombasa. He succeeded in establishing five more; one at Makongeni, two on the Sabaki River (the Athi), one at Kibwezi, and one on the Wakutukoa River. In July of that year came more import-ant issues. The Heligoland Treaty was signed, by which Uganda became a British sphere, and the Company was expected to make this effective. Accordingly in August Lugard set off from the coast with an expedi-tion. As he expected the administrator, Sir Francis de Winton, to catch him up with reinforcements, he built a fort and waited for him at Dagoretti, which was a few miles from Nairobi's present site and on the edge of Kikuyu country. Lugard got on with the Kikuyu better than any previous traveller, and regarded them as the finest tribe he had met in East Africa and well able to hold their own against their Masai neighbours. However, his stay was cut short, for he received orders to push on to Uganda with all speed and not wait for Sir Francis. By the end of the year he had reached the Kabaka Mwanga and had persuaded him to sign a treaty recognizing the Company's supreme authority. The Company on their side were to protect Uganda and treat all missionaries with complete impartiality.

The treaty was sensible enough in the circumstances, but it did little to alter the difficulties of the situation. Buganda was impover-ished and divided. The Muslim–Christian war had left many areas desolated, food was scarce, a cattle pest had taken almost all the cattle, and plague had sadly reduced the population. More serious still was the increasing friction between the Roman Catholic and Protestant parties. In fact by 1890 these parties were more commonly called the Fransa (French) and Ingleza (English) than Catholic and

Protestant, for religion was far from being the only cause of division, and each party depended not so much on the European missionaries as on the Baganda leaders. Some of these leaders were genuine Christians, some were nominal Christians, but the vast majority of both sides were chiefs and followers who were not even nominal Christians and were merely out to gain what they could as the old standards collapsed. The death of Mackay in February 1890, and of Father Lourdel three months later, made no difference to the parties, for religion was not the chief consideration. For the same reason Bishop Tucker, who arrived shortly after Lugard and was dismayed to see that his congregation brought their guns even to church, failed to stop the growing rivalry by a conference with the French missionaries. The main quarrel arose over official appointments. The political organization of Buganda included certain official appointments which carried with them much influence and much land. These appointments had been equally divided after the war so that the political power of both parties was theoretically equal, and it had been agreed, so that this equality should not be upset, that a chief who changed from one party to another should give up his appointment. But on account of the king's support the Fransa were increasing their numbers more rapidly than the Ingleza; they therefore tried to amend this last provision, while the Ingleza continued to insist that appointments must be given up when a chief changed his party. During 1890, and still more in 1891, the question became acute.

The Mohammedan defeat at Bugangadzi. After making the treaty with Mwanga Lugard built a fortress on Kampala Hill and then turned his attention to the Mohammedans. After their defeat at Bulwanyi they had withdrawn to Bunyoro, where Kalema died, but the raiding expeditions into Buganda still went on. To repel such attacks the Catholics and Protestants were ready to unite, and Lugard succeeded in raising a Buganda army under the generalship of Apolo Kagwa and recruited from both Christian parties. In May 1891 the Mohammedans were defeated at Bugangadzi, although the rains prevented a general advance into Bunyoro.

The Fransa–Ingleza War, January–March 1892. The defeat of the Mohammedans left the Ingleza and Fransa parties face to face, and it became obvious that the Company's position could not be held unless a strong central force could be established. Lugard's own force was inadequate, no help could be expected from the coast, and recruits from within Buganda would belong to one of the rival parties. Lugard solved the problem by making an expedition to Kavalli's on Lake Albert and returning with Sudanese soldiers who had been there since the time of Stanley and Emin Pasha's expedition. Some of them garrisoned a line of forts along the Toro–Bunyoro border to guard Toro from Kabarega's raids, and the remainder—300 soldiers and 600 rabble—entered Kampala on the last day of 1891.

Captain Williams had remained at Kampala during Lugard's absence and had observed with alarm the mounting excitement and the increase in smuggled arms. By the start of 1892 excitement in the armies of both parties made war a certainty, and an incident at the end of January in which an Ingleza was shot by a Fransa provoked the crisis. As the armies began to muster, Lugard offered protection to the missionaries of both missions in his Kampala fort—an offer which the Protestant missionaries accepted but which the Catholic priests did not. When fighting broke out, Lugard and his Sudanese at first watched the battle as neutrals—until the Fransa army made the mistake of swarming up Kampala Hill to attack the fort. They were driven off and then routed by the Ingleza. Weeks of confusion followed until at the end of March the Kabaka Mwanga, who had fled with the Fransa party, reappeared at his capital, 'very dirty, with scrubby beard and unwashed garments'. But grubby as he was Mwanga alone was able to sign the necessary peace treaty.

The settlement after the war. A new treaty was made to mark the end of the war. Again the Company's supremacy was recognized, and again the chieftainships were allotted between the parties. But this time there were two differences. In the first place the chieftainships were not now allotted equally, for the Fransa only received those of Buddu. Secondly, to the consternation of both Catholics and Protestants, Mbogo and his Mohammedan party were now also allotted three small chiefdoms on condition that they recognized the sovereignty of Mwanga.

The proposal to withdraw from Uganda. Now that Uganda was again at peace Lugard felt able to leave affairs in the hands of Captain Williams, while he himself returned to England, where Uganda's fate was being decided. The fact was that the Company's extension into Uganda, which had been made for political reasons and not for profit, had cost about £40,000 a year, which was more than the Company, whose income was very small, could afford to pay. By the middle of 1891 it was clear that the Company could not afford to maintain Lugard in Uganda, and therefore Sir William Mackinnon, having appealed in vain to the Government for financial aid, informed Lord Salisbury of the Company's decision to withdraw from Uganda and make Dagoretti their farthest outpost. But although the British Government was prepared to accept this with indifference, the British public were not. A quite astonishing wave of indignation swept the country at the thought of abandoning the key-point in Central Africa. On 28 September the leading article of *The Times* expressed the general feeling:

Such a withdrawal would be nothing short of a national calamity. It would mean not only the loss of a great amount of capital already expended, but the destruction of our influence and prestige throughout Central Africa, the practical defeat of our anti-slavery policy, the persecution of the numerous missionaries labouring in Uganda, and the reconquest by Mohammedan fanatics of the only African state that has shown a disposition to accept Christianity. Whether we desire it or not, the British East Africa Company must be identified for all practical purposes with national policy.

The decision to retain Uganda. The C.M.S. were as disappointed as the Company at the prospect of withdrawal, and while the Government was reconsidering its decision in view of the unexpected strength of public opinion, Sir William Mackinnon and his friends subscribed £25,000 personally, and Bishop Tucker, who was on a brief visit to England, raised £15,000 by an appeal to the C.M.S. Gleaners Union. These contributions enabled the Company to stay in Uganda for another year. When Lugard arrived in England in October of 1892 and joined in the campaign to retain Uganda the Liberal government was still undecided, but in November it temporized by agreeing to send Sir Gerald Portal, the consul-general of Zanzibar, to visit Uganda and make a report; meanwhile the Company was to be given financial aid to enable it to continue its occupation until March 1893.

Sir Gerald Portal's expedition, 1893. The verdict of Sir Gerald Portal was a foregone conclusion, for the main facts of the situation were well known in Zanzibar. On 1 April 1893, soon after his arrival, he hauled down the Company's flag on Kampala Hill, replaced it with the Union Jack, and proclaimed a provisional British protectorate over the region. He also made a new agreement with Mwanga, and signed a new agreement between the two Christian parties which was more favourable to the Catholics, for it arranged that there should be two Prime Ministers, two chiefs of soldiers, and two chiefs of canoes, so that both Catholics and Protestants should be represented. The Catholics were given several chieftainships, including the province of Kamia and the island of Sese, in addition to those of Buddu. Portal, whose brother had died in May at Kampala, and whose own health was poor, left the capital for the coast on 30 May and on arriving at Zanzibar made out his report. This was sent to the Government and emphasized again the need to protect the missions, the promise to end slave trading in the interior, and the strategic importance of Uganda in controlling the headwaters of the Nile. After much opposition Parliament confirmed the protectorate in August 1894.

The end of the I.B.E.A. Company. Thus ended the work of the Imperial British East Africa Company in Uganda. Its work throughout the rest of East Africa was almost ended, too, for during its existence it had spent £450,000 and received only a trivial revenue from the collection of duties on goods from the interior. In 1892 even this revenue came to an end when the British Government imposed free trade on the coast. Thus, the East Africa Company, which—unlike the Royal Niger or South Africa Companies—was purely administrative, was left with practically no resources except its own capital.

The directors therefore had no choice but to end the Company, and opened negotiations with the Government for that purpose in 1893. They were forced to accept a parsimonious grant of £250,000 in

Map 13. Nigeria.

compensation, a poor reward for their almost entirely philanthropic efforts. Perhaps Sir John Kirk wrote the best epitaph of the Company. 'With all its faults,' he wrote, 'it has been an honest concern, not a money-making one, and but for its work we should not now possess a footing in East Africa.'

The British East Africa Protectorate, 15 June 1895. The administration of the Company's territories was therefore taken over by the Foreign Office, and what is now Kenya became the British East Africa Protectorate on 15 June 1895.

Lugard's later career. Meanwhile Lugard, who had done more than anyone else to bring Uganda into the Empire, was busy in Nigeria, which was to be the main concern of his career. He began there by racing a French expedition through the forests to the disputed area of Nikki in 1894 on behalf of the Royal Niger Company. He retired in 1918 as governor of the whole of Nigeria, whose unity he had designed.

Perhaps, however, it is for two other things that he is chiefly remembered—'Indirect Rule' and 'The Dual Mandate'.

The system of 'indirect rule' was his answer to the difficulties arising from the shortage of European administrative staff in Nigeria. 'The Government', he wrote, 'utilizes and works through the native chiefs, and avails itself of their intelligence and powers of governing, but insists upon their observance of the fundamental laws of humanity and justice.' So successful did this system prove that it spread beyond the boundaries of Nigeria and became accepted as the basic principle of British rule in the tropical areas of the continent.

The Dual Mandate in Tropical Africa, published in 1922, was Lugard's classic book. He was sincerely proud of the general effect of British rule in Africa. He believed that it was morally right, that it was a benefit to Europe by improving trade, and that it was a benefit to Africa by improving the standard of living. 'Europe is in Africa', he wrote, 'for the mutual benefit of her own industrial classes and of the native races in their progress to a higher plane; the benefit can be made reciprocal, and it is the aim and desire of civilized administration to fulfil this dual mandate.'

Lord Lugard of Abinger, the greatest European administrator the African continent has seen, died in 1945. Twenty years later British rule in Africa, which he had helped to found and foster, had passed like the empires which had gone before; but there was this overwhelming difference—Africa was now an integral part of 'the body corporate of nations', and not just an isolated or exploited limb.

CHAPTER IX

ZANZIBAR UNDER BRITISH INFLUENCE

Accession of Barghash. In 1870 Seyyid Majid was followed on the throne by his brother Seyyid Barghash, who ruled until 1888. During this period European countries began to take a much greater interest in the development of Africa. A good deal more detail is given about this in chapter VI on 'The Scramble for Africa and the First Partition of East Africa'. Here it is important to notice that England's interest in Zanzibar, which began by being limited to the suppression of the slave trade, had gradually become enlarged, under the influence no doubt of the opening of the Suez Canal in 1869, which had brought East Africa over 4000 miles nearer to the gate of Europe. Thus in Seyyid Barghash's reign the chief British representative in Zanzibar, Sir John Kirk, came to occupy the position of an unofficial Prime Minister to the Sultan. In securing this unusual position Kirk was aided by the good reputations earned by previous British consuls, but he himself was by far the most outstanding of the British representatives at Zanzibar.

Sir John Kirk. John Kirk was born in 1832. His medical and botanical qualifications caused him to be recommended to Livingstone as a useful member of his Zambezi expedition in 1858–63. Livingstone did not find it easy to get on with Europeans and he often wished that he was alone with Africans, as he had been on his first great journey across the continent. He and Kirk, however, became real friends, and it was through Livingstone's recommendation that Dr Kirk was offered the post at Zanzibar of agency surgeon and vice-consul. He accepted this in 1866. A year later he married Miss Helen Cook, who bore him a family of five daughters and one son.

Social conditions in Zanzibar. At this time there were roughly 300,000 people in the island of Zanzibar, about two-thirds of whom were African slaves. The Arabs, Indians and Europeans formed only a fraction of the population, which included also a number of the original African inhabitants. It has been estimated that there were about 4000 Arabs, together with some 6000 Indians, the great majority of whom were Muslims, and sixty Europeans, of whom twenty-two were Englishmen. These last were the members of the Universities' Mission to Central Africa, a few businessmen and their families, the consul and the vice-consul, Kirk. As the filth and smell of the town of Zanzibar were what might be expected from a place in which there was no drainage system, and where the rotting bodies of dead slaves might be seen on the beach, there was plenty for a doctor to do. When cholera struck the island in 1869–70 and reduced the population by a tenth, there was even more than many doctors would have been able to cope with.

Kirk's work as consul. At the same time Kirk was kept desperately busy doing not only his own government work, but that of the consul as well, for the latter was sick. He was worried also about his inability to solve the problem of getting further supplies to Livingstone, who was cut off in the interior by a tribal war. However, with the help of his wife, he managed to deal with most of these difficulties, and after his appointment as consul-general (in 1873) he played a leading part in Zanzibar politics until his retirement in 1886.

Decree of 1873. The biggest problem that faced Kirk during this period was the need to get the co-operation of the Sultan in the abolition of the slave trade. When this had been largely secured by the decree of 1873, forbidding the export of slaves from East Africa and closing all slave markets under the control of the Sultan of Zanzibar, he was faced with the growing German interest in East Africa. This resulted in the delimitation treaty of 1886, dividing East Africa into British and German 'spheres of influence'. Under this treaty Zanzibar, Pemba and a narrow coastal strip were allotted to the Sultan of Zanzibar.

The importance of Kirk's influence. It was fortunate for East Africa that Kirk was acting-consul in Zanzibar when England was stirred by Livingstone's writings and actions to insist that slavery be abolished in East Africa. Only a man of exceptional character and reputation could have secured the support of the Sultan in enforcing the treaty of 1873, which, supported by the proclamation of 1876, forbade the conveyance of slaves by land under any condition. It is true that the British navy could enforce the treaty of 1873 once the consent of the Sultan, Seyyid Barghash, had been obtained, but the Sultan's active support was needed to ensure that the proclamation was obeyed. That he did give this, and was prepared to do so against the will of his subjects, reflects credit on Seyyid Barghash and on the trust which he placed in Kirk. This trust was deepened as the years went by, and from 1873-85 Kirk shared the control of the Sultan's lands. To co-operate in this way with a ruler who in theory governed as a despot demanded unusual tact, understanding and fairness. These were qualities which Kirk possessed, and it was partly due to his influence that British trade with Zanzibar increased even more rapidly than that of other nations, so that by 1878-9 it was responsible for at least one-third of the imports and more than a half of the exports. Apart from this, direct trade between India and Zanzibar amounted to £200,000.

The declaration of 1862 and German ambitions. Unfortunately Kirk was unable to convince England of the possibilities of the Anglo-Arab partnership in which he believed. English ministers were concerned with world affairs and the growing power of Germany at a time when danger threatened also from Russia. They were, therefore, prepared to conciliate Germany in East Africa (see chapter VI).

The Sultan's overlordship of much of the East African mainland had been acknowledged in the slave-trade treaties and in the 1862 declaration, signed by England and France, which stated that:

Her Majesty the Queen of the United Kingdom of Great Britain and Ireland and His Majesty the Emperor of the French, taking into consideration the importance of maintaining the independence of His Highness the Sultan of Muscat and of His Highness the Sultan of Zanzibar, have thought it right to engage reciprocally to respect the independence of these Sovereigns.

The boundaries of this land had never been defined and the danger of this was clear to Kirk. Adequate armed forces were also needed;

and in 1877 Kirk suggested that Lt. Lloyd Mathews, R.N., should be given command of a small army to see that the Sultan's proclamations were carried out. General Mathews, as he was now called, proved an ideal choice. So great was his reputation for justice and wisdom that Africans made journeys of many months to submit a dispute to him. For the rest of his life he looked on Zanzibar as his adopted home; and when Britain eventually took over the protectorate of Zanzibar he was appointed First Minister to the Sultan. When he died in Zanzibar in 1901, the son of the reigning Sultan watched by his bed during his last night. It was to the general's small army that Kirk turned when danger from German ambition threatened Zanzibar. In 1880 General Mathews was therefore instructed to set up a fortified post 120 miles from Bagamoyo on the mainland. Kirk, however, was discouraged by the British Government in his efforts to show by concrete signs that the Sultan's power extended inland. When Bismarck, the great German Chancellor, gave support to the Society for German Colonization, Kirk saw the danger that threatened Seyyid Barghash, but he was helpless because England had already decided not to oppose the Germans. He could only look on helplessly when Germany followed up the Congress of Berlin of 1884 by annexing a large area opposite Zanzibar which the Sultan had always regarded as his own. When this was followed by the news that the Sultan of Witu had accepted a German protectorate, Kirk was even ordered by England to persuade Barghash to accept the situation.

Kirk's later career. The happy partnership between the Sultan and his unofficial Prime Minister had now not much longer to run, and it was a relief to Kirk to go on leave, just before the delimitation treaty of 1886 was forced on Barghash. He never returned. His last important official service was as a British representative at the Conference of Brussels in 1890, where his long experience of Africa enabled him to play a leading part. Apart from this, he was a director of the Imperial British East Africa Company and as such remained closely linked with East Africa until the break-up of the Company in 1894. Later he was vice-chairman of the Uganda Railway Committee.

European interest in Zanzibar. It has been convenient to give an outline of the career of Sir John Kirk before that of the Sultans of Zanzibar with whom he was connected. These were Seyyid Majid and Seyyid Barghash. The latter had been exiled to Bombay for his attempts to snatch the throne from Seyyid Majid, who succeeded his father Seyyid Said. On the death of Seyyid Majid in 1870, Seyyid Barghash became Sultan of Zanzibar, and it was during his reign that close links were made between the island and Europe and Asia. To a large extent this was due to the growing interest in Africa, particularly marked in the period 1870–88 during which Seyyid Barghash ruled at Zanzibar. The great period of East African explorers, which may be said to have been from 1856 to 1873, was drawing to a close, but the interest of Europe, which had been stirred by their descriptions, was now concerned with the need to stop the slave trade. For Britain this meant concentration on Zanzibar.

Development of communications. Zanzibar's commercial possibilities had been increasingly realized since the reign of that gifted business-man, Seyyid Said. During the reign of Seyyid Barghash there was a development in communications, which in East Africa has usually been the prelude to increased material prosperity, and these possibilities became even more promising.

In 1869 the Suez Canal had been completed and although the main line of communication with the East lay across the Indian Ocean, and not down the coast of Africa, the cutting of the canal made an African branch-line practical, so that the route up and down East Africa was no longer a backwater. The value of the canal to East Africa was shown in 1871 when Seyyid Barghash was persuaded to provide a yacht to start a regular service to the Seychelles, thus linking Zanzibar with one of the mail routes. A year later this was followed up by the start of a monthly mail service between Zanzibar and Aden run by the British Steam Navigation Company (now the British India Company). This contact with Aden was a link with the rapidly improving steamship service between England and India. Then in 1879 the Eastern Telegraph Company speeded up communications further by laying a submarine cable from Aden to Zanzibar.

Barghash. Barghash's exile to Bombay had enlarged his knowledge of the world and he was quick to see the value of linking Zanzibar with the outer world. He also enjoyed the opportunities which this offered of supplying himself with European luxuries. In doing so he did not neglect the needs of his humbler subjects; he ran a line of four steamships to India, to bring food prices down in Zanzibar by importing cheaper grain. Finally in 1875 he set off to see this distant continent of Europe for himself, and paid a visit to England. He visited the Queen at Windsor, and was given the freedom of the City of London.

Domestic policy. Meanwhile in Zanzibar itself Barghash had shown himself a forceful and energetic ruler. Without his driving force the island might have suffered a worse blow in 1873 than it did, when most of its clove trees were destroyed by a cyclone. Again, his father, Seyyid Said, had originally been attracted to Zanzibar because of its sweet water. Yet there were frequent complaints of the foul drinking water which was offered in the town of Zanzibar. This was remedied by Seyyid Barghash, who arranged for a conduit to carry sweet water from the spring of Chem Chem to the town.

Suppression of the slave trade and relations with Britain. Yet to many of his subjects these benefits counted for little against the concessions he made to England in stopping the slave trade. The treaty of 1873 and the proclamations of 1876 were bitter blows at what they regarded as the main source of their prosperity, and to Seyyid Barghash at the end of his long reign it must have looked as though he had tried to secure British friendship in vain. In 1875 an unsuccessful attempt by the Egyptians to invade the northern coast of the Sultan's lands was checked by his determined attitude, supported most effectively by Kirk. But Seyyid Barghash had seen the danger to his mainland, for he well knew that Zanzibar had neither the wealth nor the population to develop the interior or to govern it effectively. If pressure should be put on him to do this, either with the object of stopping the slave trade or developing other trade, or for scientific interest, he knew that he might be forced to retire altogether from the interior. In the circumstances he decided that it was wise to risk asking the British to do what he could not do himself. In 1877, therefore, he approached Mackinnon with the offer of a trade concession under which Mackinnon and his friends were to take over the political and economic control of his mainland territories. Page 94 of chapter VI describes why this came to nothing.

Barghash's successors. Seyyid Barghash himself did not live much longer, and with his death in 1888 there followed a rapid succession of Sultans: Seyyid Khalifa 1888–90, Seyyid Ali 1890–3, Seyyid Hamed 1893–6, and Seyyid Hamoud 1896–1902. As England took over the protectorate of Zanzibar, when she signed a treaty with Germany in settlement of their territorial claims in Africa, there were a number of administrative changes during these reigns.

Anglo-German rivalry: relations in Africa. Rivalry between Germany and England had grown steadily worse in the 1880's (see chapter VI) and it was finally agreed that if England accepted some changes in the boundaries of South and West Africa and handed over Heligoland, a useful naval base off the coast of Germany, Germany would recognize a British protectorate over Zanzibar and give up her own Witu protectorate. At the same time the boundary between the British and German spheres of influence was defined as a line beginning on the north bank of the River Umba and, skirting the northern base of Mount Kilimanjaro, drawn to a point on the eastern side of Lake Victoria Nyanza. It was explained to the Sultan that in future all his dealings with foreign governments would be under British control and from this time onwards Zanzibar declined in importance. However, his claim and that of his successors to rule in Zanzibar would be supported by the British and he would be allowed to choose his own successor, subject to British approval. Seyyid Ali was well aware that if he did not accept a British protectorate his kingdom would be swallowed up by the Germans, who were showing a threatening activity. He therefore signed, but struggled to secure as much money as he could in return for handing over to Germany all rights in the coastal strip between the Umba and the Rovuma.

SULTANS OF ZANZIBAR

Said bin Sultan
(Imam Seyyid Said of Oman and Zanzibar 1806–56)

Thwain (Imam of Oman) — Muhammed — Turki — Majid (1856–70) — Barghash (1870–88) — Khalifa (1888–90) — Ali (1890–3)

Hamoud (1896–1902)

Hamed (1893–6) — Harub — Salim

Khalifa II = Matuka (1911–60)   Ali (1902–11)

Abdullah (1960–2)

Jamshid (1962–4)

Reforms in Zanzibar. In taking over responsibility for the administration of Zanzibar the British Government were concerned with the low standards accepted in many departments. The streets of the town itself were covered with filth, and it was often not possible to get through them because they were blocked by the remains of old buildings. The approaches to the harbour were dangerous. The provincial governors were paid such low salaries that they made them up by bribes. Nor was it easy to get the money to improve these things, for the Treasury itself was one of the worst-run departments. As no proper accounts were kept and there was no attempt to draw up a budget, most of the money went to those who did very little work to deserve it. If there were to be reforms, it was clear that they would have to begin with the Treasury, and at length the consul-general succeeded in arranging that the Sultan should have a fixed Civil List, but that the rest of the revenue was to be paid into a Treasury presided over by a British official. The amount of the revenue was also increased by making Zanzibar a free port, to enable it to compete successfully with Dar es Salaam. This had been developed by Seyyid Majid so that he could retire to this 'harbour of peace' if things became too difficult in Zanzibar. After this the British consul-general turned to other urgently needed reforms, some of which were to take many years to complete. A start was made, for instance, with a reform of the legal system, the harbour was improved, port regulations were issued, and the smell of Zanzibar became less unpleasant when a gang of scavengers was employed to sweep the streets.

The choice of a successor to Seyyid Ali. When Seyyid Ali died, only a beginning had been made with reforms, but the British were now able to use a weapon they had taken when the treaty was signed which gave them the protectorate of Zanzibar. This was the clause which said that, while the successor to the throne could be named by the reigning Sultan, he was to be appointed only if the British approved the choice. When Seyyid Ali died, Hamed bin Thwain was informed that he would receive support from the British Government, provided that he was guided by the consul-general in the question of slavery and in the internal administration of Zanzibar. He had also to take an oath of allegiance to the Queen of England and to accept a further reduction in the amount of the revenue which he was allowed to keep for his personal use; nor would it be possible for him to circumvent this last restriction, for the Treasury was to remain under British control. Hamed bin Thwain was quick to accept these terms. Seyyid Barghash had once said that the law of succession in Oman and Zanzibar was that he who had the longest sword succeeded. The new Sultan knew that that person in his day was the British consul-general, who had the power of the British Empire behind him.

Arab discontent. Although Seyyid Hamed bin Thwain had been eager to accept the throne on these terms, he soon became very discontented when he realized how much power was possessed by his British chief ministers. Many of the Arabs around him were eager to work on his resentment, for they hated the British attitude to slavery: it was clearly aimed at eventual abolition, and, in their opinion, at the destruction of their prosperity. Seyyid Ali had been forced to sign an anti-slavery decree which took one more step in this direction, and if the British were not turned out the future was clear. Meanwhile the restriction on the amount of the revenue which the Sultan might retain for his own use hit at all the hangers-on who reckoned to be kept in idleness by the Sultan.

The problem of compensation for I.B.E.A. In 1895 Seyyid Hamed's grievances were greatly increased. In the previous year I.B.E.A. had finally retired from Uganda, a British protectorate had been declared, and it was proposed to declare a similar protectorate over the area now known as Kenya. I.B.E.A. was asking for compensation for the Company's expenses in developing the British sphere of influence. Much against the will of General Mathews and the British consul-general the Government proposed to find the money for this by making the Sultan of Zanzibar pay over the £200,000 he had received from the Germans when he signed an agreement giving them full control of the coastline of German East Africa previously ruled by the Sultans of Zanzibar. The Sultan was told that he was to pay this sum of money to I.B.E.A., because the Company was giving up the concessions which he had previously granted to it on the coast. It was further explained that one-quarter of the money was to be paid to the Company to compensate it for the improvements it had made. Naturally enough the Sultan and the British consul-general assumed that the coastal area would now be administered by Zanzibar, but even this consolation was denied. The British considered that it would be sufficient if they paid to the Sultan the same rent which had been given by I.B.E.A. and in addition paid interest on the money that had been used to buy out the Company. The coastal area would be administered as a whole with the mainland.

In 1962 the Robertson report recommended that the 1895 agreement should be set aside and the coastal strip incorporated in the mainland of Kenya. A substantial sum of money was to be paid to the Sultan and the Zanzibar Government in compensation.

The attitude in England. There was less criticism in England of the 1895 plan than one would have expected, largely because of the slavery question. This made Zanzibar so unpopular that some of the abolitionists wanted Zanzibar itself to be annexed; the Government, too, feared that the end of slavery would mean the beginning of financial assistance to Zanzibar, and were anxious to save money before this should happen. Moreover it was, of course, more efficient to administer the coast and the mainland together.

Rebellion on the coast. The transfer of the coast from the Company to the British Government was therefore marked by a rebellion, due partly to the causes given above and partly to the zest of members of the Church Missionary Society who no longer had their energies fully absorbed by converting the heathen peoples of the interior and looking after freed slaves. Encouraged by the establishment of European administration on the coast, the missionaries were working hard to convert the Muslims to Christianity. This increase of their activities to include Muslims, as well as heathen, among those to be converted was very much resented by the followers of Islam.

A disputed succession. No sooner was this rebellion suppressed, than the death in 1896 of the Sultan caused a second crisis. The eldest male member of the royal family of Zanzibar was Seyyid Hamoud, who was a good deal more acceptable to the British as a ruler than Seyyid Khaled, the son of Barghash. This did not appeal to Seyyid Khaled, who considered his claim was the better and tried to establish it by entering the palace and there proclaiming himself Sultan. This attempt by Seyyid Khaled to secure the Sultanate was more serious than his previous effort in 1893 and was only stopped by bombardment from naval ships, after he had disregarded all warnings. After the bombardment Seyyid Khaled was rescued by the Germans, who took him down to Dar es Salaam, and Seyyid Hamoud became Sultan. He was succeeded in 1902 by his son Seyyid Ali bin Hamoud, who abdicated, on grounds of ill health, in 1911. This succession of short reigns was followed by the long one of Seyyid Khalifa, who reigned through two world wars, and celebrated his silver jubilee.

Economic progress. By far the most important event in the reign of Seyyid Hamoud was the end of the legal status of slavery in 1897, of which details have been given in chapter III. This caused very little disturbance in the economic condition of the protectorate, largely owing to the wise manner in which it was carried out. Zanzibar at this time was still dependent on the growing of cloves and coconuts which, even today, are the main cash crops produced by the island. In 1947, for instance, their combined exports sold for nearly a million pounds. In the reign of Seyyid Hamoud, however, efforts were made by the new Department of Agriculture to find fresh crops suitable for a tropical climate. These efforts were successful in that it was shown that it would pay the people of Zanzibar to experiment with a far larger variety of crops, such as coffee, tea, cocoa, cinnamon and nutmegs, but the inhabitants were not convinced that the new crops would pay them better than their old favourites, cloves and coconuts, and it was realized that nothing could be done with the older generation of Arabs. The best hope for the future lay in the education of the young. In 1907, therefore, it was decided to start a Department of Education, and primary schools were set up in Zanzibar town and some of the chief villages. Despite this the Zanzibaris continued to concentrate on their two main crops, reckoning to import foodstuffs. The Second World War shook their prejudices, and some saw the need for subsistence farming.

The development of education. Education in Zanzibar and Pemba began with the establishment of schools for the study of the Koran. These Koran schools, which were later scattered in their hundreds throughout the islands, still provided the early education of most of the inhabitants. Further developments came from Christian missions; in 1870 the Universities Mission to Central Africa started Bishop Tozer's school for the children of freed slaves. Individuals also founded schools: among these were Seyyid Hamoud who allowed the government school for the sons of his relatives and other leading Arabs to meet in one of his palaces; and by 1890 leaders of the different Indian communities had collected money for a school which became known as the Sir Euan Smith Madressa. This later received financial support from the government. However, lack of public support and the First World War resulted in little progress being made until a Koran class was formed in every government school. Greater numbers then began to come forward for the primary education which the Government provided free. However, it was not until 1935 that the Government was able to start a secondary school for boys which offered courses leading to School Certificate; in 1959 these were extended to Higher Certificate. The education of girls lagged behind and a government secondary school for them was not started until 1947. Further extension of education depended on an increase in the material economy and a change in attitude towards the education of the large African population of the island, which was relatively neglected.

The development of internal communications. In the reign of Seyyid Hamoud's son, Seyyid Ali, economic development was helped also by the improvement of communications. Not only were so many new roads built that the island had seventy-five miles of good roads by 1913, but the first electric telegraph was also opened. This linked Zanzibar town and Chake Chake. These towns also had the advantage of the good telephone system which was introduced into both Zanzibar and Pemba.

Measures of hygiene. Nor could the nickname which Livingstone gave it of ' Stinkibar' any longer be given to Zanzibar. The streets were swept regularly, precautions were taken against malaria, thousands of rats were killed every year as a check on bubonic plague, efforts were made to secure clean milk as a step in the fight against tuberculosis, which in 1909 killed 183 people in Zanzibar town alone, and the Tayabal Karimjee hospital was built. The result was a considerable improvement in the health of the population.

Judicial changes. With regard to the constitution, important changes were made at the beginning of Seyyid Hamoud's reign. The British consular court was replaced by a judge and assistant judge appointed by the Crown. These formed Her Britannic Majesty's Court for Zanzibar, and under this came subordinate courts. In all of these courts the Indian code of civil and criminal procedure was used. A number of cases were not, however, affected by this change. The Sultan's own Arab and African subjects, for instance, were still tried in his own courts, until in 1899 a regular system of native courts was set up to deal with these people, and in 1908 British judges were appointed to sit in the Sultan's courts.

Transfer to the Colonial Office. In 1913 there was a further very important change when the administration of Zanzibar passed from the Foreign Office to the Colonial Office. At the same time a Protectorate Council was set up, to enable the Sultan to take a more active part in public affairs. The posts of British Consul-General and First Minister were combined and given to one man called the British Resident in Zanzibar, under the control of the Governor of British East Africa.

Legislative Council set up and the post of High Commissioner abolished. Although it had been a wise step to transfer the administration of Zanzibar from the Foreign Office to the Colonial Office, which was better able to deal with its problems, a few years' experience showed that this also was not entirely satisfactory. For one thing, too much delay was caused by referring matters from Zanzibar to the High Commissioner who, as Governor of East Africa, was resident in Nairobi. In 1925, therefore, the post of High Commissioner was abolished. At the same time the Protectorate Council was also abolished, largely because it was out of touch with the unofficial community. In its place a Legislative Council was set up, with an official majority, but containing also unofficial members who were to be nominated after the advice of leading unofficial bodies had been secured.

Advances to self-government. Before this change could be introduced, the Sultan's consent had to be obtained, because it meant that his power of legislating by issuing decrees would be limited. As the Sultan was anxious that his subjects should have a greater share in the work of government he agreed. At the same time a small Executive Council was set up to advise him and to discuss what measures the Government should introduce into the Legislative Council.

As the British Government, the Sultan and his subjects all wanted Zanzibar to advance by suitable stages to self-government within the Commonwealth, the number of unofficial seats in the Legislative Council was increased, the Executive Council was expanded, and a Privy Council was set up to advise the Sultan.

The next step taken was to provide for common roll elections to six of the twelve unofficial seats in Legislative Council. Two parties were formed, the Zanzibar Nationalist party and the Afro-Shirazi party, the latter won five out of the six seats. By 1958 politics were absorbing the people of Zanzibar and the Senior Commissioner reported: 'Traders, cultivators, labourers, fishermen, even housewives were affected. Villagers in the rural areas argued among themselves. Funerals and religious ceremonies were boycotted by rival political parties!'

Events on the mainland seemed to have overtaken Zanzibar, and Sir Hilary Blood was appointed to review the position. In his opinion: 'a period of real ministerial responsibility, during which power in the Resident's hands will enable him to come to the rescue should anything go vitally wrong, is required before Zanzibar can complete the crossing of the great divide which separates the present non-representative from fully responsible government'.

Recommendations of the Blood Commission. In his recommendations Sir Hilary advised the creation of a predominantly elective legislature in which the official members should entirely disappear, their place being taken by elected members.

The bill giving effect to these proposals also arranged for a Chief Minister and four ministers to be appointed by the Sultan, on the advice of the British Resident, from among the elected members of the Legislative Council. These changes meant the start of responsible government in Zanzibar.

Local government. For purposes of local government Zanzibar was divided into three districts, Pemba Island, Urban Zanzibar and Rural Zanzibar. Each district was in charge of a district commissioner under the general direction of the senior commissioner, and was subdivided into mudirias and further subdivided into shehias.

Recent constitutional changes. Until 1895 Pemba was left, as far as administration was concerned, very much to itself. Since then it has had a large share of the amenities of the Protectorate, but members of the Afro-Shirazi Party who lived on the island were still not satisfied. Many of the Arabs on Pemba were smallholders who worked together with local members of the Afro-Shirazi Party to form a separate group, the Zanzibar Pemba People's Party. This led to a draw in the 1961 election, and a second election had to be held, in which the boundaries of certain constituencies were drafted so as to favour the Zanzibar

Nationalist Party and the Pemba People's Party. This coalition won eighteen out of thirty-one seats, although a majority of the electors voted against it. A constitutional conference was held in London in 1962 and independence was given on 12 December 1963 to a government representing a minority. Inadequate precautions were taken against trouble, and a month later the Sultan and his government were driven out by a revolution in which there were horrible scenes. Many lives were lost, and ships sailed from the island tightly packed with deported Arabs. Zanzibar was proclaimed a republic with Sheikh Abeid Karume, leader of the Afro-Shirazi Party, as the new President. This régime too was short-lived, and the islands of Zanzibar and Pemba are now part of the United Republic of Tanganyika and Zanzibar, which is called Tanzania. It has yet to show that it has a stable future and reliable details of its constitution were not available in August 1964.

CHAPTER X

THE RAILWAY AND
THE ECONOMIC DEVELOPMENT
OF KENYA

Brussels Conference. In 1890 the Brussels Conference at last stated its conclusions, the most important of which were directed against the slave trade. They declared that the participants intended:

The gradual establishment in the interior, by the powers to which the territories are subject, of strongly occupied stations, in such a way as to make their protective or repressive action effectively felt in the territories devastated by slave hunting.

The need for railways. The conference had stressed the need for railways, knowing that once these were built caravans would no more be used. It cost two or three hundred times as much to bring goods by caravan as it would cost to bring them by railway; moreover if there were no caravans it would not be possible to carry slaves from the interior to the coast. In addition the Imperial British East Africa Company knew that the construction of a railway to the coast would make the development of Uganda and its administration much easier. They had in fact already laid down some seven miles of a very light railway from Mombasa as a gesture of good will. They could not do more because the construction of a railway is very expensive, and the Company, owing to the cost of Lugard's administration in Uganda, was already desperately short of money. They had already tried to cut down expenses in what is now Kenya. In spite of this need for economy Sir William Mackinnon, the chairman of the Company, could show that it had fought hard against the slave trade and released over 4000 slaves in less than three years. He was also able to point out that Germany's aggressive policy under Carl Peters's leadership had forced the Company, in the interests of the empire, to attempt the effective occupation of some 750,000 square miles, and this had cost a great deal of money.

The withdrawal of I.B.E.A. from Uganda. Despite this, it came as a shock to the British when the Company announced in 1891 that it was making arrangements for the withdrawal of Captain Lugard and his entire force from Uganda. Fortunately, arrangements for the survey of the proposed railway had already begun, and the English friends of the Protestant mission in Uganda were able to collect enough money to enable Lugard to stay on in Uganda until the British Government was prepared to take over.

Difficulties of construction. It had not been easy for the Government to decide to construct a railway from Mombasa to Victoria Nyanza running through land that was known to very few people in England. No engineer, for instance, had any detailed information about the escarpments flanking the Rift Valley, although these steep rises were serious obstacles in the way of the railway. There were also the long stretches without water between Mombasa and Mtito Andei, the tsetse-fly country, and the dense bush and rock through which a way had to be hacked. To these difficulties must be added the problem of labour, for the Africans in this area had no experience which would enable them to build a railway and had not even used a pick and spade. It was not long before another difficulty appeared, the danger from wild animals. The House of Lords was told of a party of man-eating lions which had halted the work for three weeks, during which time two of them had killed twenty-eight Indian coolies and scores of Africans. The two lions were killed by Colonel Patterson, who described his adventures in *The Man-Eaters of Tsavo*. It is not surprising that many of the Africans believed these lions were possessed by the spirits of their dead chiefs, who had come back to warn them against the railway. Nor did the lions flee when the railway was completed: they would still occasionally stroll on to the platform and set the station master a problem.

By now, however, the Foreign Office was determined that the line should run through to Victoria Nyanza. They knew that the Germans would construct a railway to the lake if the British did not, and that communications must be improved if England was going to be responsible for Uganda. Nor was the strategical importance of the

Map 14. The railway and agricultural products of Kenya.

country overlooked. It was realized that it dominated the northern and western shores of Lake Victoria and held almost the only exit to Lakes Albert and Edward, thus controlling the headwaters of the Nile. One by one the obstacles in the way of its construction were cleared. Parliament agreed to meet its cost, and coolie labour was imported from India. The interests of the coolies were carefully guarded by the British Government of India. It was stipulated that, if a coolie wished to remain in East Africa at the end of his contract, he could do so, provided he forfeited his right to a return passage. In this way the number of Indians in what is now Kenya rose to just over 13,000 in 1898. By the next year the rails had reached Nairobi, the headquarters of the railway being moved there from Mombasa. No one in that year had thought of Nairobi as the site of the future capital; it was merely regarded as the last stretch of flat land on which to prepare for the long climb to the top of the Rift Valley escarpment; and it took its name from the Masai word for the cold stream which ran there.

The next step was to run steamers on the lake. These had to be brought from England in sections, which were assembled at Kisumu. The first steamship, the 'William MacKinnon', was launched two years before the railway opened, having been carried up from the coast on the backs of porters. Before the lake was reached further obstacles had to be overcome. The Kikuyu escarpment was one of these. There was trouble, too, with the Nandi, who first saw in the railway a free supply of iron for making weapons and wire for brace-lets, and later ambushed the escorts of railway survey parties. But in 1901 all these difficulties were past and the 572 miles of railway line from Kilindini to Kisumu carried the first train on its triumphant passage, festooned as though for a party.

Costs. The railway had cost Great Britain £9500 a mile and it ran at a loss of nearly £50,000 a year, excluding interest on the capital cost. At the time this cost seemed overwhelming, yet before the railway reached Nairobi it had saved countless lives and made the 'famine of the rice' the last great famine in the history of the Kamba people. In 1898–9 famine due to an evil trinity of locusts, drought and rinderpest had struck the Kamba. It was halted by the free distribution of rice brought up from the coast by the railway to the starving people round Machakos.

In 1897, the year in which the Uganda railway, as it was then called, was begun on the mainland of East Africa, slavery was finally abolished throughout British East Africa, and with the construction of the line the last threat of the slave trade was silenced. The cost of carriage had also dropped from 7s. 6d. per ton per mile (the old charge by caravan) to 2½d. per ton per mile. It has been said that Kenya was conquered by a railway, and its modern history may well be said to have begun in 1901; for the railway has been the basis for subsequent development.

Extension of the railway. To those responsible for the development of the new colony it seemed to have been weighed down by a load of debt before it had a chance to succeed; and the critics of the railway felt justified in their prophecies that it would never pay its way. Yet not only did it make a working profit in 1905, its later profits eventually helped the Treasury to pay the general expenses of government. Moreover, by 1936 the original 572 miles of railway had grown to 1625 miles, which included major extensions, as well as several branch lines including that from Nakuru to Eldoret which was a forerunner of the later extension to Uganda.

Later extension to Uganda. The solitude of the Rift Valley was also gone. Trading had begun, wrote Johnston

with shy and astonished natives, who had scarcely realized the existence of a world outside their own jungle, for the beef, mutton, fowls, eggs, and vegetable foodstuffs which are to assist in feeding this invasion. Far away on Baringo natives are extending their irrigation schemes and planting twice as much as they planted before, knowing that there is a market where their spare food can be exchanged for rupees. Further north still, in the Suk countries, Englishmen, Scotsmen, Goanese, Arabs, Swahilis and Baluchis are pushing into deserts to buy donkeys, are trading for ivory which the railway will carry to the coast at a rate cheaper than the cheapest porter caravan. The Nyando Valley, for years without human inhabitants other than the shiftless Andorobo, is filling up with Masai, Swahili, and Nandi inhabitants.

Indian traders. Today the story of the development that followed is impressive. In 1901 it would have been described as impossible; and those who had the task of making the railway pay looked out bleakly on a land in which the native inhabitants had never seen a wheel, used a plough or exchanged goods for money. Along the coast were to be found Indian traders who had been established there for centuries, for the link with India was an ancient one and the Indians had helped to finance and organize the trade caravans in the days of the Arabs. With the coming of the railway the Indians penetrated inland into the present-day Kenya for the first time, although Alidina Visram, the leading Indian merchant, had extended their business up to Uganda more than twenty years before the coming of the railway. They had used bullock-carts and porters to carry supplies and had set up small centres of trade. Two other Indian traders, Adamjee Alibhoy and M. G. Puri, were also established at Machakos before the coming of the railway, but with these exceptions it is generally true to say that it was not until about 1900 that the Indians effectively spread into the interior. They then practically had a monopoly of the trade in the small township of Nairobi. Although the Indian community was active in developing the early trade of Kenya, they were not so concerned about developing the natural resources of East Africa. Sir Charles Eliot, the Commissioner for the East Africa Protectorate, considered that, if these were to be developed, European settlers would have to be encouraged to take up land in East Africa.

The land problem and the Kikuyu. The British Government was anxious that this should not mean that any Africans were dispossessed of their land, but the settlers came at a time when four disasters had struck the land—smallpox, rinderpest, drought and locusts. In Kitui the rinderpest epidemic struck with such speed that the Kamba stockments were surrounded by thousands of rotting carcasses, and as the full force of the disasters developed the Kamba population dwindled until, at a place like Nazi, it is believed that about half the population died or moved to other parts. There was a similar fall in the population of Kikuyuland, and this at a time when the Kikuyu had been expanding across the Chania into the lands occupied by the Wanderobo. This was a tribe of hunters who supplemented their livelihood by collecting honey. Numerically they were inferior to the

Kikuyu, who could therefore have driven them out if they had felt that this would have secured for themselves an undisturbed title to the land. According to Dr Leakey in his book *Mau Mau and the Kikuyu*, the Kikuyu believed that this was not possible, because 'The Spirits of the owners would make it impossible for the new occupiers to carry out their agricultural activities with any hope of success, or with any hope of the blessing of Ngai, the god of the Kikuyu'. For this reason negotiations had to be carried on between individual Kikuyu and Dorobo with a view to 'mutual' adoption before the actual transfer of property rights. In this way the good will of the departed Dorobo spirits would be secured for the Kikuyu who took over the land. A religious ceremony would then be held to mark the boundaries. In this manner the Kikuyu had been steadily advancing across the Chania River from about the middle of the sixteenth century. At the same time they retained a fringe of forest, secured by fortified villages against attack from their neighbours the Masai. The disastrous close of the nineteenth century put an end to these interesting developments, and many Kikuyu moved back to the Nyeri and Fort Hall districts. By tribal custom these people still retained their claim to the land they had vacated.

The need for European settlers. Difficulties began with the need for European settlers, if the railway was to pay. The British taxpayer had invested millions in building a railway on which every train ran at a loss. This could not go on for ever: somehow the railway must be made to pay for itself. Yet the Africans, it was thought, would never be able to supply enough traffic without assistance. Sir Charles Eliot, the new Commissioner for the East African Protectorate, believed the answer was to attract European settlers who would also help the indigenous population by introducing the ways of western civilization. This view was typical of an age in which the right of civilized men to develop resources and their duty to teach a code of behaviour and scientific knowledge were not questioned. With this object in view, the East Africa (Lands) Order in Council was issued in 1901, defining Crown lands as land not already occupied by Africans, and arranging the terms on which it could be purchased. The next step was to secure the settlers, and Sir Charles Eliot arranged for the attractions of East Africa to be made known in South Africa, where he hoped that the unsettled, poverty-stricken state of the country at the end of the Anglo-Boer War might mean that South Africans would be tempted by the opportunities offered in East Africa. The good response surprised the Government, who allowed insufficient time for defining unoccupied land available for settlement. This was the beginning of the clash between European and African claims on land which was to extend over a much wider area.

The Masai agreements. Linked with the coming of the early settlers was the problem of the Masai. According to a rough estimate, in 1904 they owned 50,000 head of cattle and 600,000 sheep, they themselves being about 45,000 strong. They roamed over a vast stretch of country which included the land north and south of the new railway line. In view of the danger of clashes between the Masai warriors and the white settlers, it was suggested that the Masai be moved into two reserves linked by a corridor, half a mile wide. The northern reserve was Laikipia and consisted of some 4500 square miles, and the southern, which was of about 4350 square miles, ran down to the border of German East Africa. The area provided was, therefore, generous, but the Masai were given no alternative, and there is evidence that the tribe were unwilling to abandon their claims to the grazing grounds in the Rift Valley.

The agreement covering this move was made in 1904. In a few years it was seen to be working badly: the presence of tick-borne disease in the corridor resulted, for example, in the tribe becoming split into two. Lenana, the great Laibon of the Masai, suggested, therefore, that the tribe should be reunited in one reserve. If the Masai moved from the northern reserve it would mean that Laikipia would be freed for European settlement. Hence the tribe were offered an increase of the reserve in the south to 15,177 square miles, or approximately one and a half square miles of land for each Masai household, which averaged five people. There were complications, however, in carrying out the move, and during this time Lenana sent the following message from his death-bed: 'Tell my people to obey the government as they have done during my life. Tell the Laikipia Masai to move with their cattle to the Loieta plains.' This message had considerable influence, and the northern Masai expressed their wish to move south. In 1911 a new agreement was drawn up and orders were given a year later for the move to be completed, but when the time came some of the northern Masai changed their minds and asked for the move to be cancelled. Eventually, after considerable further agitation, it was completed in 1913. The manner in which the move was carried out has often been strongly criticized as it appeared to create a pattern which favoured European settlers at the expense of African needs.

The Carter Land Commission. The Masai were not the only tribe for whom reserves were suggested. There was even a recommendation from the Land Committee that a European reserve should be made. This was not done, but after 1904 native reserves were set aside. Unfortunately, they were created without adequate information, and in a number of cases some tribes were unwittingly deprived of watering places and grazing grounds, while others received lands to which their claim was doubtful. Despite this, the reserves were declared Crown land in 1915 and their boundaries defined by the Crown Lands Ordinance of 1926. Afterwards it was claimed that some of the land which had been included in these reserves had later been taken for European settlement. In 1932 the Government, therefore, appointed a Royal Commission, known as the Carter Land Commission, to investigate the question of native lands. The report of this commission led to adjustments in land which were accepted by the Government as the final settlement of claims based on past injustice. A substantial area of land was also added to the native reserves to meet permanent economic needs. The native areas were then transferred from the Crown to the Africans themselves. Their rights to these lands were guaranteed for ever and a Native Lands Trust Board was set up to watch over them. The boundaries of the Highlands area, in which Europeans were to have a privileged position, were also defined and safeguarded by a Highlands Board. These changes created native areas of 52,097 square miles. By comparison the extent of the Highlands in 1950 was 16,173 square miles including 3979 square miles of forest reserve, which was not considered to be available for settlement. The difference between these figures and the total area of Kenya was largely made up of the Turkana and Northern Frontier districts, which were inhabited by nomad tribes observing no fixed boundaries.

Lord Delamere. When the dust raised by the arguments over land has blown away, it will be seen that the coming of the European settlers changed the country as profoundly as Peter the Great changed Russia, for democracies may administer a land, but under their rule profound economic changes are often initiated by the individual. Initiative, self-reliance, determination, courage, all these were called for and possessed in some measure by the settlers who came up from the south or from Great Britain. Even a short history cannot overlook one man in particular: Lord Delamere, who lived from 1870 to 1931. His colourful career cannot be compressed adequately into the limited space which is all it can be given here. Only the main outline of the story is indicated, leaving the details to be filled in by subsequent reading, and argued over both by those who admire and by those who hate him. Few would deny that he was a man of intense vitality and volcanic temper; as such he came in for a great deal of criticism, which was not lessened by his high-handed procedure on occasion. There was the time, for instance, when two Indian policemen arrived at his farm when he was away, and had to spend the night there. Seeing an empty tent pitched conveniently, they went to sleep on the camp bed inside. Unfortunately Lord Delamere returned late that night and went to look for Sammy McCall, to whom the tent belonged. Finding the police inside he sent for some Masai to make threatening noises behind the tent, and when the police shot out he hit them on the head with a heavy African club which he had borrowed from the Masai.

Early career and contribution to stock farming. By the time he was twenty-one Hugh Cholmondeley had become the third Baron Delamere and inherited Vale Royal, Cheshire, the estate whose finances were to be drained to provide the money for his East African ventures. He soon decided that hunting in the winter and shooting in the autumn did not provide him with sufficient excitement, and went off big-game hunting in Somaliland. After this he returned there every year until 1896, when he extended his journey into the Northern Frontier District, and so into Kenya, where he was entranced by the country. He returned to England, married and tried to settle down at home, but it was no good, his heart was in East Africa. Finally, in 1903 when he was wondering whether to live there permanently, he met with his third serious accident. By the time he was able to get up he had thought things over. Lying on his back for nearly a year in Nairobi he had decided that the Highlands were potentially good farming land, well suited for white settlement. First, however, someone had to prove that first-class stock could be bred there and give good returns, and that crops could be grown which would lift the land from the level of subsistence farming. Even for a wealthy man this would mean risking all his capital, but Delamere was prepared to take the gamble to show that East Africa was a place where the English way of life could flourish. His first venture emphasized the price he would have to pay, for the concession of 100,000 acres which he obtained at Njoro cost him several thousand pounds in capital before he proved that sheep could not be run there successfully. This was land over which the Masai had never grazed their flocks, and because it was totally unoccupied the Government had been ready to rent it to Lord Delamere for £200 a year, provided he spent £5000 on developing it within the next five years. When four-fifths of his flock of imported ewes died, owing to a mineral deficiency in the soil, Delamere turned to cattle, but here again his imported stock was doomed, for the tick which carries East Coast fever abounded in his land and in those days no one dipped cattle to safeguard them from the disease.

Wheat. Equator Ranch, as Lord Delamere called his home, had proved a failure as a stock farm; it remained to be seen whether wheat could be grown there. First the land had to be ploughed, and there were no trained oxen or horses available. Next, fences had to be put up to keep out the wild animals. These tasks finished, Delamere looked forward to the first big crop of wheat on which he had staked so much

money, but the wheat was riddled with rust. With this third failure
Lord Delamere would have been ruined if he had not been able to
raise a mortgage on his estate in England. Even so, his life for the
next six years was a bleak one in a windowless, mud-floored shack.
The money he was able to raise went on tracking down the remedy
for rust. To do this he called in the help of a scientist, for whom he
built a simple laboratory. Here research was done on the breeding of
a rust-resistant variety of wheat. Three years later Lord Delamere
harvested his first successful crop.

Summary of achievement by 1914. Now Delamere could give his
mind to his stock, the remnants of which he had transferred to a farm,
'Soysambu', which he had bought near Gilgil. By 1914 he had proved
that stock could be graded up in Kenya and the land improved. The
years of struggle were over. That they had been hard can be read in
Lord Delamere's own words. He summed up his experience at
Equator Ranch as follows:

I had 3000 acres under cultivation—mostly wheat—on the Njoro farm
alone.

The result after a few years working was that sheep had proved a
failure and big losses had been incurred; that the land had been proved
unsuitable for improved cattle until the East Coast fever menace was
dealt with; the wheat was proved to have come to stay. That the possibility of ploughing large acreages in a country where the plough had
never been seen was proved to be an economic proposition; that large
numbers of natives had been taught ploughing and working with other
implements; and that I had managed to get rid of £40,000 in cash
which I had invested in the country.

Leader of the white settlers. By now Lord Delamere was looked on
as a leader by the other settlers, who felt the need of a spokesman in
a land where the Government was in the unique position of having
preceded the settlers, and therefore claimed that 'All actual or potential sources of wealth—land, minerals, forests, rivers, lakes—belonged
to the state'. All forms of transport—railways, roads, lake steamers
and accessories such as wharves and harbours—were state-built and
state-owned. Private trading in the most important commodity in the

country, land, was prohibited. This position was peculiarly irksome to the many settlers who had hoped for a freer life overseas and who relied on their own initiative to carve out a future which should be beneficial to themselves and the country of their adoption. In other parts of the empire, such as the New England and plantation colonies, England had only taken over responsibility for the administration when there were already settlers there who had begun to develop the land and organize themselves. In East Africa, however, the Government was there first, and it was primarily concerned with political administration, and not economic development. There was, therefore, a good deal of friction between the Government and the settlers, which could not result in official discussions until the first Legislative Council was authorized in 1907.

It was not long before Lord Delamere became convinced that the unofficial members of the Legislative Council should be elected, and not nominated, as a step towards ultimate self-government for the Europeans, and he was working to secure this when the First World War broke out.

Services, 1914–18. British East Africa was now faced with the Germans along the whole of its southern frontier, which lay right through the middle of Masailand. Delamere, quick to see that his knowledge of the Masai was the best gift he could give his country, offered to organize the Masai warriors for intelligence duties along the German border. This was to be at his own expense. It was a hard life and eventually the strain proved too much for his strength and he collapsed. His war service, however, was not over, for in 1917 he was elected to the War Council and was in office when the German General von Lettow was driven out of German East Africa.

Elections to the Legislative Council. In both England and East Africa the end of the war brought an extension of the franchise to those on whose support their country had relied, and in 1920 the first election was held to the Legislative Council, which was now to include eleven unofficial members chosen by the European community. Two Europeans were also chosen as unofficial members of the Executive Council, one of whom was Lord Delamere. In this position he was to have a degree of influence which often surprised those who did not realize the value of his experience in a land where officials were not permanent residents.

Devonshire White Paper. The grant of elected representatives to the Europeans alone did not long go unchallenged, and in 1920 the Indians demanded the vote on the same terms. With this they linked the rights to acquire land in the Highlands and to have an unchecked entry into East Africa. Both these claims were strongly opposed by the European settlers, who looked to Lord Delamere to lead them. He accepted this responsibility and led a deputation to England to lay their case before the Secretary of State for the Colonies. When a settlement was finally reached in 1923 the following important statement was issued with the terms:

Primarily, Kenya is an African territory, and H.M. Government think it necessary definitely to record their considered opinion that the interests of the African native must be paramount, and that if and when those interests and the interests of the immigrant races should conflict, the former should prevail.

This was qualified by the further statement that:

Obviously the interests of the other communities, European, Indian and Arab, must generally be safeguarded. Whatever the circumstances in which members of these communities have entered Kenya, there will be no drastic action or reversal of measures already introduced.

Dairy farming. After the publication of the Devonshire White Paper, Delamere developed a third branch of farming. Before the war he had shown that stock and wheat could be profitable assets to Kenya. Now he concentrated on dairying, and in addition to building up his own herds established a co-operative creamery in 1925. The next year saw the export of the first butter from Kenya, and in 1930 the Kenya Co-operative Creameries were formed. This was followed by the establishment of the Kenya Farmers Association.

Staple commodities. Agriculture is the basis of Kenya's economy, and Lord Delamere had played the leading part in its early development. The search for staple commodities, the development of coffee, sisal, wattle, tea, and pyrethrum, the growth of African production, and the start of secondary industries, have still to be described. At the close of the last century the first fast-growing wheat, passion fruit, tomatoes, Cape gooseberries and potatoes to be grown in the hinterland of East Africa were planted at Machakos by a missionary, Stuart Watt, in an effort to make the little mission station he had established there self-supporting. He also experimented with eucalyptus and wattle trees. From this tiny beginning a fruit and vegetable canning plant has been set up which exports throughout the world.

Coffee. Missionaries were also responsible for the introduction of coffee into Kenya, for the French Fathers of St Austin's mission planted the first coffee near Nairobi in 1896. It throve there and was developed by many of the early settlers to such an extent that the yield is now 14 cwt. per acre. In 1945 it was only 1·8 cwt. In 1963, when it was being extensively grown by Africans, coffee was worth twice as much as any other single export from Kenya.

Tea and sisal. Two other valuable Kenya crops were introduced early in the century—tea and sisal. The former was first started at Limuru in 1904, and three years later an enterprising district commissioner raised one plant in the prison garden at Kericho. It was not, however, until two planting companies came from India in 1925 that any real progress was made: today tea is Kenya's second most valuable export. Sisal found its way to Kenya from Tanganyika, where it had been introduced by the Germans in 1893.

Probably the most valuable crop to be introduced since the First World War has been pyrethrum. The fact that it was not grown in the country until 1930, although today Kenya leads the world in first-class products of this plant, tempts one to encouraging forecasts about the agricultural potentialities of East Africa. On the other hand, soil erosion throws a menacing shadow.

Erosion, of course, is a threat common to other parts of Africa where the earth is trodden hard by stock and baked by the sun; for heavy rains then wash away the unprotected soil, leaving deep channels. After the First World War, the soil was further weakened by the heavy planting of maize, which was encouraged by official recommendation. It was mistakenly considered a suitable crop which would also provide bulk for the railway to carry to Mombasa. By the 1950's the soil had recovered, but since 1960 there has nevertheless been a steady increase in the acreage under maize, which is a tempting crop for small farmers with large families and little capital.

Scientific farming. If a country makes use of science, it becomes easier to plan its farming wisely. Much can be done for livestock, for instance, through the veterinary department. The first veterinary officer to come to the mainland was Captain Haslam, who was posted to Ukambani at the time of the great rinderpest plague at the end of the nineteenth century. Although he himself was murdered when he went to Kikuyuland to deal with the rinderpest there, his work was continued, and since the Second World War scientific research into the problems of farming has increased considerably. Much of it now covers the whole of East Africa, not only one territory, and the high standards of research maintained by both the Kenya Government and the East African Common Services have done much for East African agriculture.

By the beginning of the twentieth century, too, the first schools, hospitals and 'vets' had appeared on the mainland of East Africa. Development had begun. It could only go on if the wealth of East Africa could be increased. Here the European settlers were an asset; but they could not run their farms without labour and the Africans were reluctant to change the habits of centuries. The old way of life provided most of them with what they wanted and they saw no reason to alter it. Many of the Europeans were shocked, for they came from lands where food was much harder to get and clothing was essential. They took it for granted, therefore, that most men must earn their living by work, and felt that it was not unreasonable that they should expect the Government to tell the Africans that the young men must find work on the settlers' farms, and generally to help in recruiting labour. The governor would have preferred to let things alone; this led to the characteristic attempt which Lord Delamere made to put pressure on the governor by unruly behaviour, which led to his suspension from the Legislative Council. A board was appointed to go into the question and suggest ways of easing the situation. The crisis was solved when they recommended the removal of some of the restrictions on African movements to which the settlers had objected, together with certain improvements in the labourer's living conditions.

Economic development, 1895–1914. It remains to look at the effect of world affairs on events in the East Africa Protectorate. In Britain the period 1895 to 1914 was one both of material prosperity and of strain due to the growing friction between Britain and Germany and Austria. In the East Africa Protectorate it was a period of economic development during which the country passed from the stage of receiving a grant-in-aid to that of financial balance.

Taxation. Until the railway was built the Government considered that its work was to administer the country and not to develop it. Departments of Agriculture, Forestry, Public Works, Customs, Land, Education, Medical Services, a Treasury and a railway were, therefore, all started early in the twentieth century, and naturally they cost a good deal of money. Yet the country was not sufficiently developed for the Government to be able to collect large sums in taxation. In 1902, for instance, it cost over £200,000 more to govern Kenya than was collected from the country. Nor was it easy to see how Kenya could quickly make more money, because her exports were worth less than half her imports. It was clear that the protectorate would have to receive help from England, and it was given a grant-in-aid of some £250,000 a year. It received this until 1912, when the increasing prosperity of the country in general, and of the railway in particular, enabled it to do without it. Since that time the country cost the British taxpayer nothing, until a State of Emergency was declared in 1952.

Problems caused by the First World War. In the 1914–18 war a very great strain was put on a country which had only just begun to develop on new lines. In 1914 the total European population of the East Africa Protectorate was about 3000. Of these, 1987 joined up during the war, leaving a bare minimum to carry on the government and run the farms. A vast army of African porters was also required to supply the troops in the field. Nearly 60,000 were recruited in Uganda and the great majority of the rest came from the East Africa

Protectorate. Losses in both groups were heavy; and the end of the war saw a sadly impoverished country.

The veterinary services had been too busy keeping transport animals alive to be able to spare much time for producers' troubles; African stock had been shifted about according to military needs, and without due regard to quarantine restrictions. Disease had, therefore, spread and in 1916 rinderpest reappeared. Nor was this all: weeds and grass had spread over the ploughed land and through the coffee plantations. For many men, years of hard work had been wiped out by four years' absence. There was hunger, too, for in 1918 there had been a drought and a bad famine. Finally, the administration of the country, the roads and the railway had all been seriously weakened by the war.

The soldier settlement scheme. In 1919 a new governor, Sir Edward Northey, arrived to deal with these difficulties. During his period of office the railway finances were separated from those of the Protectorate and the soldier settlement scheme, which resulted in the second large flow of settlers to East Africa, was introduced. To carry out this scheme 17½ square miles were taken from the Nandi reserve, and this grievance was not remedied until the Carter Land Commission's Report in 1934.

By 1919 the European population of Kenya had increased by 200 per cent to over 9000. The African population, for which there are no exact figures available, had been reduced by war, famine and the influenza epidemic which swept through East Africa. The demands on the labour supply by both private employers and the Government were, therefore, difficult to satisfy, especially as the damage done by the war had to be repaired and the population fed. The problem was acute and there was much bitter discussion in England and East Africa over the degree of pressure which might be justly put on Africans to persuade them to leave the reserves and work outside. Eventually a further amendment was made to the Native Authority Ordinance, to the effect that the consent of the Secretary of State must be obtained before any compulsory labour was called out.

No sooner had Kenya steered her way past these difficulties than she was involved in a currency crisis which was eventually settled by the introduction of a new coin, the shilling.

Depression. In Europe the end of the First World War was followed by a slump. The same thing happened in Kenya, where the problems described above added to the difficulties. This was followed from 1925 to 1929 by years of expansion and lavish expenditure. In the 1930's depression again set in. The world prices for primary products were steadily falling, and Kenya was an agricultural country, and as such badly hit when the forward-on-rail value of maize fell from Shs. 11/10 a bag to Shs. 3/20 a bag, and coffee from Shs. 89/50 a hundredweight to Shs. 46/50. All over the world the mid-1930's were a time of falling prices, unemployment and general distress. In Kenya, where this was made worse by locusts and droughts, it is not surprising that the budget could not be balanced. A new source of revenue had to be found and in 1937 income tax was introduced. This was a tax which fell particularly heavily on the European community— Africans in practice were exempt—and for that reason was much criticized.

Outbreak of war. From this point onwards things began to improve, although over in Europe people were growing increasingly concerned about Hitler's plans for world domination. Knowing the close understanding between Hitler and Mussolini, men assumed when war with Germany came on 3 September 1939 that Italy would attempt to invade Kenya from her base in Abyssinia. Fortunately Italy did not declare war until May 1940, by which time East Africa was assured of support from South Africa. As in 1914, a high proportion of the population enlisted to serve their country; in addition the East African Railway's Nairobi workshop was the centre from which motor ambulances, mortars, lorries, stretchers, etc., came to help in equipping the East Africa Command.

Conduct of the war. Once Italy entered the war, fighting began in the Northern Frontier district and British Somaliland. By the autumn of 1940 the position had improved to such an extent that it was possible to move from the defence of Kenya to the attack on Italian Somaliland. South African, Nigerian, Northern Rhodesian and Gold Coast brigades were now serving with the East African forces, and after the successful attack on Italian Somaliland these forces pushed on into Abyssinia. Here their progress, once they had begun to use the roads the Italians had built, was extraordinarily rapid, and with the fall of Abyssinia British arms secured their first complete success on land.

East Africa's contribution. The nature of East Africa's contribution to the war effort then changed. Guards for prisoner-of-war camps and garrisons for the conquered lands had to be provided. Troops were sent also to help in the defence of Ceylon and India and to other theatres of war. East Africa was also a training base and a place of asylum for refugees from the Middle East and Poland. All this meant that greater emphasis had to be placed on agricultural production.

As a country producing vitally needed foodstuffs, Kenya flourished at the end of the war, especially as she could now draw on capital and people who turned, with the withdrawal of Britain from India, to Kenya.

The Swynnerton Plan. Since the war African agriculturalists have taken a much greater interest in the production of export crops. In 1952, for example, Africans sold three times as much wattle bark as Europeans. A plan was therefore made to intensify agricultural production in the African areas, commonly known as the Swynnerton Plan—named after its author—by which the United Kingdom Government made a grant of 5 million pounds with which to engage specialist staff, to purchase special equipment and to introduce special training and investigation centres for agricultural, veterinary, forest and water development. This large investment, coupled with widespread land consolidation and enclosure, greatly increased the production of tea, coffee, pyrethrum, rice, cereals, sisal and animal products in the African areas. In the opinion of a recent mission by an international bank the results were unique and stand as a model for future development in other countries besides Kenya.

The Swynnerton Plan was published in 1954 and in the following year the Royal Commission outlined the problem of land tenure:

The African way of life and sense of security have always been bound up in the land and his stock. Memories of famine deter him from

178

changing his way of life until the success of the new ways has been demonstrated. Most land is held on customary tenure and farmed accordingly. In the last two decades this type of land tenure has shown itself to be ill adapted to modern conditions.

Land tenure. On the coast customary land tenure had come under Arab influence and individual rights to land were, therefore, recognized. Inland, customary land tenure still prevailed. Among the good things that came out of the Mau Mau movement was the opportunity to consolidate the fragmented holdings of the Kikuyu. Some owners of three or four acres had their land scattered in twenty different places, yet suggestions of land consolidation and individual titles to land were regarded with suspicion. Africans, especially those from Nyanza, felt that a handicapped class of landless men might be created, as they were in England by the agricultural revolution there. On the other hand, the agrarian changes in the England of the eighteenth century had helped the country to feed a rapidly rising population, which was absorbed in the growing towns by the industrial revolution. Kenya also had the problems of a rapidly rising population: in 1948 it was 5,405,966; by 1962 it had increased to 8,636,263.

By 1957 many people in the Kikuyu districts had come to understand the immense economic advantages of land consolidation and individual tenure of land. As a result the process of registration and consolidation was greatly speeded up and has spread to Nyanza Province. At the same time there was a steady increase in land registration in such districts as Kipsigis, Nandi and Elgeyo; but in 1964 the Kamba people were still reluctant to consolidate their land. This immense revolution in land tenure was recognized by the Kenya Legislative Council, which in 1959 introduced proposals which ensured that the decisive considerations governing the ownership or occupation of land in the Highlands should only be those of the economic use of land, sound agricultural development and good husbandry, and not those of race.

Settlement schemes. In 1960 settlement schemes were introduced to help Africans to purchase and develop land in the scheduled areas which had previously been restricted to Europeans. Only part of the former 'White Highlands' is subject to the scheme, the areas around Kitale and Nakuru being excluded for the first five years so that they may continue to produce grain and dairy products to feed the non-farming population. In 1962 the Government said that there would be a big extension of the smallholder scheme for those with little money. Increasing emphasis is being put on the number of men who can be settled on the land. The suitability of the land-holding for efficient production is considered less. Yet efficient production is most important, for agriculture still provides between 85 and 90 per cent of the money earned for Kenya by exports. Moreover, about 80 per cent of the population work on the land, and their standard of living also depends on efficient production. An answer may lie in the development of African socialism, including farming co-operatives. These might take over land that is unsuitable for subdivision and would help in marketing. These too would need money, in addition to the cost of the revised smallholder scheme proposed in 1962, which will be between 13 and 18 million pounds. It is being contributed in the form of loans and grants by Britain. It was Britain who provided a large part of the cost of the original scheme.

Post-war industrial development. Although Kenya's wealth is always likely to be in its agriculture, manufactures are growing in importance. During the years 1954–62, manufactured goods increased and their value rose from 14·1 million pounds to 23 million pounds. The biggest increase took place in the textile industry, which makes Nakuru blankets and similar goods. This industry produced so much that its goods went up in value by 430 per cent. Matches, brewing, bricks, plastics and metal boxes are also among Kenya's developing industries. Some of these already produce nearly all the articles required by the local market, cigarettes and cement, for example. Construction industries, such as woodwork, have also developed. Then there is the industry connected with garages; this too is going ahead.

In 1945 there were very few Africans in the retail trade. Since then their numbers have grown considerably and they are replacing many of the Asians who once had a monopoly. Finally, all races are finding that the development of air and motor travel has changed their lives.

Now that adequate transport services are available, tourists are coming to the country in increasing numbers. Tourism is a valuable source of income to the Kenya of 1964 and is looked after by a minister, who is also responsible for information and broadcasting. Travel will mean an increasing demand for petrol and oil. The opening of a large oil refinery near Mombasa in 1963 was, therefore, an important event: Kenya had a new source of revenue and employment, and an asset worth millions of pounds.

Subsistence agriculture often results in too little thought about the future; industry needs planning, and it can happen that too many urban affairs are settled by drift; Kenya has few natural resources. These are some of the economic problems that lie ahead. To solve them Kenyans have experience in living together in a multi-racial community. They also have the African tradition of working together as a team, which may well be the characteristic twentieth-century way of tackling problems.

The Prime Minister's views were given at the Commonwealth Conference in 1964 when he said, 'We plan not only to strengthen the old economic institutions but to establish new ones, freely choosing our models from the successful economies of the world, adapting the old institutions to suit Kenya's conditions; and in the process to develop new concepts of economic organization.'

CHAPTER XI

THE SOCIAL AND CONSTITUTIONAL DEVELOPMENT OF KENYA

Introduction. On 12 December 1963, Kenya became an independent country and its leaders joined in the councils of the world. This was the culmination of some sixty years of dramatic social change and constitutional development, which were interwoven with the economic development outlined in the last chapter; the two types of development should be studied in conjunction with each other.

Before the coming of the British there was no central government in Kenya; that is, no one person or body controlled the whole country and could give orders which had to be obeyed throughout the land. There were, however, local governments which could make themselves obeyed within limited areas, and the tribes who shared the land had their own customs for their particular areas. These were usually enforced by councils of elders, but were effective only in the nearby settlements from which members were drawn. It is not possible in this book to describe the different forms these councils took, so those of one tribe, the Kamba, have been taken as an example. This particular tribe has been chosen because the headquarters of the British Government on the mainland was originally at Machakos and the commissioner there was probably influenced by their organization. This tribe did not have chiefs, but was broken up into a number of small groups, in even the largest of which the members lived within easy walking distance of each other. Each group was presided over by the Nzama ya Ndua (Council of Elders), which was made up of the chief elders of the group, each of whom had to pay for admission to it. The chief function of this council was to act as a court of law; but it was also responsible for religious observances. That is why these councils usually centred upon places of sacrifice. Nowadays a council like this might be expected to pass new laws, but the Kamba did not think this was necessary. This was partly because laws only come in with change. If there are no big changes, men will expect their neighbours to be guided by the established customs of the tribe or group. Men thought of themselves as members of a group rather than as individuals with differing aims. Within this group they had specific duties and privileges as warriors, elders or wives. In this tradition-directed society status was usually indicated by dress or ornament. Riddles and proverbs reflected tribal opinion and conveyed the wisdom of experience; songs and stories told of the history of the tribe.

Policy of the British Government. In 1895, the British Government took over from I.B.E.A. the responsibility for the government of the area between the Tana and the Umba, stretching as far to the west as a line drawn from Lake Rudolf to the east of Lakes Baringo and Naivasha, down to the German East Africa border. In 1902 this also included the territory to the east of the lake. This whole area was henceforth to be known as the East Africa Protectorate. The very name showed that England was thinking of the country as a whole and not as a collection of entirely separate tribes. It had therefore to be administered as a whole. To do this, communications had to be improved and order kept over a wide area. The Government also aimed at raising the standard of living of the people as a whole. Recurrent famine had therefore to be checked, health improved and education started. When this was done the number of Africans greatly increased, because fewer were killed in battle or died of disease or famine. Apart from anything else, this increase in population had made it essential to develop the country more than in the days before the coming of the British. Development of the country meant that money had to be collected, and the fairest way to do this was thought to be a hut tax of 2s. per annum, which was introduced in 1903. The amount collected by this in the province of Ukamba in 1903–4 was £3400. Change also meant laws and in 1902 the Village Headman's Ordinance became law. It was difficult at first for the Government to choose headmen wisely, and cases were reported of the oppression of the African people by headmen and police. So, in 1908, the more reliable government servants were appointed as chiefs and given authority over wider areas. In 1924 a further big step forward was taken when Local Native

Councils were started; these may be said to have grown out of such bodies as the Nzama of the Kamba.

Beginning of central government. Central government began with the appointment of a Commissioner for East Africa. He recognized that there were a number of matters which affected the whole country; and by 1902 Departments of Agriculture, Forestry, Public Works, Trade and Customs, Land, Judicature, Medical Services, a Treasury and a Post Office had been set up. In 1905, when the Executive Council was formed, the members were chosen from the heads of these departments. This body was similar to the advisory council which governors usually had to help them in the nineteenth century.

First Legislative Council. In 1907 it was thought by the Colonial Office that the East Africa Protectorate was ready to take another step forward; and the new governor was given instructions to form a Legislative Council. There was no question at the time of the election of anyone to the Council; the governor nominated eight men. Six of these were officials, that is men who were in the employment of the Colonial Office, and two were 'unofficials'. These last two included Lord Delamere, who hoped that his appointment meant that the settlers' opinions would be seriously considered. He soon found that its meetings were only to give formal consent to laws, estimates and supplies, and he sent in the first of his many resignations.

Introduction of the franchise. After the First World War the loyal support which had been given by British East Africa was rewarded by several constitutional changes. In 1918 it was announced that two European unofficials would be placed on the Executive Council. In the following year it was also announced that the long-awaited franchise would be granted to the Europeans, eleven of whom were to be elected to the Legislative Council. Eleven electoral areas were defined and the first elections to be held in the country took place the following year.

The Indian community—Devonshire White Paper. During these years prolonged and bitter discussions went on between the British Government and the European and Indian communities in Kenya. The end of the war had meant for India, as well as Kenya, an advance in self-government; and Indians everywhere were proudly aware of the aid their country had given during the war. A deputation was sent to England asking for equal representation on the Legislative Council, the end of segregation in the townships, the right to hold land in the Highlands and promotion on merit, not race, to the highest posts in the police, army and civil service.

This deputation was soon followed by one from the settlers putting the opposite point of view. After a stormy interlude the Devonshire White Paper of 1923 was issued, as a result of which Indian members were elected on a communal basis to the Legislative Council and the Nairobi Town Council. There was now an official majority of only two in the former. In this respect, there were no further changes until after the outbreak of the Second World War.

Advances in self-government. The First World War had been followed by the grant of representative government to Kenya; and the advance to self-government was further accelerated by the Second World War, in which Africans gained experience in a wider world. In 1944 the first African, Mr Eliud Mathu, took his seat in the Legislative Council. There were now two representatives of African interests. In 1948, when this number was increased to four, all of whom were Africans, there was for the first time an unofficial majority in the Legislative Council. In other words the majority of the members of the Council were there because they had been elected and not because of their position as officials.

Urban development. The coming of the railway in 1901 led to economic development and towns began to grow around the shops and offices of Europeans and Asians. In 1903 the East African Township Ordinance was issued. This stated that certain areas were to rank as townships. Rules were made for their health and good administration, and their cleaning, lighting and policing were declared to be the responsibility of the district commissioner. At the same time it was stated that a rate could be levied to supply the money needed. Nairobi, however, was declared to be in a special position, as it was the only town of any size in the interior, and its affairs have been managed since 1900 by a committee.

Except on the coast, towns in Kenya were created by Europeans needing administrative centres who wanted to live under conditions resembling those they had left in Europe. Here they were joined by Asians, a number of whom lived above their shops. Africans were in a different position. In most of East Africa legislation restricted non-Africans to living and running businesses in gazetted townships. Africans, therefore, found it cheaper to live and trade outside these areas. Gradually an increasing number came to get jobs in the towns. These men were faced with many problems. Few were able to bring their families with them and many found they had lost a sense of security. It is usually only skilled labour that commands good wages and these men found themselves with very little money. When Africans began to spend longer periods in towns a serious situation arose. For one thing housing schemes had failed to keep up with the increasing population.

By 1952 the drift to the towns had reached proportions which history indicates cannot be checked by government action. During the industrial revolution England went through similar suffering, and although problems that have occurred in the past may be better understood when they appear again today, it is not always easy to solve them.

A new way of life. In the early days of the twentieth century primitive conditions restricted the increase of people and animals. The slave trade, moreover, took a heavy toll of life, and epidemics which ravaged the country at the end of the century have been referred to. By the beginning of the twentieth century the slave trade and slavery had been abolished, tribal warfare stopped and European medical and veterinary techniques were being introduced. Thus the death-rate decreased and the population rose; this increased pressure on the land. In addition, certain land was subject to increased pressure, owing to the introduction of cash crops and the change from barter to cash systems of transaction. These changes made it difficult to follow the old system of moving from place to place to rest the land. Villagers were beginning to live in a world which had no contact with the past. In the last fifty years new ways of life had been opened in employment in government service, in forestry, on European farms, in towns and in the competitive worlds of commerce and industry. These occupations required skills and knowledge for which the young showed their aptitude in schools and colleges and which their elders, by tradition the wise men of the people, were too old to acquire. Old men had moved through life as members of an age-set which was a unit; as such they had served first as warriors, next as junior elders and later as elders in power. Within the age-set individuals were equal, although in some peoples there were provisions for the rapid promotion of men of promise. If individuals in an age-set are equal, they have as much right to the vote as others in their group. The slogan 'one man, one vote' appealed, therefore, very strongly to the great majority of the nation who had not yet got the franchise.

Problems created by social change. Approximately one-quarter of the African population of Kenya belong to the Luo and Luhya peoples. The next largest group are the Kikuyu, who are approximately one-fifth of the total; a further one-tenth belong to their kindred peoples, the Meru and Embu. They live close to Nairobi, where the problems of an industrial society were particularly difficult. These problems included slums, low wages, insecurity of employment and the relatively high cost of living.

At one time it was estimated that there were 10,000 unemployed Africans in Kenya, out of an African population which in 1948 was reckoned to be five and a quarter million. Many of these were disappointed because they had either sought education and been unable to obtain it, or obtained it and found it did not lead to the kind of job they had hoped for; most of the junior technical and clerical posts in commerce, industry and the Government were held by Asians. In 1947, in reply to a question in the Legislative Council, it was stated that the Government and the railway between them paid salaries of Shs. 300 a month or more to only nine Africans. The racial discrimination which checked Kikuyu economic, social and political ambitions showed itself in such ways as the restrictions on the planting of cash crops, like coffee, and on the acquisition of land in the White Highlands, as well as in differences in wages.

Some Europeans understood these difficulties but did not realize their full significance to the Africans, whose real needs were not met by the paternalism which many of the Europeans showed. And many Africans thought Europeans treated them as inferiors, depriving them of their land and making them work on other men's farms. It was the Kikuyu who had come into closest contact with Europeans and their way of life; and they turned to the concept of tribal unity, making a show of reverence for their god 'Ngai' and their ancestors, Gikuyu and Mumbi. Leaders in African society without indigenous chiefs are not elected but appear to come to the front supported by their group as a whole. They are usually gifted speakers and men of ability who hold views not very different from those of the group they lead. One African's name was known throughout Kenya at this time. Mr Kenyatta was a brilliant orator who had been chosen as a spokesman on the land question before the Carter Commission of 1933. After studying for a post-graduate diploma in anthropology at London University, he had published a book called *Facing Mount Kenya*. He had also played a prominent part in African political organizations, and soon after his return to Kenya in 1946 was made President of the Kenya African Union.

A State of Emergency. For some time there had been references to a new movement, Mau Mau. The Government was slow to admit its existence and was also reluctant to recognize the strength of the demands of African nationalism. Mau Mau was in the direct line of descent from previous Kikuyu political societies, and was first recognized officially under the name of Mau Mau in 1949. It appeared to be a spearhead force for those who believed in the need for violence. In its early stages the new organization bound itself together by oaths. By 1952 it had been forced underground and increasing numbers of Kikuyu had been bound up with it, some as a result of threats. Those who refused were, in many instances, killed. There is a story that an African who had served his European employer for many years was forced to take an oath that he would kill her. His genuine devotion to her and his genuine respect for the oath he found irreconcilable, so rather than do either he committed suicide by drowning himself.

Despite the growing crime-wave in Nairobi, the Government hoped that the situation was not as serious as it seemed. Then, in October 1952, Chief Waruhiu was murdered in broad daylight and the new governor, Sir Evelyn Baring, declared a State of Emergency. Mr Kenyatta, with other suspects, was detained and later tried with five others and convicted of managing Mau Mau.

The struggle that followed was mainly confined to the region of the Aberdares and Mount Kenya, and to the Nairobi district; it centred on the land. Kikuyu condemned to death would strive to scratch up a little earth in their prison cell and hold it out, when bravely facing their end, saying, 'For this I die.' On the other hand, many, but not all, Christians refused to take the oaths, claiming, like the early martyrs in Rome, that they were already bound to their God; and in so doing died for their faith. Many of the old people also rejected this new perversion of the old ways.

At the beginning of the emergency Nairobi was the headquarters of the Mau Mau movement, but by 1956 the city was cleared. The last struggles of the movement were in the Aberdares and on the slopes of Mount Kenya, where it is generally held to have ended in 1956 with the capture of Dedan Kimathi, who had become the real leader of the militant movement. By that time thirty-two European civilians and more than 2000 African civilians on both sides had been killed; some were burnt alive, others were tortured (even cases of cannibalism were known). Nor were Mau Mau attacks restricted to men; women and children, contrary to tribal custom, were included. Asians also were involved—twenty-six Asian civilians were killed, mostly in Nairobi. The State of Emergency was not declared at an end till January 1960.

After the emergency. During the time of Mau Mau isolated huts were fired and families slaughtered. In order to protect their supporters and prevent the gangs from commandeering supplies they needed, the Government compelled the Kikuyu to live in villages under strict discipline and to farm their lands under supervision. By 1957 it was possible to develop what had been little more than labour lines as villages with social services, piped water and so on, which could not be provided for isolated land-holdings. Closer administration was also possible as the villages were near the road and, therefore, easier to reach. Many of these villages have become permanent towns for those with very little land; at the same time a large number have been abolished to enable the inhabitants to go and live on their consolidated farms. By 1960 the Kikuyu were able to return to Nairobi, from which most of them had been excluded. Although great efforts had been made to increase and improve the accommodation available, it was strained by the influx that ensued. The problems of the capital, though, were dwarfed by those of Kenya itself: social services had to be expanded and the productivity of the land increased to pay for them, yet Kenya now had a public debt of 47 million pounds as compared with the 16 million pounds owed by Tanganyika.

Changes in local government. In 1950 Nairobi had become a city and was followed by Nakuru; later Kisumu, Eldoret and Mombasa developed municipal councils with mayors. Nairobi thus continued to lead the group of developing townships, as she had ever since the railway headquarters had been transferred to her as the growing capital of the colony. A more important step was taken in 1950 when the African District Councils Ordinance was passed, which gave these councils a position similar to those of the municipalities. The new councils were able to provide a variety of services. They could also pass by-laws, some of which would be binding on people of all races who lived in their area. In 1955 a constitution was also given to the locational councils, which had proved very successful. In 1952 an effort was made to fill an important gap in this system and an ordinance was passed which allowed districts in the scheduled areas to set up county councils. These corresponded roughly to the African District Councils and replaced the European District Councils, which had been little more than glorified Road Boards.

The Lyttelton Constitution and the Council of Ministers. Before the State of Emergency was officially at an end, Mr Lyttelton, Colonial Secretary at the time, had seen the need to grant Kenya fuller powers of self-government. The most important change he made was the introduction of a Council of Ministers, which became the chief instrument of government in Kenya. It is worth noting that the Legislative

Council could not, at this stage, control the Council of Ministers in the way in which the House of Commons controls the Cabinet in England. It really replaced the Executive Council, which had always consisted almost entirely of officials, and was abolished soon after the introduction of the Council of Ministers.

Further changes were introduced by the next Colonial Secretary, who increased the number of Africans in the Legislative Council, so that for the first time Asian and African elected members outnumbered European elected members. In 1957 the first African elections were held in Kenya.

That year Ghana reached independence and thus became the first African member of the Commonwealth to achieve the target which Britain had worked towards in her colonies. The Mau Mau movement had focused attention on the demand for independence in Kenya also; and the pace of advance to self-government was now set. The State of Emergency was declared at an end in 1960 and a conference called at Lancaster House.

Lancaster House Agreement. In January 1960 all the elected members of the Legislative Council, plus a small number of nominated members, were asked to a conference at Lancaster House in London. The chairman was the Colonial Secretary, Mr Macleod, who said, ' Independence—I hope within the Commonwealth—is the ultimate objective, but it is not the task of this conference.' Afterwards a new constitution was introduced.

The executive was to consist of a council of twelve ministers with an unofficial majority, and an Arab representative should have the right of attendance. No restrictions were, however, put on the Governor's power to nominate ministers and members of the Legislative council. Unofficial posts were to be filled on a racial basis.

The Legislative Council was to consist of sixty-five elected members. Twenty of these seats were allotted on a racial basis in order to safeguard the interest of minorities. For these seats candidates had first to secure the support of not less than 25 per cent of the members of their own race in their constituency. Those who obtained this quota would be candidates in a second election in which members of all races would vote. The sixty-five elected members would then proceed to elect a further twelve members on a racial quota. The governor retained the right to nominate members.

Judges were to continue to be appointed by the governor.

Between conferences at Lancaster House. The absence of political parties had long been a characteristic of political life in Kenya. Candidates stood as individuals and not as members of parties. Shortly before the first Lancaster House conference, though, a multi-racial party, the New Kenya Group, had been formed under the leadership of Sir Michael Blundell; this was opposed by the United Party with its European supporters. After the conference the ban on country-wide African political parties was removed. Both the Kenya African National Union (commonly known as Kanu) and the Kenya African Democratic Union (usually known as Kadu) were now registered. The 1961 election was, therefore, a keenly fought contest on party lines. When this was over the 'caretaker' government under the leadership of Mr Ngala, who had acted as spokesman for the African elected members at Lancaster House, resigned.

In the 1961 election a large number of Independents were returned; but it was clear that Kanu, with eighteen supporters, had defeated Kadu, with only eleven. Mr Mboya was therefore asked to form a government, but refused until the real leader of the country, Mr Kenyatta, was released. Kadu then agreed to accept office and held it until 1962, when a second conference was held at Lancaster House. This was attended by Mr Kenyatta, now released through pressure by African members. After a further short period of coalition government, elections were held; as a result of these Mr Kenyatta became Prime Minister and Mr Ngala leader of the opposition.

Independence. After the second Lancaster House Conference, the pace of the advance to independence increased rapidly and a 'crash programme' of Africanization of the administration was introduced. On 12 December 1963 Kenya became an independent country and chose to remain within the British Commonwealth.

In August 1964 it was announced that Kenya would become a Republic on the first anniversary of independence. A day earlier the

Map 15. The provinces of Kenya, 1 January 1963.

Prime Minister, in his capacity as President of the Kenya African National Union, had announced that 'From now on we will work toward a one-party state'. The essence of democracy is the rule of law and respect for individuals. In so far as it means the right of every man to be heard, this is a basic concept in East African thought. In the old days in an African meeting both sides of an argument would be heard, but the final result was expected to be accepted unanimously. In this it differs from the two-party system of 'Westminster' democracy.

Outline of government, 1964. In August 1964 the head of the Government was the governor-general, representing Her Majesty, and the National Assembly, consisting of two Houses—the Senate and the House of Representatives. The leader of the largest party in the House of Representatives, Mr Kenyatta, had been appointed Prime Minister by the governor-general, who had appointed the other ministers on his advice. In Kenya, as in England, ministers are responsible for the different departments. There was, for instance, a Minister of Finance, whose task it was to introduce the Budget into the House of Representatives. Under the December constitution the Prime Minister will be replaced by a president, who will be Head of State with an executive cabinet of ministers. These will be appointed by the president from amongst the members of Parliament and will be responsible to them. The President will be the leader of the largest party or group in Parliament; but it is not clear whether Parliament will continue to consist of two Houses, and in future it is possible that there may only be one party. The fundamental rights and freedom of the individual, together with the independence of the judiciary, will continue to be guaranteed in the proposed constitution.

In August 1964, local government was in the hands of seven Regional Assemblies. These were: Coast, East, Central, Rift Valley, Nyanza, Western and North Eastern. In addition the Municipal Council controlling the Nairobi area was specifically stated to be the City Council of Nairobi and its area was defined. These regions could be divided into such local government areas as the Regional Assemblies decided; 'each such area shall be either a municipality or a county and be further subdivided'. According to proposals put forward by the Prime Minister in August 1964,

the Regional Assemblies are to have no exclusive executive authority or legislative competence in any matter which should be planned and directed on a national scale, for example, education, agriculture, health, economic and social development and the utilization of land. The Government would employ the Regional Authorities and the Local Government Authorities as its agents to such extent, and subject to such administrative and financial control, as the Government may decide.

Regional Assemblies are elected by the districts and those who live in an area may vote for members of the local councils. Councils are expected to levy rates but, according to the 1964 proposals, the central government will decide on the amount and on what services the local government authorities should provide.

Post-war social development. Since the end of the Second World War in 1945, there has been a shift from mission control of social services to Government control. This is shown in the increase (from 7068 in 1953 to 10,617 in 1962) in the number of beds in government hospitals. It shows also in the growth of government schools. In addition, the Government has developed a network of health centres and rural clinics. Youth clubs have been sponsored and community development schemes introduced. One of the most successful of these schemes was at Machakos, where by 1958 the whole district was included. Adult education was encouraged and courses held for African leaders at the Jeanes schools at Kabete and Maseno. These courses were for both men and women; and by 1958 there were over 30,000 members of women's clubs in Kenya. There are many more today. The Kenya Women's Seminar is another sign of the growing part women are playing in the public life of the country. The post of matron-in-chief, for example, is held by an African woman. Again, in the 1961 election men were surprised by the enthusiasm with which the women voted—there was even pressure for women to be included in the Legislature.

A changing way of life has led to the spread of dress and customs common overseas among the younger people; there are examples of this in housing and furniture. Ways of eating have also altered. An increasing number of Africans go to hotels and restaurants when travelling. Many women have more to do in their homes, which gives less time for their work on the land. Changes are likely to increase now that many more girls go to secondary schools; especially as the young, both men and women, have greater opportunities to travel beyond the boundaries of Kenya. Within the country, cars and motor bicycles now carry their owners to areas that were once far beyond their reach. The older people have also benefited from adult literacy campaigns and the effects of broadcasting and television (the latter was introduced in 1962). Changing interests are shown in the figures of books borrowed from the East African postal library service, which now lends over twice as high a proportion of fiction as it did in 1954.

Another important feature has been the spread of trade unionism among African industrial workers, and of co-operative societies among farmers. Wages have risen substantially since the Carpenter Report advocated that African urban wages should be adequate to support a family and not just a single man. This report was followed by the introduction of the Lidbury scales of pay in the civil service, when it was announced that salaries would be based on the work done and not on the race of the person doing it. Wages in fact have risen very substantially since 1946. On the other hand there is a growing number of unemployed, which it is hoped will be reduced by the recent tripartite agreement.

The population is increasing at the alarming rate of 3 per cent per annum; but the number of Africans attending primary school is increasing even more rapidly. Between 1953 and 1962 it roughly doubled and seven years' primary education for all boys is in sight. School leavers find it hard to get a job and there is heavy unemployment among them. At the same time, only about 10 per cent of those completing the primary school course are able to go on to secondary schooling. Higher School Certificate classes were started in African schools in 1961 and the number of entrants is expected to be nearly double (i.e. 1100) in 1967; yet there is an acute shortage of teachers with university degrees. Part of the demand for further education is met at the Royal College, which was founded as a multi-racial institution. Fifteen years earlier a multi-racial college would have seemed impracticable, but the old barriers are becoming blurred and single-race schools (secondary ones at any rate) seem an anachronism today. In *Facing Mount Kenya* Mr Kenyatta pointed out that to the Europeans 'the individual is the ideal of life, to the Africans the ideal is the right relations with and behaviour to other people'. Today this distinction also is less marked.

CHAPTER XII

THE LATER HISTORY OF UGANDA

When Sir Gerald Portal hastened from Kampala in 1893 he left Captain Macdonald to act as commissioner in his place. The problems of Uganda had now begun to change, for the hostility between the political-religious groups was subsiding, and with the arrival of Bishop Hanlon in 1895 to take over the new Roman Catholic diocese which had been allotted to the Mill Hill Fathers, hostility between the two factions practically ceased and the number of Christian converts multiplied at a remarkable speed.

The Mohammedan rising of 1893. But during Macdonald's brief period as acting commissioner one of the old parties revived and made its last effort. This was the Mohammedan Party, which in 1893 began to demand a greater share of territory than the three small chieftainships allotted to them in the previous year. What made this agitation a particular danger was the fact that the Sudanese troops under Selim Bey, who had been introduced by Lugard from Kavalli's, were openly sympathetic, for they too were Mohammedans—and it was feared that there would be a general rising of the Mohammedan party supported by the Sudanese. This was prevented by the defeat of the Mohammedans by the Baganda Protestants, the disarming of the Sudanese garrison at Port Alice (now Entebbe), and the arrest of Selim Bey. Macdonald's prompt action almost certainly prevented another civil war.

The invasion of Bunyoro. The next trouble came from Bunyoro. The line of forts left along the Toro–Bunyoro border by Lugard rapidly became centres from which the Sudanese garrisons raided the surrounding country, and Sir Gerald Portal had accordingly moved these garrisons into Buganda, where they could be effectively supervised. No sooner had they been withdrawn than Kabarega of Bunyoro took the chance of resuming his raids into Toro and drove Kasagama, whom Lugard had reinstated, back into the Ruwenzori Mountains.

197

For this reason, and also because Bunyoro had long been regarded as a refuge for revolutionaries from Buganda, the new commissioner, Colonel Colvile, decided that Bunyoro must be taken if there was to be peace. The invasion of Bunyoro was launched on the last day of 1893 when Baganda and Sudanese troops crossed the Kafu River and overran the country. To make the occupation more effective a line of forts was built from Kibiro on Lake Albert southwards to Hoima and Baranwa. Kabarega, for all his faults, was a courageous leader; he withdrew northwards into the forests and a series of campaigns was necessary before he was finally captured five years later. The southern portion of his kingdom was divided in 1894 between the Protestant and Catholic Baganda chiefs, while Kasagama returned to Toro.

The years of peace, 1894-7. With the subjugation of Bunyoro and the Mohammedan Party, and with the old Protestant and Catholic feud dead and buried, the next three years were unusually peaceful and prosperous ones for Uganda. Apart from guerrilla warfare against Kabarega, the only cause for apprehension was the approach of the Belgians from the west. This was settled by the Anglo-Belgian agreement of 1894, by which the boundary between the British and Belgian spheres was fixed at 30° E. and along the Nile–Congo watershed. Meanwhile Portal's report had been considered by Parliament, and on 18 June 1894 the British Government officially accepted the protectorate of Buganda. And although it did not yet officially accept responsibility for Bunyoro, Toro, and Ankole, the British maintained garrisons in the first two and the commissioner agreed to protect Ankole.

The rising of the chiefs, 1897. The formal acceptance of the protectorate in 1894 came as a great relief to both Catholic and Protestant missions. It did not, however, to Mwanga. He did not like the restrictions on his power which the protectorate involved, or the high standard of conduct advocated by the missions. He was not alone in these dislikes. Several of his chiefs also wanted a return to the bad old days. In 1897, therefore, these chiefs, probably aided by Mwanga, planned a revolt, which was fortunately discovered. The chiefs concerned were arrested and Mwanga fled across the lake to Buddu, where he raised a large army to support him. The acting commissioner, Major Ternan, had just led a punitive expedition against the Nandi, who were raiding along the caravan route. He marched out to meet

Map 16. Uganda.

Mwanga with Baganda and Sudanese troops. After a sharp battle ending in a bayonet charge the rebels were defeated, and Mwanga fled. The rebel troops did not give up so easily, however, for they went to Marongo on the Ankole frontier, which was notorious as a hideout for criminals from Buganda, known as the 'colony of bhang smokers'.

Together with these criminals they made a second stand against Major Ternan, but were again defeated, and by August the rebellion was over. Meanwhile, in place of Mwanga, Daudi Chwa, his infant son, was proclaimed Kabaka, with a regency of three leading chiefs.

The Sudanese mutiny: the causes. No sooner had Mwanga's rebellion been dealt with than a mutiny broke out among the Sudanese troops. In view of the trouble these troops caused it would be easy to get too evil a picture of them. As their behaviour in the Toro forts showed, they were certainly not angels; on the other hand they had many good qualities—their courage was beyond question—and in 1897 their grievances were very real. Having fought against Kabarega in Bunyoro they had been marched several hundred miles east against the Nandi. As soon as the Nandi campaign was over they had been marched west again to Buddu to deal with Mwanga, and immediately that rebellion was crushed they were ordered to march back east again to Eldama Ravine. This time it was for an expedition under Major Macdonald to explore the headwaters of the Juba River and also to be ready to give assistance against French expeditions from the Congo and Abyssinia, and against Mahdists in the southern Sudan as General Kitchener advanced upon Omdurman. Had the Sudanese been well led they might have accompanied the expedition loyally, but in fact their European officers, who were good and popular, were continually changing, and this unsettled the troops. Above all, their pay was far less than that of Sudanese troops at Machakos or in German East Africa, and even so it was six months in arrears. On the other side of the picture there is little doubt that some of the leaders, such as Mabruk Effendi, wanted to create trouble in order to gain control of Uganda for the Sudanese, and that they used the very genuine grievances of the soldiers simply as a means to achieve this end.

The events of the mutiny, 1897–8. The mutiny started on 23 September 1897 near Eldama Ravine, which was the collecting centre for Macdonald's expedition. Macdonald and Jackson who was with him were in no position to grant all the Sudanese requests, as they themselves had strict orders from Britain concerning the expedition. When the troops did not receive satisfaction they marched back towards

Buganda, killing and looting as they went, and finally took up their position in Luba's fort. Major Thruston, who was in military charge of Uganda, went to Luba's to negotiate with them, but while there he was imprisoned with two other Europeans and later all three were killed. Meanwhile Macdonald, with Swahili and Baganda troops, besieged Luba's, which held out determinedly from October 1897 to January 1898. Constant attacks were made upon it and in one Macdonald's brother was killed with G. L. Pilkington of the C.M.S., whose translation of the Bible into Luganda had made him one of the most popular missionaries in the country. The situation was now critical. Indian troops had been sent for from Jubaland and from Bombay but could not arrive without considerable delay. Meanwhile it was feared that the other Sudanese garrisons in Bunyoro, Toro, Buddu, and Kampala might join the mutiny. To make matters worse Mwanga reappeared in Buddu in January declaring himself a Mohammedan, and raised 2000 armed troops. Macdonald had to take part of the force besieging Luba's in order to deal with Mwanga, who was quickly defeated. But while Macdonald was away the mutineers took the opportunity to escape from Luba's, and began to march towards Bunyoro, where the Sudanese garrisons were showing signs of joining the mutineers. The immediate danger was averted by the arrival of Lt. Scott with Indian and Swahili troops, who marched sixty-five miles in three days, disarmed the Sudanese garrisons in Bunyoro, and prevented the mutineers from joining them. The last major stand of the Sudanese was at Kabagambe on the central part of the southern shore of Lake Kyoga, where they were successfully attacked in February 1898. A number of them fled across Lake Kyoga and carried on local skirmishes until the last were dispersed by the Lango expedition of 1901, but the real danger had ended with the storming of Kabagambe.

The exile of Kabarega and Mwanga. Meanwhile two royal troublemakers had at last been caught—Kabarega and Mwanga. Mwanga had fled to Kabarega after being defeated by Macdonald. When captured in 1899 the two prisoners presented a remarkable contrast. Mwanga was despondent in the extreme, but Kabarega was a proud monarch to the end. While in hospital he kicked a European doctor's bottom for attending to a sick man of humble origin before himself. Both kings were exiled to the Seychelles, where Mwanga died in 1903, and although Kabarega returned to Jinja twenty years later he died of influenza almost at once.

The need for reorganization in Buganda. Throughout the Uganda mutiny the three regent chiefs of Buganda had shown remarkable loyalty and good sense, and had been supported by the great majority of the Baganda people. But the country was exhausted, disorganized, and full of troops. This led to difficulties between the military and civil authorities, and the home government decided to send out a Special Commission to reorganize the administration.

Size and condition of the protectorate in 1900. The man selected as Special Commissioner was Sir Harry Johnston, whose period of office was the turning point in Uganda's history. In 1894, as we have seen, the British had assumed a protectorate over Buganda (known as the Kingdom of Uganda until 1908 when it was changed to the current word Buganda) but by the end of the nineteenth century the protectorate of Uganda had come to include a much greater area than just the Kabaka's kingdom. In fact the area which comprised the protectorate of Uganda when Johnston arrived was about double the present size of the protectorate. Its boundary extended from Gondokoro eastwards to Lake Rudolf and then southwards through Naivasha to the northern border of German East Africa, along which it extended from Kilimanjaro to Lake Victoria at 1° S. and then was continued westwards to the 30th meridian of longitude. This marked the western boundary, following the Nile–Congo watershed. The only non-Africans were the Protestant and Catholic missionaries, apart from a very few European, Indian, and Arab traders. The only external trade which could pay for the enormous cost of porterage to the coast was ivory, and until the arrival of the railway at Port Florence (Kisumu) at the end of 1901 communication was difficult and extremely slow.

Sir Harry Johnston. Johnston already had a very wide experience of African affairs when he arrived. Besides being a doctor of science,

an author, and a painter, he also was a great administrator and
traveller. In 1882 he had visited the Congo area; two years later he led
an expedition to Kilimanjaro; in 1887 he was in the consular service
in West Africa, and two years later he was appointed consul-general
for Portuguese South-East Africa, where he followed up Lugard's
work in stopping the slave trade in Nyasaland and establishing a settled
administration there. From 1897 to 1899 he was consul-general in
Tunis. He left this post to take up his appointment in Uganda.

The 1900 agreement: the land settlement. The three main questions
he was called upon to deal with were concerned with land ownership,
taxation, and government. As Buganda was the most advanced of the
provinces under his jurisdiction, it was with Buganda that he made
the first, and most important, agreement on these points. The land
question was the one which aroused the greatest controversy and
which had the deepest effects. Before 1900 all land had been regarded
as belonging to the Kabaka, who had the power to turn a chief out of
office and out of his land at a moment's notice. After discussions
with the three regents, the leading chiefs, and the missions, Johnston
put forward the suggestion that assuming the area of Buganda to be
about 19,000 square miles—which was actually an overestimate—
about 10,000 square miles were to be Crown land, 1000 square miles
were to be allocated to the royal family and principal chiefs, and the
remaining 8000 square miles were to be divided between all existing
landowners. The 9000 square miles which were not allocated to the
Crown were known as the 'mailo' lands (from the English square
mile), and the division of them was a gigantic task, which Johnston
wisely left the Buganda Council (Lukiko) to settle. The effect of this
land arrangement was to break down the old feudal organization, and
the security given by the new system of absolute ownership provided
a great incentive to increase production.

The financial settlement. The second question to be decided by the
agreement was that of finance. The cost of administration had hitherto
been paid by Britain through Parliament, and during the previous
three years had cost a million pounds. By the agreement of 1900 the
Baganda were asked to help to pay for the administration by a hut tax

of three rupees a year. As they had paid tribute to the Kabaka from time immemorial, this was accepted without difficulty, although at first the people did not find it easy to raise the money. This was chiefly due to the shortage of rupees. Many of the population had never seen one. For a while the Government accepted 2400 cowrie shells instead, and wild animals were also accepted, if brought to Entebbe alive, at the rate of 1000 huts for an elephant, 100 huts for a hippopotamus and so on, until the streets of the little township became so like a zoo that the Government insisted again on rupees. The effect of the tax upon Baganda life was startling, for it made the earning of wages a necessity and spurred even the slothful into taking some sort of work. Unfortunately, however, it also led to overcrowding, and in 1909 was replaced by a native poll tax, which is now the chief source of revenue.

The constitutional settlement. The assumption on which Johnston based his proposals concerning the government of Buganda was that the old forms of government should be retained and modified under the supervision of the British administration. It was, in fact, the principle of indirect rule, which was particularly suitable to Buganda, where native government was already strong. By the 1900 agreement the Kabaka, assisted by the Lukiko, was to continue to rule in Buganda over the Baganda, his decisions being subject to the approval of the commissioner or governor. Daudi Chwa was recognized as Kabaka, the succession to the throne being confined to the family of Mutesa. The Parliament was to contain the Prime Minister (Katikiro), the chief justice (Omulamuzi), the treasurer (Omuwanika), twenty county or saza chiefs, three important men from each county, and six other important people. All were to be appointed by the Kabaka and approved by the British Government. In addition a committee of the Lukiko was appointed to act as a court of appeal. Besides having its central government, Buganda was divided into counties supervised by a saza chief, each county was divided into gombololas according to its population and size, and in each gombolola were villages, also with chiefs.

Such were the essentials of the 1900 agreement with Buganda. No other kingdom in the protectorate was given such extensive control of its affairs, but agreements were also made with Toro in 1900, with Ankole in 1901, and much later with Bunyoro in 1933.

Boundary alterations in the twentieth century. Johnston left Uganda in 1901, having laid the foundations on which the protectorate developed. In the twenty-five years which followed his commission the size of the Uganda protectorate was practically halved. The first portion to be lost was the eastern area, lying between the Sio River and Naivasha, which was ceded to the East Africa Protectorate in 1902. In 1914 the Gondokoro and Nimule districts were also ceded —to the Anglo-Egyptian Sudan—but at the same time the present West Nile district was acquired by Uganda. In 1926 yet a third adjustment was made, by which the Rudolf Province, lying between the Turkana escarpment and Lake Rudolf, passed to Kenya. But although Uganda's size has been halved, there still remains a compact and fairly well-populated territory, which has been brought under organized administration so peacefully that the Foreign Office was able to transfer control of the protectorate to the Colonial Office as early as 1905.

The development of the central government, 1900–54. The government, as well as the boundary, of Uganda has changed since Johnston's time. The agreement of 1900 was followed in 1902 by the Uganda Order in Council which established the constitution of the protectorate. By this order the administration of the whole of Uganda was put into the hands of a commissioner, whose title was changed in 1907 to that of governor; he was the direct representative of the British sovereign. The next major step in political development came in 1921, when the first Executive and Legislative Councils sat in Uganda. When this first Legislative Council began no one seems to have realized the crucial part it was later to play. In any case it consisted of only six members—four officials and two European unofficials. The Indians were interested enough to agitate for two officials like the Europeans, and they eventually got these members in 1933; but their agitation was not as fierce as the agitation in Kenya. The Buganda leaders also were sufficiently interested to inquire whether the new council would affect their position in the protectorate by the 1900 agreement. They were assured it would not. Apart from this the new Legislative Council caused hardly any interest and had very little effect.

The main development of the council did not in fact begin until the 1940's, especially after the Second World War. From that time representation grew rapidly, as the council became a focus of political and national advance. In 1945 Africans were represented for the first time and the council was reorganized with seven government members and seven unofficial members (two Europeans, 2 Asians, three Africans) besides the governor, whose vote gave the government side a majority. Membership of the council was further increased in 1947, 1948 and 1950, when African representation was made equal to that of the Asian and European unofficials combined. An even bigger change was announced in 1953, and became operative in 1954, when the council was reconstituted with fifty-six members, half being officials and the other half unofficials (fourteen Africans, seven Europeans, seven Asians).

Local government. The governor, the Executive Council and the Legislative Council were the central government and dealt with affairs concerning the whole protectorate. Local affairs were dealt with by means of local government.

This was based on the division of the country into four provinces (Buganda Province, Northern Province, Eastern Province, Western Province) which were subdivided into districts. Although the constitutional position varied between the 'agreement' kingdoms and other parts of Uganda, a general pattern of local government developed with the executive powers carried by the provincial commissioners, district commissioners, and chiefs assisted by advisory councils. The main characteristics of development were the increasing responsibility given to the local authorities and the increasing degree of election to their councils.

Local government also developed in the towns. In 1958 Kampala and Jinja, the two largest, were given municipal councils with power to levy rates and administer their own social services. At the same time Mbale and Masaka, which were next in size, were given town councils, while the remaining towns were administered by town boards.

Buganda and the central government. The difficulties which may arise between local and central government were well illustrated by the relations between Buganda and the protectorate government in the 1950's and early 1960's. They were of particular importance because Buganda contained between a third and a quarter of the total population of the protectorate, in the main commercial and administrative centres of Kampala and Entebbe.

For about forty years following the 1900 agreement the relations between the Buganda and protectorate governments were, generally speaking, good. Following the Second World War, unrest came in the shape of riots and strikes in 1945 and 1949, in which economic discontent was mixed with an agitation for a more democratic Lukiko. Some years later the Lukiko was democratized and the Kabaka's influence on it somewhat decreased. These affairs, however, were local within Buganda. It was not until 1953 that a major clash occurred between the Buganda and the protectorate governments.

As the Legislative Council developed from a small ineffective body into an increasingly representative political power on the protectorate level, it appeared to threaten the prestige and position of the Buganda kingdom. The Lukiko feared that by supporting the council it would undermine its own position, and it was therefore reluctant to send representatives. There was also a lurking fear—not so real, but treading the pages of East African history like a persistent ghost—that federation with other East African countries would be enforced, leading to domination by Kenya. It so happened that a chance remark on this topic by the Colonial Secretary in 1953 provoked a major collision between the Buganda and protectorate governments.

It was unfortunate that circumstances should have forced two such men as the governor and the Kabaka into political collision, for both were sincerely anxious to promote the interests of the African people. Sir Andrew Cohen had come to Uganda as governor in 1952, when his achievements as head of the African Department of the Colonial Office had already made him famous. He had been closely associated with the rapid progress of the West African territories towards self-government, and he came to Uganda with the aim of democratizing not only the government of Buganda but also the government of the protectorate; he aimed also at a great expansion in education and industry. His faith in the ability of Africans to develop self-government was beyond question. The Kabaka Mutesa II, who had succeeded Daudi Chwa in 1942 at the age of eighteen, had been one of the first to welcome the appointment of Sir Andrew, for they were old friends. Frederick Mutesa himself was no illiterate despot but a man of education faced with a powerful Lukiko. Educated at King's College, Budo; Makerere College, Kampala; and at Cambridge University; and serving for a time with the Grenadier Guards (becoming a Captain), the Kabaka was a man with European as well as African attachments. Nevertheless, when the fears of an East African federation were revived in 1953 he decided to support his ministers and the Lukiko in demanding, among other things, that the federation issue should be dropped, and that Buganda should become independent within 'a short, stated space of time'. Sir Andrew, after consultation with the Colonial Secretary, gave a speedy assurance that a policy of federation would not be followed, but he refused to grant the request for immediate independence, which was considered impractical, for Uganda had always been developed as a united territory whose main centres— Kampala and Entebbe—were situated in Buganda. The Kabaka, in accordance with the 1900 agreement, was expected by the governor to support these views in the Lukiko. The Lukiko stated later that 'If he had chosen to do the Governor's bidding, we, the Lukiko would have expelled him'. As it was, the Kabaka refused to comply and announced his intention to oppose the governor's decisions publicly and to advise the Lukiko to reject them. After persistent attempts at compromise had failed, recognition was withdrawn from him by the British Government in November 1953 and he was deported to Britain.

The 1955 Buganda Agreement. The deadlock was ended by the Namirembe Conference (1954), presided over by Professor Sir Keith

Hancock. The conference suggested that Buganda should remain an integral part of the protectorate of Uganda and that the Kabaka himself should become a constitutional monarch retaining the right to sign laws passed by the Lukiko, although ministers were to be responsible for every Act. As these suggestions were acceptable to both the Lukiko and the governor, the Kabaka was able to return amid tremendous rejoicing and sign the new treaty himself in 1955.

The central government of the protectorate. While the Namirembe Conference was working out the problems of Buganda, Sir Andrew Cohen, despite the recent enlargement of the Legislative Council to fifty-six, was pushing ahead with further schemes to make it more representative and responsible. As a result of this policy the British Government recommended the introduction of a ministerial system which was to include five ministers from the general public, three of whom would be Africans. In view of the 1954 changes the size of the Legislative Council was only slightly increased to a total of sixty, but the proportion of African members was increased to half the total. As far as Buganda was concerned the Lukiko Committee had at last agreed to let the Baganda representatives sit in the Legislative Council and it was agreed that no further constitutional changes should be made until 1961.

This temporary harmony of outlook on constitutional advance was disturbed, however, by the refusal of Buganda to take part in the elections for the Legislative Council of 1957. Again the basic reason was that the Buganda leaders feared that their own kingdom and authority would be swamped by the growing power of the Legislative Council and protectorate, but the occasion of their protest was the appointment of a speaker instead of the governor as Chairman of the Council. This, claimed the Baganda, was a breach of the agreement to avoid constitutional changes until 1961. However, despite the lack of co-operation from Buganda, elections were held in 1958 and the experiment of direct elections proved generally popular.

In 1959, while Buganda was still troubled by disturbances, and while the African parties of the protectorate agitated increasingly for political independence, the Government appointed a committee to suggest the constitutional developments which should follow the end of the time pause in 1961. It was important that the committee consisted almost entirely of unofficials from the Legislative Council, thus giving the African members a great measure of responsibility. It was also important that the committee recommended that the 1961 Legislative Council should be renamed the National Assembly and should have a vast majority of African members directly elected. It also recommended that the Executive Council should be appointed mainly from the elected members of the Legislative Council. Most of the people in Uganda welcomed these suggestions and accordingly elections were held in March 1961. These were won by the Democratic Party led by Mr Benedicto Kiwanuka, who became chief minister, while Mr Milton Obote, the leader of the Uganda People's Congress, was recognized as leader of the opposition.

To these constitutional changes Buganda remained rigidly opposed. The 1961 elections were boycotted; the Lukiko passed a resolution in favour of immediate secession; something had to be done.

Uganda becomes independent. In fact something had been done already, for a Relationships Committee had been appointed to suggest a solution to the Buganda problem, and in September 1961 its recommendations formed the basis for a constitutional conference in London. Here the long-awaited agreement was reached on a time-table for independence. Internal self-government was to begin in March 1962 and complete independence in October that year. The Buganda problem was settled by arranging that Buganda's relationship with the central government should be a federal one.

This time-table was kept, and Uganda thus became a constitutional monarchy with the Queen, represented by the governor-general, as Head of State. By its constitution Uganda was to consist of five federal states, ten administrative districts, and the territory of Mbale.

The supreme central legislature became the Parliament of Uganda, consisting of the Queen and the National Assembly. This assembly had sixty-one members elected by universal adult suffrage, twenty-one representing Buganda, and nine elected by the assembly. Elections for a new assembly were normally to be held every five years.

The 1962 elections were won by the Uganda People's Congress supported by the Kabaka Yekka (the Kabaka's party). The U.P.C. leader, Mr Milton Obote, was therefore appointed Prime Minister. A year later, in October 1963, Uganda's constitutional position altered when the governor-general was replaced as Head of State by a President elected by the National Assembly. The Kabaka, by election, became the first President and Uganda remained in the Commonwealth as an independent sovereign state.

With Uganda's federal arrangement, local and central government begin to shade into one another. The largest of the five federal states is the kingdom of Buganda, whose internal government resembles the central one. Its head is the Kabaka, who has a Council of Ministers led by the Katikiro and a Lukiko which is mainly elected. While some subjects, such as foreign policy, security and citizenship are reserved for the Uganda Parliament alone, the Lukiko has wide powers over most of its kingdom's affairs. The other four federal states are the kingdoms of Ankole, Bunyoro, and Toro, and the territory of Busoga. Each has, besides its ruler, provision for a Council of Ministers and a Legislative Assembly with a majority of elected members.

The ten administrative districts are Acholi, Bugisu, Bukedi, Karamoja, Kigezi, Lango, Madi, Sebei, Teso, and West Nile. The constitution provided for each a council with at least nine-tenths of its members elected, and made it possible to establish the office of 'Constitutional Head' which would be similar in function to the rulers of the federal states.

Since 1962 all the large towns have had their own councils which can levy rates and administer certain social services, but they are controlled by the central protectorate government. The Buganda towns are exceptions here for they come under the Buganda Government. Kampala, as the capital, has city status and is controlled by the central government with an advisory committee.

Economic development. The economic history of Uganda is one of steadily increasing prosperity. Sir Harry Johnston had found a country where ivory was the only export, and he foresaw that the most likely method of increasing prosperity would be the encouragement of

Map 17. Administrative districts of Uganda, 1962.

plantations of rubber, coffee, and cocoa under European management. It was Sir Hesketh Bell, who was Commissioner and later Governor from 1905 to 1909, who was mainly responsible for the decision that Uganda should be developed as an African state.

Cotton. A major factor leading to this decision was the astonishing success of African farmers in growing American upland cotton. This had been introduced into Uganda almost simultaneously by Mr Borup of the C.M.S. and by the protectorate government in 1903–4. After 1915 the output of cotton had grown sufficiently to enable the protectorate to dispense with the assistance of a grant-in-aid. In the early 1950's cotton exports alone brought in 15–30 million pounds annually, making cotton easily the greatest single product. This great development was steadily increased by the Government, which carefully controlled the type of seed used, supplied it free to African growers, and generally supervised and assisted the industry throughout. The area now occupied by cotton is over a million acres, and cotton is grown on plots which range from the size of a tablecloth to fields of several acres where hired labour is necessary. The world importance of Uganda's cotton production lies in its quality rather than in its quantity, for its production is only 1 per cent of the world's total. Its price depends mainly on the cotton markets of Egypt, the Mississippi Delta, South Carolina, Peru, and Brazil, whose staple is of similar length.

Coffee. Coffee has recently rivalled cotton in importance. As early as 1903 coffee was exported from Uganda, but it was during the slump following the First World War that the Agricultural Department began to encourage Africans to grow coffee as an alternative cash crop. During the early 1950's the crop brought in 11–12 million pounds annually and today Uganda is the greatest coffee producer in the Commonwealth. By far the greatest part of the crop is of the Robusta variety. Again, production is encouraged and controlled by the Government.

The Five-Year Development Plan and agriculture. In the first Five-Year Development Plan 1961–6, it was clearly recognized that Uganda is an agricultural country with 90 per cent of all her exports coming from the land. It was also recognized that coffee and cotton were 'the most important determinants of the size of the national income', as they alone accounted for over 60 per cent of Uganda's export earnings. Sugar, sisal, groundnuts, tea and livestock account for most of the remaining agricultural produce.

However, three other factors besides agriculture must be mentioned in connection with Uganda's economy.

Transport. The first of these factors is transport, especially the railway on which all development has depended. Without it, transport costs would have made profitable production impossible. For example, before the railway was built the cost of head porterage from Uganda to Mombasa might be as much as £300 per ton, whereas the rail freight on cotton lint for that distance is now about £5 per ton.

At first the cotton-growing regions of Uganda were linked to the rail-head at Kisumu by steamers across Lake Victoria. In 1912 the Busoga railway, joining Jinja and Kakindu, was completed and later extended to Namasagali. In 1927 it was joined to the main line from Kenya. However, it was not until the Nile bridge was built at Jinja in 1931 that the main line reached from Kampala to the coast. In the early 1950's the Western Uganda extension carried the railway still further into the interior, and by 1955 it reached Nkonge, almost exactly 1000 miles by rail from the coast. In 1956 the extension was completed to the railhead near Kilembe. In the north a further extension of the railway is planned into West Nile district.

With this development of the railway has gone a remarkable extension of road transport to feed the railheads, and today Uganda's road system has made possible the production of cotton in all parts of the country where the climate is suitable. The steamer services on the lakes also provide an essential link in Uganda's communications.

Mining. The second factor is mining. The mining possibilities of Uganda were not seriously considered until after the First World War, and minerals still do not provide a major part of Uganda's exports. However, copper deposits were found at Kilembe in 1927 and following the arrival of the railhead there has been a considerable export, which in 1962 was valued at over $3\frac{1}{2}$ million pounds. In 1961 a new and detailed survey for minerals was started.

Hydro-electric power. The third factor which should be mentioned is the Owen Falls Hydro-electric Scheme. It was Sir Winston Churchill who wrote in 1907 that 'it would be perfectly easy to let the Nile begin its long and beneficent journey to the sea by leaping through a turbine'. In 1954 his statement became a reality when the Queen opened the great dam built across the Nile at Jinja. The electrical power from the Owen Falls is carried to Kenya as well as Uganda and has made possible the establishment of further industries.

The sleeping sickness outbreak. The chief setback to Uganda's economic development was the appalling outbreak of sleeping sickness which was first noticed at the C.M.S. hospital at Namirembe in 1901. Fortunately it did not spread over the whole country but was confined

214

to certain areas of Buganda, Busoga, and the islands of Lake Victoria. In these regions two out of every three people died of it. In 1903 the disease was traced to a trypanosome carried by the tsetse fly, but this was only the beginning. From 1906 the drastic step was taken of evacuating all the affected areas, and this, together with constant medical attention, had a definite effect. By 1910 the worst of the epidemic was over, but in the meantime nearly a quarter of a million people had died.

Social development: the African population. The social history of Uganda was not complicated by the presence of a large number of European landowners as it was in Kenya. The African population, which in 1900 was concerned chiefly in producing enough food for itself, and measured its wealth mainly by head of cattle, has adjusted itself to a money economy based on the export of agricultural products. This has not meant, however, that the unit of family life has been broken or that the towns have become over-full. The majority of the population still prefer to live upon their homesteads of perhaps eight acres, being largely self-supporting and having a certain amount of cotton and coffee for sale.

Meanwhile there has been a clear realization of the need to develop social services, and especially education. In this field the missionary societies played a leading part and are still of importance, although the financial burden is now carried by the Government—in the 1961–6 Development Plan education was granted over 5 million pounds, or more than half the total expenditure for social services. The educational facilities range from primary schools to Makerere University College, which became part of the University of East Africa in 1963.

Another major drive has been made on health, and as well as the dozens of existing hospitals, both government and mission, a large new teaching hospital, costing about $2\frac{1}{2}$ million pounds, was opened at Kampala during the independence celebrations.

The European and Asian populations. The Asians and Europeans have never been more than a very small proportion of the total population of Uganda. Nevertheless they have played, and in many cases still are playing, important parts in the country's life.

The Asians, in the early years of the century, replaced the Arabs as the chief traders. In the early 1950's they also provided a successful mayor of Kampala.

Until recently the Europeans provided most of the administrators and specialist aids, but with the development of education it has become increasingly possible to replace them, so that Uganda may feel self-supporting in every sense.

CHAPTER XIII

THE LATER HISTORY OF TANGANYIKA

General outline of development. The area comprising German East Africa, according to the 1886 and 1890 Partition Treaties, was substantially the same as that of Tanganyika today, except that German East Africa included the Ruanda and Urundi areas, which are now under Belgian trusteeship. Its history since 1886 may be divided into four main periods. The first lasted until 1907 and was chiefly occupied in suppressing the numerous rebellions which occurred; the second period lasted until 1914 and was characterized by a sincere, but only partially successful, attempt by the German Government to develop the country by paying particular attention to the African population and to communications; the third period was that of the First World War from 1914 to 1918, during which the present Tanganyika suffered more than any other part of Africa; the fourth, and happiest, period is that of British administration shaped by the outstanding governorships of Sir Donald Cameron and Sir Edward Twining. We shall look at each in turn.

The Germans and colonization. It was unfortunate for Germany, and still more unfortunate for East Africa, that the man who set the pattern of early colonization there was Carl Peters, generally known by the Africans as 'Mkono-wa-damu' or 'the man with the bloodstained hands'. But the Germans were not all like Peters, and the achievements of Germany in East Africa have not all been military. The first missionary to East Africa was Krapf, who was a German; the most thorough early agricultural research was done by Germans, whose research station at Amani was a model; and the greatest early advances in African education were made by Germans. When all its achievements are reckoned Germany has much to its credit. The disastrous early period, which was largely due to Peters's influence, should not lead us to the conclusion that the Germans and their administration were wholly evil. There was good as well as bad.

Aims and methods of British and German companies. As we have already seen, the development of German East Africa after the 1886 Partition Treaty was undertaken not by the German Government but by the German East Africa Company, started in 1888; like the British company it received from the Sultan a concession to administer the mainland opposite its sphere of influence, but the aims and methods of the British and German companies were in sharp contrast. The British had accepted their sphere of influence reluctantly as a political and moral necessity, and were mainly concerned with developing the trade of the region, stopping the slave trade, and encouraging the missions; no major alterations were made in administration, nor at first was there any alienation of land for European settlement. The general result was that in the British sphere the Africans and Arabs accepted the company peacefully. To the south the story was different. The Germans had acquired their region partly in the hope that an empire in Africa would bring them prestige, political power and wealth, and partly to provide an outlet for the large number of German emigrants without losing their attachment to the fatherland. The company came, therefore, with the intention of making sweeping changes, and the clear aim of establishing German plantations. It is not surprising that their arrival met with opposition, while that of the British company did not.

The end of the company's administration. The first opposition came from the Arabs, whose trade and administrative functions the German company intended to replace. Bushiri's rebellion and its suppression by Captain Wissman have already been described. In East Africa the effect was to create widespread anti-European feeling, in Germany to convince the Government that the company was incapable of administering the region; in 1891, accordingly, the company handed over its administrative powers to the imperial government. But the situation did not improve, for the simple reason that the same officials with the same ideas still remained, including Carl Peters, who became imperial high commissioner for the Kilimanjaro district. In 1892 he was indicted by a German judge for excessive cruelty to natives, but it was not until 1897 that he was officially dismissed from the German colonial service for 'misuse of official power'. He died in 1918. It is a sad commentary on the Nazi régime that Hitler spoke of him as a 'model, if stern, Colonial administrator'.

The German method of administration. The imperial administration was similar in many ways to the earlier Arab system. Only in three areas—Ruanda, Urundi and Bukoba—did the Germans consider that tribal authority was strong enough to be worth preserving. In these three they allowed the native chiefs to retain their administrative authority under the supervision of a German Resident. These, however, were exceptions; elsewhere they considered that tribal institutions were too weak to be useful, and a system of direct rule was set up. The whole country, apart from the three Residencies, was divided into nineteen civil and two military districts, each under a district administrator or 'Bezirksamtmann'. Each district was then divided into groups of villages, consisting of twenty to thirty thousand people, in charge of which were officials known as 'Akida', and in charge of each village was an official known as a 'Jumbe'. The system was never satisfactory. There were only about seventy German officials, many of very poor quality, to administer the population of perhaps seven million, so that the actual working of the administration depended chiefly on the Akidas, who were usually Arab or Swahili. They were neither liked nor respected by the Africans whom they governed, and generally their only qualifications were that they could read and write and therefore obey orders. They had both executive and judicial powers and were responsible for the collection of taxes, but they were not properly supervised, and an official German report later admitted that 'the Akidas were in the habit of resorting to oppression and fraud, which made the administration detested by the people'. The general effect of the system was to further the breakdown of tribal institutions and to create a state of suspicion and enmity between the administration and the people. The bomas in which the Bezirksamtmänner lived at each provincial capital tell their own story. They were not built as civil dwellings. They were forts, with thick, square walls, windowless lower storeys, and machine-gun emplacements commanding fields of fire cleared in case of attack.

The German land policy. Meanwhile settlers were arriving: for the Germans, like the British later, assumed that the best chance of prosperity lay in the encouragement of European plantations. By 1888 about thirty such plantations had been started, and the number rose as colonists took up land in the North-east Highlands around Moshi and Arusha, and on the coast at Tanga and Pangani. In view of this colonization Germany declared its land policy in the Land Law of 1896, by which the whole of Tanganyika became Crown land except for the areas already claimed by chiefs, native communities, and individual landholders. It was also realized that most of the land was poor, and that its cultivators depended on a shifting cultivation; the *Land-Kommission* which marked out the reserves therefore reckoned to keep free from native cultivation four times the amount of land already cultivated. Unfortunately the boundaries were not strictly observed. Unfortunately also, time proved that the size of the reserves meant serious congestion, especially in the Meru and Kilimanjaro areas. This, combined with the constant demands for forced labour by the planters, and by the Government for public works, seriously increased the discontent.

Early rebellions. It is not surprising, therefore, to find that the early history is marked by a series of rebellions and punitive expeditions, mostly originating in the south. The Arab rebellion on the coast was scarcely over before war began with the Hehe of the Southern Highlands, who resented German intrusion into their areas. In 1891 they killed a quarter of a German column of 1000 men which had penetrated into their territory. Vengeance followed. In 1894, Kalenga, the court town of the Hehe, was stormed and taken by the Germans despite the massive stone walls by which it was surrounded. But Mkwawa the chief escaped. For four years the Germans tracked him. They offered a reward of 5000 rupees for his head, but so great was his influence that his followers refused to desert or betray him. When at last he was caught he had apparently died by his own hand rather than be taken alive. Trouble also occurred with the Chagga, the Nyamwezi, and the Gogo.

The Maji-Maji rebellion, 1905-7. The bloodiest rising of all, known as the Maji-Maji rebellion, was still to come. There were

Map 18. Tanzania.

tribes south of the Rufiji River who remained warlike and hostile despite the German attempts at pacification. They hated the Akidas, they hated the demands for forced labour, and they particularly hated the hut tax of three rupees which was imposed on the African population. Encouraged by witch doctors, who scattered water mixed with millet and maize over the warriors and assured them that this was proof against all bullets, nearly all the tribes between North Nyasa and the Kilwa coast rose in 1905, in a last great attempt to drive out the Germans. It was the most widespread revolt East Africa has ever seen. Mau Mau in comparison is a local affair concerning mainly one tribe. The Maji-Maji rebellion began with the murder of all Europeans in the area, and officials, missionaries, planters, and traders were killed almost to a man, so complete was the surprise. The revenge was equally horrible, for the Germans, finding themselves unable to end the rebellion simply by force of arms, decided to destroy the villages and crops of the affected area. By 1907 the entire south of German East Africa had been devastated, 120,000 Africans were dead, mainly from starvation, and the region was again at peace—the peace of complete exhaustion.

The reform of German colonial affairs. This rebellion was the end of the first phase of German colonization. Missionaries had sent home to Germany reports of atrocities, and the Social Democrats had supported them in the Reichstag. In 1906 their exposures shattered the happy dreams of empire which the German people had treasured. They exposed corruption and cruelty in every colony, and they gave facts to show that all colonies ran at a heavy loss to the fatherland. The Maji-Maji rebellion of 1905-7, a rising in the Cameroons in 1904-5, and the Herero War in South West Africa drove home their arguments. Reform now became the order of the day. A separate Colonial Office was created and Dr Dernburg was appointed as the first Secretary for the Colonies.

Changed official attitude to African population. The change of policy, for which Dernburg was largely responsible, was especially noticeable in two respects. The first was the change of attitude towards the Africans. During the old régime little importance had been attached to the economic possibilities of the African population. The chief hope had been placed in the development of European plantations, and the Africans were regarded chiefly as useful labour for these. Dr Dernburg took a different view. He saw the colonies as a source of raw material for German industries, and the African population as the most valuable asset of the colonies, whose economic development should be encouraged and whose rights should be guaranteed. Learning from Uganda, he encouraged cotton growing among the Africans and by 1914 the export of cotton from German East Africa was ten times greater than in 1902. In addition, the granting of lands to companies and settlers was tightened and forced labour was made illegal except for public works. Such measures were not popular with the settlers, however, and their influence not only made Dernburg's reforms largely ineffective, but also drove him from office in 1910.

Extension of the railway system. The second change in policy which coincided with the reform period was the increased attention given to communications. By 1900 the only railway in German East Africa was a 25-mile stretch of the Usambara railway which had been built in 1893 and was later extended. It was originally intended to run from Tanga to Lake Victoria, but the completion of the Uganda railway forestalled this plan. The next plan had been to build a trunk line from Dar es Salaam to Lake Tanganyika; this was actually started in 1905, but by 1907 had only reached as far as Morogoro From that date railway construction went ahead at a much quicker pace. In the north the Usambara railway was extended to Moshi by 1911; this provided transport for the European plantations there, and was also of strategic value by reason of its position near the boundary of British East Africa. More important still was the extension of the Central Line, which was pushed forward to Tabora by 1912 and to Kigoma on Lake Tanganyika by 1914, the previous arrival of the Lukuga railway through the Belgian Congo to Lake Tanganyika having acted as a strong incentive. Further plans were interrupted by war.

Economic condition in 1914. By 1914 the European population was about 5000, mainly Germans, and was concentrated chiefly in the North-east Highlands. The most important European crop was sisal, which had been introduced in 1893. Other crops which had been found profitable were coffee, cotton, rubber and groundnuts. Much assistance had been given by the Agricultural Institute founded at Amani in the Usambara Mountains in 1902, and much by the extension of the railway system. Nevertheless, at the outbreak of war German East Africa was not a profitable concern, for her exports totalled only £1½ million pounds and subsidies from Germany were necessary.

Education. In many ways the German administration may be criticized, but in one respect the Germans fulfilled their obligations to the African population very fully. This was in education. The Government, and more especially the missions, provided education for well over 100,000 Africans, which was more than in any other Germany colony and was an example to the British after the war.

The World War, 1914–18. The World War of 1914–18 affected Tanganyika more than any other part of Africa, for elsewhere in the continent fighting had ceased by the end of 1915, while in Tanganyika it lasted until the armistice. It was tragically unnecessary, for all areas in Africa might have remained neutral like the Belgian Congo. But this was not to be. The German Commander, von Lettow-Vorbeck, wanted to occupy as many British troops as he could in East Africa, while the British were afraid for the safety of their Uganda railway. In August British ships shelled Dar es Salaam and a German patrol attacked Taveta. A few days later the German Government suggested that possessions in East Africa should be considered neutral. But it was too late; the fighting had begun.

In British East Africa there was an immediate rush of settlers to Nairobi anxious to volunteer for the forces. Farms were left, families were left, and a disorganized medley of units tried to sort themselves out in the camps formed on Nairobi race-course, in the grounds of Government House, and at the other available spots. There was at first plenty of cause for worry, for the Germans had an overwhelming superiority of soldiers, arms and ammunition. But this superiority was of limited duration; for, as the British had complete naval supremacy, the Germans could receive no fresh supplies and were dependent on the land over which they fought. In fact there was no major attack by von Lettow-Vorbeck, and until 1916 most of the activity consisted of raids and patrols by both sides along the border. The British also made an attack on Tanga, but von Lettow-Vorbeck was given time to bring up reinforcements and the attack was repulsed. An interesting feature of the Tanga attack was the appearance of fierce swarms of bees, which stung both the British and German troops with painful impartiality. There was some naval excitement also in 1915 when the German cruiser *Koenigsberg*, which had been raiding British shipping, was driven up the Rufiji River—where her hulk still lies—and put out of action. But it was in 1916 that the main assault began on German East Africa. From British East Africa a force led by General Smuts, who had just finished a successful campaign against the Germans in South West Africa, advanced across the frontier, defeated the Germans near Kilimanjaro and in March occupied Moshi. Meanwhile an army from the Belgian Congo advanced into Ruanda and by September had reached Tabora, while a Uganda force had crossed the Kagera River and in July occupied Mwanza. By the end of 1916 British and Belgian troops had occupied the northern part of German East Africa and established a provisional administration there, while von Lettow-Vorbeck and his forces were confined to the area south of the Central railway. General Northey, advancing from the south, drove them from the Northern Rhodesian frontier, and in November 1917 the little German army was driven over the Rovuma River into Portuguese territory. From there they were pressed northwards again by British troops from Nyasaland, but von Lettow-Vorbeck, harassed and without supplies, still had sufficient genius and determination to turn to the offensive and actually advanced into Northern Rhodesia and captured Kasama in November 1918. At that point the armistice was declared.

The effects of the war on Tanganyika. No armistice, however, can turn the wasteland into productivity or restore the sacrifice of lives which war demands. In 1918 Tanganyika looked as though it could never recover. The military campaign which had cost Britain 72 million pounds had cost Tanganyika misery such as no other East African territory experienced. Most of the campaign did not take place on the green and pleasant highlands of the country but in its waterless and fly-infested scrubland, where the army sickened and the Africans of the porter corps died of malaria and dysentery by tens of thousands. Disease and famine followed the army across Tanganyika, reducing the population, reducing production, breaking to pieces the whole economic pattern as effectively as the retreating German army broke to pieces the Central railway. And as the war ended the influenza epidemic of 1918–19 also claimed its tens of thousands. 'Chiefs', wrote Cameron later, 'were without people, and people without chiefs. Thirty thousand natives were said to have died of famine. . . . Amongst those remaining great numbers had pawned their children for food, husbands had left their wives, mothers had deserted their children, family life had very nearly ceased to exist.'

The 'mandates' system. By the Treaty of Versailles Germany renounced all her claims to overseas possessions, but they were not handed over to the victors in full sovereignty. Instead, it was decided that the territories previously owned by Germany should be classed as 'mandates', and that the country responsible for their administration should be responsible to the Permanent Mandates Commission of the League of Nations, to whom annual reports were to be made of progress in each territory. In all mandated territories slavery was to be abolished entirely, and forced labour was forbidden except for public works, in which case adequate payment was to be made. The mandatory power was also obliged to 'promote to the utmost the material and moral well-being of its inhabitants'.

The work of Sir Horace Byatt. Britain was given the mandate to administer the former German East Africa except for the areas of Ruanda and Urundi, which were given to Belgium. Tanganyika, as the British area was renamed, was given a governor and an Executive Council in 1920. The governor appointed was Sir Horace Byatt. His task was to restore order and restore trade and, despite the after-effects of war and the world slump of the early 1920's, he did both. When he left in 1925 Tanganyika was exporting twice as much as she had exported before the war, and from 1923 no longer needed British grants-in-aid. It was a remarkable achievement and provided a firm foundation on which Sir Donald Cameron could build.

The policy of Sir Donald Cameron. Sir Donald Cameron, who had been chief secretary in Nigeria, succeeded Byatt in 1925. He was the architect of modern Tanganyika and the administrative policy which he adopted was the exact opposite of that of the Germans. They had ruled mainly through alien administrators, who had encouraged the disintegration of tribal authority. Cameron's policy was to revive that authority and allow it to rule. There were two main considerations on which he based his policy. The first was that he had too few European officials to set up an efficient administration dependent on them alone. The second was that the mandate itself implied that the aim of government should be to enable the people of Tanganyika to stand by themselves, however distant the time might be when they would be able to do so. Sometimes Cameron's administration has been described as indirect rule; he himself preferred to call it native administration.

The reorganization of administration. Tanganyika, as he organized it, was divided into eleven provinces, each under a provincial commissioner whose area was divided into districts under district commissioners. In this there was nothing unusual, except Cameron's insistence on obtaining frank opinions from his subordinates and co-ordination of policy. The striking change was his deliberate revival of African institutions. In each district he sought to discover not who claimed to rule but who in fact was accepted by the tribe—or group of tribes—as the rightful ruler. The only cases where he failed to choose a satisfactory authority were in the coastal districts of the extreme south, where Ngoni invasions, the disruptions caused by the Arab slave traders, and the Maji-Maji rebellion had broken tribal life into smaller fragments than elsewhere. But throughout the rest of Tanganyika, except the Bukoba district where the chiefs' authority had never been destroyed, Cameron chose his authorities so well that the system rapidly proved a success. Generally the native authority was made responsible for the maintenance of good order and government among the Africans in its area. To enable it to enforce its powers it was given a native court with limited powers of punishment and imprisonment. In addition the native authorities were made responsible for the collection of taxes.

The Legislative Council and independence. It was to Cameron also, who always valued criticism highly, that the early introduction of a Legislative Council in 1926 was due. Until recently all its members were nominated by the governor and there was a majority of officials. In 1955 an interesting experiment was made when the council met on the basis that unofficial members should represent the various races equally (ten Africans, ten Asians, ten Europeans). However, this expedient was unlikely to provide a lasting solution in a country where the overwhelming majority of the population were Africans, and in any case most of the council members were still officials and there were no elections. It was in 1958 that the first general election took place, and this resulted in the Tanganyika African National Union (T.A.N.U.) winning an overwhelming majority of the elected seats. T.A.N.U. urged that the speed of advance towards self-government should be increased, and as this was the goal the Government had always been working towards, and as Dr Nyerere—the leader of T.A.N.U.—had widespread support and was able to co-operate on friendly terms with the governor, the next advance came in 1960, when a new and larger Legislative Council was created with, for the first time, a majority of elected members. Meanwhile the Executive Council had been replaced by a Council of Ministers. As Dr Nyerere's party won all the elected seats except one (his majority was certain before the election as most of the T.A.N.U. candidates were unopposed) the governor asked him to be the chief minister and choose ten of the fourteen members of the Council of Ministers. Tanganyika thus reached responsible government. Full independence came in December 1961. Dr Nyerere then became the first Prime Minister and the Legislative Council was renamed the National Assembly. In December 1962 Tanganyika became a Republic with Dr Nyerere as president, but remained within the Commonwealth.

The Tanganyika Constitution of 1962 laid down that the executive power of the Republic should be vested in the president. His position was made elective, normally after five years in order to correspond with the elections for each new National Assembly. This assembly, together with the president, comprised the legislature of the Republic.

The National Assembly was essentially democratic, consisting of 107 members elected by universal adult suffrage with one member for each constituency, and with an Electoral Commission to ensure that the constituencies were of roughly equal population. On the other hand, the president was given extensive powers which included control over the armed forces, and authority to choose his cabinet and to summon or dissolve Parliament, besides the power to nominate up to ten members of the National Assembly over and above those who were elected.

In the early part of 1964 events in Zanzibar began to impinge upon the Tanganyika Republic. First came the Zanzibar revolution, which caused general military unrest throughout East Africa, including a short-lived army mutiny in Dar es Salaam. Then, in April, Tanganyika and the new régime in Zanzibar agreed to join together, and a few months later—after Dr Nyerere had offered a prize for a suitable name—they became the United Republic of Tanzania.

Local government. The organization of local government in Tanganyika has also developed. In 1953 a Local Government Bill was passed introducing local councils at various levels as a necessary development from the native authorities devised by Sir Donald Cameron. These new councils were given increased responsibilities and a training school giving courses on local government administration was started for chiefs and those recommended by the native authorities. Nevertheless, the pace of development in local government was slow in comparison with the extremely rapid advances on the national level, partly because there was no general agitation for it. Following independence, the weight of responsibility in local government has moved increasingly towards Regional Councils supervised by T.A.N.U.

Economic development. Tanganyika is about the same size as Nigeria, or, to take another comparison, it is roughly equal in area to France and Germany combined. From the economic point of view its size is its handicap, because the fertile areas are on its edges—on the coast, the lake, the highlands—whereas the centre is mainly arid bush often inhabited by the tsetse fly. Moreover, enormous communication problems arise.

9-2

In view of these difficulties the economic development has been remarkable; the value of exports in 1960, for example, was thirteen times greater than in 1938. Like those of the other East African countries, Tanganyika's economy is based on agriculture and live-stock, which together provide 80 per cent of the exports. The most important crop since the beginning of the century has been sisal, which was introduced by the Germans; and since before the Second World War Tanganyika has been the world's greatest producer. As a plantation crop sisal requires a large capital outlay and easy access to communications, so it was chiefly developed by Asians and Europeans near the railways or the sea. But by 1960 cotton and coffee, which were grown almost entirely by small African farmers, were together nearly as valuable as sisal. Unfortunately the groundnuts scheme run by the United Africa Company, and later by the Overseas Food Corporation on behalf of the British Government, which was intended to encourage African prosperity and production while providing raw material for margarine and cattle food in Britain, was not a success.

Although Tanganyika is primarily an agricultural country, it has the most valuable mineral resources of any of the East African countries. Until the 1930's these were not seriously developed, but by the early 1960's they provided about 13 per cent of the exports. At first gold was the most valuable mineral but in 1940 Dr Williamson, a Canadian geologist, discovered an extremely rich diamond pipe near Shinyanga, and since then diamonds have become by far the most important mineral export. The most valuable stone yet discovered in the Shin-yanga mine, valued at over £10,000, Dr Williamson gave to the Queen (then Princess Elizabeth) as a wedding present.

Transport. Together with increased production have gone improved methods of transport. In 1928 a branch line from Tabora to Mwanza was completed, which opened up the valuable producing areas around Lake Victoria and provided closer links with Kenya and Uganda through the lake steamers. In order to facilitate economic develop-ment in the south, especially in connection with the groundnuts scheme, the Southern Province railway was constructed and by 1954 had been opened to Nachingwea. Originally the railway began from

Lindi, but when the new port of Mtwara was opened in 1954 that became the main outlet. By 1964 a line joining Ruvu to Korogwe at last made it possible to travel by rail from Dar es Salaam to Nairobi and Kampala, instead of having to use the steamer link across Lake Victoria. A railway line to Zambia is also anticipated.

The road system of Tanganyika is also being developed and includes long stretches of tarmacadam, but to overcome the country's geographic problems it would be necessary to have a road network far out of proportion to the traffic that would use it and pay for it.

Development plans. The rapid economic development of Tanganyika has been due, in great measure, to the series of development plans. These have been financed partly by loans and partly by the British Colonial Development and Welfare Acts. One ten-year plan was launched in 1947, and in 1961 another three-year plan was started. This was guided to some extent by the World Bank Mission, and the planners came to the conclusion that the most urgent objectives for Tanganyika's growth were the development of agriculture and live-stock (and therefore of water supplies as well); the improvement of communications; and the development of secondary and technical education. Measures to implement these decisions were taken, but those responsible emphasized that they would not bring a great increase in prosperity overnight; they were primarily laying the foundations for future growth.

Social development. The African population of Tanganyika is probably over nine million, in addition to which there are about 100,000 Asians and Arabs, and perhaps 20,000 Europeans.

The vast majority of the Africans are peasant farmers, and in 1962 only half a million were recorded as being in paid employment. The Sukuma are the largest of the 120 tribes in the country, the next largest being the Nyamwezi, Ha, Makonde, Gogo, Haya and Chagga, and they live mainly on the highlands, the lakeside and the coastal plain. In these regions most of them graze their cattle, cultivate their land, and hope to produce enough food for themselves besides a small cash crop of cotton, coffee or groundnuts. Some tribes, like the Masai, are purely pastoral.

The education pattern in Tanganyika has been similar to that in the other East African countries. The missions and Government have combined and have increasingly realized the importance of the task. By 1960 secondary schools were preparing pupils for Higher Certificate, and the first University College of Tanganyika opened in 1961 with a law faculty. This, together with the colleges of Uganda and Kenya, formed part of the University of East Africa, which was inaugurated in 1963. However, despite these advances, in 1961 only half the African children in Tanganyika went to school and only 8 per cent reached their fifth school year. Dr Nyerere, knowing this, said, ' I have so few graduates that I shall want them as soon as they graduate. I cannot wait for them to become nuclear physicists and chemists.'

European population. Under the German administration most of the Europeans in Tanganyika were Germans, but after the First World War all Germans were forced to leave and their properties were sold. Most of their mission stations, however, were taken over by missionaries of the same, or similar, denominations. In 1925 German settlers were allowed to return. Most of them were financed by the Usagara Company, which was in practice, although not in name, an instrument of the German Government, and almost all the settlers were Nazis. During the Second World War they were interned. Later, most of them were repatriated, and since the 1950's Germans have been far less numerous than either the Greeks or the British. With independence, many of the posts previously held by Europeans, especially in administration, were taken over by Africans, although the value of the specialist aid which Europeans could still give was recognized.

Asian population. The Asian community has played an outstanding part in the country's economic life, because they have not only controlled the petty trade of Tanganyika for many years, but recently they have also taken a major share in large commercial undertakings. In addition they are considerable landowners, much of the land having been purchased from the Germans who were forced to sell after the First and Second World Wars. Today not only is much of the town property, especially in Dar es Salaam, owned by Asians, but Asians are also among the greatest sisal producers.

Inter-territorial co-operation. It has been shown that local government bodies have expanded to cover much wider areas than the ridges which the tribal councils ruled. In a similar way the powers of the central government developed, and it became necessary to consider how common problems should be solved by Uganda, Tanganyika and Kenya.

The East African High Commission. Before the Second World War there had been talk of federation, and proposals to bring this about were put forward by the Hilton Young Commission. When these were discussed by a Joint Select Committee of both Houses of Parliament in England it was decided that they were premature. At the same time, the three countries shared many problems which it was wasteful to consider separately. From 1926 onwards, therefore, there was always a conference twice a year between the governors of the three countries, together with the British Resident of Zanzibar. It had no authority and its decisions could be carried out only after they had been referred to the various governments. During the Second World War the need for this co-operation was seen even more clearly, and it was agreed that an East African High Commission should be set up, consisting of the governors of Kenya, Tanganyika and Uganda. At the same time, in 1948, the East African Central Legislative Assembly was created to provide a means of discussion of the common interests of the three territories. This met two or three times a year in each of the territories in turn, and its membership was increased from twenty-three in 1948 to thirty-three in 1956, although only nine of these members were elected. The services controlled by the High Commission included the East African Railways and Harbours, the Posts and Telecommunications, Customs, Research, and Income Tax.

The East African Common Services Organization. The benefits which co-operation brought made Tanganyika anxious that it should continue when independence came. Therefore, after a conference in London and an investigation by the Raisman Commission, the High Commission was reconstituted in December 1961 as the East African Common Services Organization. In this organization responsibility was to rest with the principal elected ministers of the three countries, who were the East African Common Services Authority. The authority was to be supported by four groups: one for communications, one for finance, one for commerce and industry, and one for social and research services. There were to be three ministers in each group, one from each country.

The new Central Legislative Assembly was also made very different from the old because from the outset its forty-one members were nearly all elected.

So far the association has been primarily an economic one, but many people anticipated that its importance might go beyond the economic sphere, and that it would provide a basis for co-operation in other ways, perhaps even providing the foundation for a federal parliament. A statement issued jointly by Dr Nyerere, Mr Obote and Mr Jomo Kenyatta in June 1963 encouraged this idea and talked of establishing a federation in the same year. A year later, however, federation remained a possibility but was still at the discussion stage.

POSTSCRIPT

This book was first published in 1957, which is not very long ago. At that time none of the East African countries was self-governing and the problems in the path of each towards that goal looked formidable. Yet, by the time this edition is published only seven years later, all the countries have reached independence.

In many ways they are still a patchwork of contrasts. Their paths towards independence have varied greatly and their forms of government have differed too. In Tanganyika there is one central government and in it the T.A.N.U. party have such overwhelming support that there is practically no opposition. In Uganda there is a federation and the two leading parties are both considerable. Other contrasts abound.

The routes to independence and the results have varied. In Kenya great emphasis was placed on the need for a strong central government; in Uganda a federation was considered the most suitable pattern to follow, and in Uganda alone has government with more than one party been retained. Tanganyika, where progress to independence was particularly remarkable for its rapidity and co-operation, has joined with Zanzibar where revolution followed the independence celebrations.

It is hoped that this book, by giving the background of the peoples and territories of East Africa, may help towards the solution of those problems, and that by showing how much has been achieved in the past it may give some reasonable hope for the future.

SUGGESTIONS FOR FURTHER READING

The titles given are of books recommended for schools that are building a reference library. A few of these books are out of print and can only be purchased second-hand at the current market value, which in the case of some of the earlier works may be considerable.

Books which appear more than once are starred (*) in the later entries.

GENERAL

SIR R. COUPLAND, *East Africa and its Invaders*. (Detailed standard authority on early history.)

SIR R. COUPLAND, *The Exploitation of East Africa*. (Detailed authority following on *East Africa and its Invaders*.)

K. INGHAM, *A History of East Africa* (strongly recommended at sixth-form level, embodying the latest research).

ROLAND OLIVER and J. D. FAGE, *A Short History of Africa*. (An inexpensive readable outline.)

ROLAND OLIVER and G. MATHEW, *History of East Africa*. (A scholarly work.)

LORD HAILEY, *An African Survey*. (Very detailed and authoritative survey of African affairs.)

J. D. FAGE, *An Atlas of African History*. (An historical atlas showing the development of the continent.)

J. HORROBIN, *An Atlas of Africa*. (A series of clear maps illustrating historical topics interleaved with short explanatory matter.)

Z. MARSH, *East Africa through Contemporary Records*. (Provides illustrative historical material.)

B. DAVIDSON, *Old Africa Rediscovered*. (An illustrated readable account of the archaeological background of Africa south of the Sahara.) Published 1959.

R. E. WRAITH, *East African Citizen*. (A very good handbook for discussion groups. It gives economic and social background to recent East African history.) Published 1959.

G. W. KINGSNORTH, *Africa South of the Sahara*. (An introduction to the history of the continent as a whole.) Published 1961.

L. HOLLINGSWORTH, *The Asians of East Africa*. (The only comprehensive historical account of the part played by the Asians in East Africa.)

G. DELF, *Asians in East Africa*. (Supplements Hollingsworth, *The Asians of East Africa*.)

CHAPTER I. EARLY HISTORY OF EAST AFRICA

*SIR R. COUPLAND, *East Africa and its Invaders*.

L. W. HOLLINGSWORTH, *A Short History of the East Coast of Africa*.

J. H. PARRY, *Europe and a Wider World*. (Outline of European discovery and settlement up to 1715. Hutchinson's University Library, No. 31.)

E. PRESTAGE, *Portuguese Pioneers*. (Authoritative detailed account of Portuguese discovery.)

C. D. LEY, *Portuguese Voyages*. (Useful source book. Everyman series.)

HART, *Sea Road to the Indies*. (An interesting account of the Portuguese maritime explorers.)

GENESTA HAMILTON, *In the Wake of da Gama* and *Princes of Zinj*. (Colourful account of the Portuguese pioneers in East Africa.)

Apart from *Akamba*—Lindblom, *Akikuyu*—Father Cagnolo and *The Social Institutions of the Kipsigis*—Peristiany, most of the detailed studies of tribes are out of print and very scarce. There is, however, a new series of detailed East African Tribal studies by the International African Institute. In addition the East African Literature Bureau has produced two cheap, useful series: (1) 'The Peoples of Kenya' (titles still in print are *The Kamba* and *The Nandi*); (2) 'Custom and Tradition in East Africa' (titles still in print are *Nandi Customs and Law*, *Kamba Customs and Law*, *Home Life in Kikuyuland*, *The Ntemi*).

J. KENYATTA, *Facing Mount Kenya*. (An anthropological study of considerable interest.)

L. S. B. LEAKEY, *Adam's Ancestors*. (Authoritative and readable guide to the prehistory of East Africa.)

J. DUYVENDAK, *China's Discovery of Africa*. (Lectures given at London University.)

S. COLE, *The Pre-history of East Africa*. (Penguin book. Easily obtainable.)

C. R. BOXER and C. DE AZEVEDO, *Fort Jesus and the Portuguese in Mombasa*. (A detailed study of the history and architecture of Fort Jesus.)

Chapters II and IX. Earlier and Later Zanzibar

*Sir R. Coupland, *East Africa and its Invaders*.

*Sir R. Coupland, *The Exploitation of East Africa*.

*L. W. Hollingsworth, *A Short History of the East Coast of Africa*.

L. W. Hollingsworth, *Zanzibar under the Foreign Office*. (Standard book on the period.)

R. H. Crofton, *Zanzibar Affairs 1914–1933*. (Contains specialized source material.)

G. E. Tidbury, *The Clove Tree*. (General account of clove industry.)

Chapter III. The East African Slave Trade and Abolition

Sir R. Coupland, *The British Anti-Slavery Movement*. (A general outline of the movement. Home University Library series.)

*Sir R. Coupland, *East Africa and its Invaders*.

*Sir R. Coupland, *The Exploitation of East Africa*.

W. E. Ward, *Africa and European Trade*. (Longman's African Histories, Bk. 2. Cheap and simple outline.)

J. D. Fage, *An Introduction to the History of West Africa*. (Contains the best available account of the West African slave trade.)

E. A. Loftus, *Elton and the East African Coast Slave Trade*. (Cheap abridged version of Part I of *Travels and Researches among the Lakes and Mountains of Central Africa, 1879*.)

J. A. Williamson, *Builders of the Empire*. (Contains useful biography of Wilberforce.)

J. Mbotela, *The Freeing of the Slaves in East Africa*. (A translation from the Swahili account by the son of one of the slaves freed by the British.)

Chapter IV. Europe Hears of Africa

J. I. Macnair, *Livingstone's Travels*. (An account of Livingstone's travels in his own words, with a brief explanation.)

J. I. Macnair. *Livingstone the Liberator*. (Collins' pocket series biography.)

D. Middleton, *Baker of the Nile*. (Draws largely on Baker's own account.)

J. M. Synge, *Book of Discovery*. (Interesting detail for school work.)

M. Perham and J. Simmons, *African Discovery*. (Extracts from explorers' accounts, with brief explanations.)

'Early Travellers in East Africa'. This series of cheap, useful books includes:

> *Early Travellers in Acholi.*
> *Charles New.*
> *Johnston on Kilimanjaro.*
> *Gregory: the Great Rift Valley.*

(These books cover explorers whose work it was not possible to treat in chapter IV.)

J. A. HUNTER and D. MANNIX, *African Bush Adventures*. (This includes an account of Tippoo Tip and some of the early East African settlers.)

The works of some explorers themselves are listed below but may not be easily obtainable:

L. KRAPF, *Travels and Missionary Labours in East Africa.*

J. H. SPEKE, *Journal of the Discovery of the Source of the Nile.*

SIR R. F. BURTON, *First Footsteps in East Africa.*

D. LIVINGSTONE, *Missionary Travels and Researches in South Africa.*

D. LIVINGSTONE, *Narrative of an Expedition to the Zambezi and its Tributaries.*

H. M. STANLEY, *Autobiography.*

H. M. STANLEY, *Through the Dark Continent.*

H. M. STANLEY, *In Darkest Africa.*

J. THOMSON, *Through Masai Land.*

J. THOMSON, *To the Central African Lakes and Back.*

C. RICHARDS and J. PLACE, *East African Explorers.*

H. SCHIFFER, *The Quest for Africa*. (A readable and comprehensive account of exploration in Africa which is brought up to date in 352 pages.)

CHAPTER V. MISSIONS

R. OLIVER, *The Missionary Factor in East Africa*. (Detailed authoritative account of missionary development.)

A. R. TUCKER, *Eighteen Years in Uganda and East Africa*. (Bishop Tucker's work in East Africa.)

H. R. A. PHILP, *A New Day in Kenya*. (Account of Protestant missionary effort up to 1935.)

*L. KRAPF, *Travels and Missionary Labours in East Africa.*

FORBES, *Planting the Faith in Darkest Africa*. (An account of the work of Père Lourdel.)

GLENN KITTLER, *The White Fathers.*

SUGGESTIONS FOR FURTHER READING

CHAPTER VI. SCRAMBLE AND PARTITION

R. ROBINSON and O. GALLAGHER, *Africa and the Victorians*. (A modern study of the partition of Africa.)

*SIR R. COUPLAND, *The Exploitation of East Africa*.

P. L. MCDERMOTT, *British East Africa or I.B.E.A.* (An account of I.B.E.A. and its work.)

F. JACKSON, *Early Days in East Africa*. (Jackson's travels and work in East Africa.)

SIR A. R. COOK, *Uganda Memories 1897–1940*. (Provides interesting contemporary material.)

E. LEWIN, *The Germans and Africa*. (An account of the German Colonial Movement.)

E. R. VERE-HODGE, *Imperial British East Africa Company*. (In 92 pages this gives an outline of the history of the company.)

R. OLIVER, *Sir Harry Johnston and the Scramble for Africa*.

CHAPTER VII. UGANDA TO 1890

H. B. THOMAS and R. SCOTT, *Uganda*. (Standard work on Uganda giving history and general survey.)

H. B. THOMAS, *The Story of Uganda*. (Small, simple school history.)

R. P. ASHE, *Two Kings of Uganda*. (Account of events by early missionary. Not easily obtainable.)

C. W. HATTERSLEY, *The Baganda at Home*. (Account of the Baganda. Not easily obtainable.)

C. NORTHCOTT and J. REASON, *Living Names. Six Missionaries in Africa*. (Small, cheap book giving useful outline of Mackay. Fuller biographies are not easily obtainable.)

K. INGHAM, *The Making of Modern Uganda*. (A history of Uganda dealing mainly with this century.)

CHAPTER VIII. KINGDOMS AND LEADERS

Tippu Tib, published by the East African Swahili Committee. (Very useful.)

F. D. LUGARD, *The Rise of our Empire in East Africa*. (Account of work in East Africa.)

M. PERHAM, *Lord Lugard*. (An authoritative and readable two-volume biography.)

*H. B. THOMAS and R. SCOTT, *Uganda*.

*H. B. THOMAS, *The Story of Uganda*.

*R. OLIVER, *The Missionary Factor in East Africa.*
*A. R. TUCKER, *Eighteen Years in Uganda and East Africa.*
J. V. WILD, *The Story of the Uganda Agreement.* (Cheap, useful account in the series 'A Treasury of East African History', published by the East African Literature Bureau.)

CHAPTER IX. (See Chapter II)

CHAPTER X. RAILWAY AND ECONOMIC DEVELOPMENT OF KENYA

E. HUXLEY, *White Man's Country.* (Lord Delamere's biography, with background history of Kenya's early development.)
M. F. HILL, *Permanent Way.* (Detailed account of the Uganda Railway with fairly full historical background. There is a very much smaller version by Patrick Pringle, *The Story of a Railway,* published by the East African Literature Bureau.)
*F. JACKSON, *Early days in East Africa.*
J. H. PATTERSON, *The Man-Eaters of Tsavo.* (An exciting account of difficulties caused by lions in the building of the railway.)
F. H. GOLDSMITH, *Ainsworth, Pioneer Administrator.* (Provides interesting local background.)
E. HUXLEY, *A New Earth.* (This deals with recent agricultural development in Kenya.)
East African Royal Commission Report 1953–5. (Readable; supplies economic and social background.)

CHAPTER XI. CONSTITUTIONAL DEVELOPMENT OF KENYA

G. BENNETT, *Kenya: A Political History. The Colonial Period.* (A detailed and clear account.)
Books giving relevant detail further to that included in this chapter are not easy to obtain.

CHAPTER XII. THE LATER HISTORY OF UGANDA

*H. B. THOMAS and R. SCOTT, *Uganda.*
*H. B. THOMAS, *The Story of Uganda.*
J. V. WILD, *The Uganda Mutiny.* (Cheap, useful account in the series 'A Treasury of East African History', published by the East African Literature Bureau.)

*M. F. HILL, *Permanent Way*.

SEMPA, *The Buganda Government and its Constitutional Functions*. (Cheap small book in English and Luganda, published through the East African Literature Bureau.)

*K. INGHAM, *The Making of Modern Uganda*.

L. A. FALLERS, *The King's Men: Buganda on the Eve of Independence* (Topical.)

CHAPTER XIII. THE LATER HISTORY OF TANGANYIKA

STEER, *Judgement on German Africa*. (Contains very readable account of Tanganyika's background and development for the general reader.)

V. L. CAMERON, *Across Africa*.

P. H. C. CLARKE, *A Short History of Tanganyika*. (A clear history of Tanganyika written within a vocabulary of 2000 words.)

M. F. HILL, *Permanent Way*, vol. II. (This is the illustrated story of Tanganyika's railways and contains useful information on the history of Tanganyika as a whole.)

Handbook of Tanganyika. 1958 edition. (It has useful history chapters.)

INDEX

Chief references in italics

INDEX